Sledgehammers

Strengths and Flaws
of Tiger Tank Battalions
in World War II

Christopher W. Wilbeck

THE ABERJONA PRESS
Bedford, PA

Technical Editor: Keith E. Bonn
Production Editor: Patricia K. Bonn
Cartographer: Tom Houlihan
Printer: Mercersburg Printing

The Aberjona Press is an imprint of Aegis Consulting Group, Inc.,
      Bedford, Pennsylvania 15522
Printed in the United States of America
10 09 08 07 06 05 04   6 5 4 3 2

ISBN: 0-9717650-2-2

Contents

Acknowledgments

In a world where so much information is so easily obtained and so readily available, I am continually amazed at how many nuggets of history are still hidden on a shelf in the dark corner of some library or archive. For their great assistance in helping me to find these nuggets, I would like to thank the librarians at the Combined Arms Research Library in Fort Leavenworth, Kansas. I would especially like to thank research assistant Michael Browne who kept his eye out for me for over two years while this book was being written.

For their advice and input during the formative stages of this work, I would like to thank three members of the faculty of the Combat Studies Institute at the U.S. Army Command and General Staff College, Fort Leavenworth, Kansas: Dr. Curtis King, LTC John Suprin, and Dr. Sam Lewis.

I would like to thank the publishers of this book, specifically the editor, Kit Bonn, and the chief of production, Patti Bonn, for believing in it from the first time they saw the manuscript. Their suggestions, recommendations, and good ideas all contributed to making it a better book, and helped to refine my thoughts and ideas in many areas.

For kindly granting me permission to include most of the photos in this book, I would like to thank the Patton Museum of Cavalry and Armor at Fort Knox, Kentucky, especially Candace Fuller, for helping me in searching the files there. Mr. Dale Ritter, an author, veteran soldier, and educator in Alburtis, Pennsylvania, shared both photos from his exceptionally extensive private collection and his expertise in precisely identifying the subject matter in others. I am grateful for his truly collegial attitude and willingness to cheerfully share his formidable knowledge of Tiger tanks and units. I would also like to recognize and commend the exceptional professionalism, expertise, and responsiveness of Mr. David Fletcher of the Tank Museum, Bovington, Dorset, in the United Kingdom, who provided important photos on short notice. Mr. Wilfred Rogers of Helion Books in Solihull, Warwickshire, was instrumental in quickly scanning and transmitting those photos, making their inclusion in the book possible.

Several World War II veterans shared their thoughts and recollections that comprise the Prologue and Epilogue of this book. Famed Tiger commander

Otto Carius very graciously agreed to contribute the former, and an officer who could easily have been across the battlefield from him, Colonel Viktor Iskrov, formerly of the Red Army, kindly provided part of the latter. Bob Holt, webmaster and creator of the very fine site telling the history of the 752nd Tank Battalion in WWII (www.752ndtank.com) contributed the gripping story that comprises the other part of the Epilogue on behalf of his veteran father, the late Ray Holt, former Sherman tank driver and commander in B/752nd. I am indebted to all of them for adding color and personal insights in reinforcing the themes of the book. I am also grateful to Hans Roepke of Frankfurt, Germany, for eliciting and coordinating Herr Carius's thoughtful contribution. I am similarly grateful to Lars Gyllenhaal of Rosvik, Sweden, and Bair Irincheev of St. Petersburg and Helsinki for facilitating our receipt of Colonel Iskrov's vivid anecdote.

Staff Sergeant Tom Houlihan, USMC (Ret.) of Aegis Consulting Group, Inc., created the outstanding maps which so vividly portray the action in the case studies which are central to this study. A true professional in every way, he was a real partner in the process of fashioning these exceptional graphic aids. Lieutenant Colonel Mark Reardon, US Army; Mr. Terry Poulos, Toronto, Ontario; Mark Rikmenspoel, Fort Collins, Colorado; and Lawrence Frappier, Houston, Texas also all contributed to the information contained on various maps.

I owe a lasting debt to my close friend Andrew Harris, who read the initial draft and has always provided me valuable suggestions, for this book and in life, usually over a late-night whiskey or a bottle of wine. Perhaps that is why his advice always seemed so sage at the time.

I am grateful to my parents, Warren and Corlynn Wilbeck, for always supporting me in whatever I have done and for somehow instilling in me a thirst for knowledge and a passion for history. Thanks to my children, Jonathan and Abigail, for helping me in a variety of ways during the production of this book, from taking on increased responsibility in yard and household chores to simply being great kids.

Finally, a heartfelt thanks to my wife and best friend, Lizzie. Her support during the writing of this book and also during many extended deployments away from home have always been a source of strength.

—*Chris Wilbeck*
March 2004

A Guide to Tactical Unit Symbols

Types of Units

⊠	Infantry
⊗	Armored Infantry/ *Panzer-Grenadier*
▢	Tank/*Panzer*
⬭	Armored Recon
⊠	Parachute Infantry
✕	Motorized Infantry
TD	Tank Destroyer*
△	Antitank (Towed Guns)
⊙	Armored Field Artillery or *Assault Guns* (*Sturmgeschütze*)
⫟	Engineers

Sizes of Units

● ● ●	Platoon/British Tank or Recce Troop
I	Company/Battery/U.S. Cavalry Troop/ British Tank or Recce Squadron
II	Battalion/U.S. Cavalry Squadron
⎢II⎥	Battalion-sized task force or *Combat Group*
III	Regiment
⎢III⎥	Regimental-sized task force or *Combat Group*
X	Brigade/Group/ Combat Command
XX	Division
XXX	Corps
XXXX	Army
XXXXX	Army Group

Example

```
        II
      ┌────┐
      │ ▢  │ 501
      └────┘
```

Heavy Tank Battalion 501

▢	US, Soviet, or British Forces	▨	German Forces

*The German equivalent, *Panzerjäger* units, is symbolized by "PZJG" in the unit box.

Note. If the specific subelement of a unit is not known, only its size is graphically indicated on the left of the unit box.

Thus, Bn⊗12 would be an unspecified battalion of Panzer-Grenadier Regiment 12.

Rank Equivalences

US Army	German Army	Waffen-SS
General of the Army	Generalfeldmarschall	
General	Generaloberst	SS-Oberstgruppenführer
Lieutenant General	General (der Infanterie, der Artillerie, etc.)	SS-Obergruppenführer
Major General	Generalleutnant	SS-Gruppenführer
Brigadier General	Generalmajor	SS-Brigadeführer
		SS-Oberführer
Colonel	Oberst	SS-Standartenführer
Lieutenant Colonel	Oberstleutnant	SS-Obersturmbannführer
Major	Major	SS-Sturmbannführer
Captain	Hauptmann	SS-Hauptsturmführer
1st Lieutenant	Oberleutnant	SS-Obersturmführer
2nd Lieutenant	Leutnant	SS-Untersturmführer
Sergeant Major*	Stabsfeldwebel	SS-Sturmscharführer
Master Sergeant/ First Sergeant	Oberfeldwebel	SS-Hauptscharführer
Technical Sergeant	Feldwebel	SS-Oberscharführer
Staff Sergeant	Unterfeldwebel	SS-Scharführer
Sergeant	Unteroffizier	SS-Unterscharführer
Corporal		
Private First Class	Hauptgefreiter Obergefreiter Gefreiter	SS-Rottenführer
	Obersoldat (Obergrenadier, Oberkanonier, etc.)	SS-Sturmmann
Private	Soldat (Grenadier, Kanonier, etc.)	SS-Mann

*Not a rank in the US Army during WWII. NCOs serving as sergeants major during that era were usually Master Sergeants.

Prologue
Through the Eyes of a Tiger Ace

As a "Tiger-Man" from the design's earliest days, I am having difficulties appreciating the phenomenon of such immense interest in a weapon of which only a little over a thousand units were used by the German armed forces. There is no doubt that the Tiger was a technical masterpiece, in spite of insufficient production sites during this phase of the war. This was a situation that was less than optimal, particularly in view of the bombing.

Unfortunately, the front line activities of the Tiger battalions' crews were mostly unpleasant, but they were eminently necessary. We were to act as the backbone of the defensive lines of the rather weak infantry units, in order to prevent a major catastrophe on the Eastern Front.

Operation ZITADELLE and the action in the Kursk Salient were more or less the only events when Panthers and Tigers could really demonstrate their preeminent offensive strength, acting as sledgehammers to clear the path for units equipped with Panzer IIIs and IVs.

The attack was doomed, however, because the order had been given too late, thus forfeiting the desired surprise effect. Ten times as many Tigers would not have altered the situation, since our infantry forces had been much too weak.

The failure of Operation ZITADELLE turned the tide toward ultimate German defeat. The only task left was to try to keep the Russians from forcing their way into Germany proper. In this, too, Tiger units played a major role, although it was not one for which they had been designed. Our Heavy Tank Battalion 502 mastered its task with outstanding efficiency.

My own 2nd Company, Heavy Tank Battalion 502 participated in numerous defensive battles against the Russians. Tigers proved themselves superior against Soviet tanks countless times, even when greatly outnumbered. One such occasion was during the defensive battles around Dünaburg in the summer of 1944. On 22 July 1944, Soviet forces broke through our front lines north of the city. My company was ordered to advance along the Rollbahn north of Dünaburg to hold open the important road to Viski. Along this road, at the small town of Malinava, my company encountered a Soviet force of 20 tanks, comprised of T-34s and Josef Stalins, their new heavy tank. We attacked immediately, using only two of our company's eight operational tanks, to limit exposure to enemy fire. In a battle that lasted about 20 minutes, my crew and the other, commanded by Feldwebel (later Oberfeldwebel and Knight's Cross recipient) Albert Kerscher, destroyed 17 of the enemy tanks.

Even successful engagements like these were unable to stop the Red Army. No amount of skill or courage could stem the tide, and no tank ever designed could perform miracles. Still, I wouldn't have wanted to go into battle with any other tank but the Tiger, because it was superior in every aspect to all other tanks fielded by the German military.

A brief word about this book: As former frontline soldiers, my comrades and I do appreciate every author who holds discipline, chivalry, and readiness to fight in esteem. I have personally given up hope that politicians who never experienced war first hand will ever realize that war is the worst of all possible alternatives.

Otto Carius
Former Commander, 2nd Company, Heavy Tank Battalion 502
Herschweiler-Pettersheim, February 2004

AUTHOR'S NOTE: Otto Carius was born in Zweibrücken, Germany, on 27 May 1922. He enlisted in 1940 and saw his first combat during Operation BARBAROSSA as a crewman aboard a Czech-made Panzer 38(t) with the 20th Panzer Division's Panzer Regiment 21. Following about a year of combat against the Soviets in the central sector of the Eastern Front, Carius attended an officer candidate course in Germany and was commissioned a lieutenant in the Panzer branch. He was assigned to Heavy Tank Battalion 502 in April 1943, and deployed with the unit to combat in the vicinity of Leningrad. Over the next 14 months, his unit fought mostly defensive actions, ultimately withdrawing to the Narva Pocket before being transferred to the Dünaburg (Daugavpils, Latvia) sector. There, Oberleutnant Carius and his men participated in several spectacular tank duels; subse-

Otto Carius

quently, he was awarded the Oakleaves to the Knight's Cross of the Iron Cross.

In August 1944, Carius was transferred to the armor center at Paderborn to assume command of a company in Heavy Tank Destroyer Battalion 512. This unit, equipped with the heaviest armored vehicle to ever see combat (even to this day, in 2004!), the Jagdtiger *("Hunting Tiger"), later conducted defensive operations along the Rhine in March and April 1945, before capitulating to the Americans.*

During his wartime service, Otto Carius earned the Wounds Badge in Gold; the Armored Combat Badge in Silver (for 100 engagements); the Iron Cross, 1st and 2nd Classes; and the Knight's Cross of the Iron Cross with Oakleaves. Since the war, he has pursued a career as a pharmacist, and continues in this profession even at the time of this book's publication.

Chapter 1

Introduction to
Heavy Tank Battalions

Armored units are not intended for mopping up. They constitute a
sledgehammer for striking at decisive points.[1]
Militärwochenblatt, 11 November 1936

The only instrument of armored warfare which German commanders
regarded as qualitatively different from the rest was the Mark VI Tiger,
which was not allotted to divisions but organized in independent battalions, kept under central control, and committed to crucial offensive
and counteroffensive missions.[2]
John Keegan, *The Second World War*

German Tiger and King Tiger tanks are legendary armored fighting vehicles.
They were arguably the most feared weapon developed by the Germans during World War II. Many of the commanders and crewmen who fought from
these tanks accomplished extraordinary feats. This book analyzes the combat
effectiveness of German heavy tank battalions (*schwere Panzer-Abteilungen*)
Although they were rarely used in the role for which they were originally conceived, namely breaking through prepared enemy defenses, these units effectively destroyed enemy tanks, whether employed in offensive or defensive tactical situations. Results varied between different battalions, however, and German doctrine and tactical decisionmaking sometimes limited these heavy tank
battalions' effectiveness. The analysis includes the performance of doctrinal
and assigned missions from both the Western and Eastern Fronts, and it considers the impacts of doctrine, force structure, equipment, leadership, and
personnel.

Although there is a great wealth of information available on many aspects
of the heavy tank battalions, no literature to date exists to answer whether
these units were viable forces that achieved the doctrinal mission for which
they were conceived. Also, there has been no inquiry into whether they were
able to effectively accomplish the missions assigned to them while the German
Army was on the defensive—counterattacking, reinforcing other units in the
defense, or as a mobile reserve. This book fills that void by examining unit histories and engagements from all perspectives while analyzing the different

3

organizations developed, types of equipment employed, and the missions of the heavy tank battalions.

Background

After World War I, the best minds of the major armies of the world wrestled with solutions for avoiding the linear, stalemated, deadly, positional combat that characterized World War I. With the construction of the Maginot Line through the late 1930s, the French actually *embraced* the idea of fighting from fixed, linear positions, but the objective of other major armies was to avoid the massive attrition introduced by trenches, high explosive shells, and machine guns by restoring maneuver to war. A mechanism by which enemy defenses could be penetrated had to be found. Many military theorists tried to conceive a doctrine to rupture and exploit the enemy defensive line. The military thinkers of Great Britain, Germany, and the Soviet Union all published material in their professional military journals that put forth the idea of attacking in waves of tanks. In these theories, the lead wave consisted of the "heavy" tanks, while the follow-on waves included lighter, faster, armored vehicles to exploit the breach made by the first wave. Although the German Army planned for heavy tanks and development of the *Durchbruchswagen* (breakthrough tank) began in 1937, no heavy tanks were fielded before World War II began.[3]

The German Army ultimately developed their own concept of mobile warfare that was very successful during the first part of World War II. Their success in Poland, France, and during the first year in Russia was generally the product of envelopment or even encirclement, which precluded the necessity of having to "break through" a continuous line of fortified defensive positions. Thus, the Germans did not suffer from the absence of heavy tanks in their armored forces. The German Army's encounters with the Soviet T-34 medium and KV-1 heavy tanks during their advances near the end of 1941, however, reinvigorated the development of their dormant heavy tank program.

The German Army created the first two heavy tank companies on 16 February 1942 and assigned them to the first heavy tank battalion, officially created on 10 May 1942.[4] These heavy tank battalions were not assigned to panzer divisions; rather, they were used as army-level units (*Heerestruppen*). From this point forward, the *Oberkommando des Heeres* (Army High Command, hereafter referred to as *OKH*) allocated these units to army groups whose commanding generals were free to subordinate them further to armies, corps, or even to divisions for tactical employment. Before the war was over, the Army fielded 11 and the *Waffen-SS* fielded three heavy tank battalions.

These organizations had several different Tables of Organization, but were always centered around either the Tiger or the King Tiger (also known as the Tiger II or Royal Tiger) tank.[5] In continual service from 16 September 1942, they saw their first action against the Russians near Leningrad, and fought until the end of the war.[6] During this time, they fought in almost every region of the European theater against Russians, Americans, and British forces.

Historical Literature

There are many books available that discuss the technical characteristics of Tiger and King Tiger tanks. There is also a vast amount of literature about many of the soldiers who attained incredibly high kill totals while commanding these tanks. Very little, however, is written about the actual units in which these tanks and individuals operated. The biggest shortcoming is in literature concerning the effectiveness of the heavy tank battalions. At best, there are several books covering the combat histories of heavy tank battalions using combat reports of these units. These books do not attempt to analyze any of these combat actions and do not include conclusions on their role in combat.

Although there are weaknesses in the literature of heavy tank battalions, there are some works that provide useful insights. Two of these accounts are by Generaloberst Heinz W. Guderian. Guderian played a very important role in the development of armored doctrine before World War II as a leading theorist and as the *Chef der Schnellen Truppen* (Chief of Fast Troops, as the Germans called their motorized and mechanized forces in general). During the latter half of the war, he served as *Generalinspekteur der Panzertruppen* (Inspector General of Armored Forces). Any exploration of Germany's doctrinal development and use of armored forces is deficient without including Guderian's two books. His first book, *Achtung-Panzer! The Development of Armoured Forces, Their Tactics, and Operational Potential* provides a background on doctrine prior to World War II. His second book, *Panzer Leader,* was written after the war and provides information concerning changes in the doctrine and employment during World War II. Because *Achtung-Panzer!* was written prior to the development and fielding of any heavy tank battalions, it contains no specific analysis of these units, but it does provide the foundation for defining the doctrinal role envisioned for heavy tank battalions. *Panzer Leader* contains several reflections on the correct employment of heavy tank battalions, but its insights focus on the initial fielding of the heavy tank battalions prior to the battle of Kursk.

In terms of combat histories of the heavy tank battalions, Wolfgang Schneider's *Tigers in Combat I* and *Tigers in Combat II* are good sources of information obtained from personal interviews, unit histories, and battle reports. The first book covers the ten separate Army heavy tank battalions and the second book covers the *Waffen-SS* battalions and the heavy tank battalion of Panzer-Grenadier Division *Grossdeutschland*, and other units that included a heavy tank company. These books provide brief overviews of these units' equipment, organization, camouflage, and vehicle markings. The main source of combat history comes in the form of a sentence or paragraph describing each unit's actions on a particular date, similar to a daily log or diary. The type and amount of information provided varies from unit to unit and from time period to time period. Although providing a great deal of data, Schneider's books do not include an analysis of heavy tank battalion combat actions. The daily log entries, however, do contain information on the changes in the battalion's combat power and the operational status of its Tigers. His books provide a table for each unit, detailing the date and cause of each Tiger lost. They also contain information on the number of enemy tanks and equipment destroyed during stated time periods so that an evaluation of tank kills and losses can be ascertained through the unit's log. These books are very helpful starting places for a study of heavy tank battalions' combat effectiveness.

Three unit-specific heavy tank battalion combat histories provide combat details, but little analysis. They are *The Combat History of schwere Panzer-Abteilung 503*, *The Combat History of schwere Panzer-Abteilung 507*, and *The Combat History of schwere Panzer-Abteilung 508*, and they recount the respective unit histories from the officers and soldiers that served in these units. These books, published in 2000, 2001, and 2003 respectively by J. J. Fedorowicz Publishing, contain personal accounts of these units in combat from a variety of sources, from common mechanics to company and battalion commanders. Together these units were involved in important battles at Kursk; Normandy; Italy; in the attempt to relieve the encircled German forces in Cherkassy; and in Operation BAGRATION. As a compilation of logs, diaries, and personal accounts, these books are very valuable for gaining insights into the combat actions of the heavy tank battalions, but they do not attempt to analyze the effectiveness of the units. Some of the diary entries are from the battalion and company commanders and include records of losses and casualties inflicted on the enemy on a daily basis, along with narrative accounts of the action. These expand, clarify, and add personal color to the information included in Schneider's books.

There are many books that address technical aspects of the Tiger and King Tiger tanks. The single most important author in English on Tiger tanks in general is Thomas L. Jentz. Based purely on primary sources, his books *Germany's Tiger Tanks, D. W. to Tiger I,* and *Germany's Tiger Tanks, VK45.02 to Tiger II*, provide a great deal of information regarding the design, production, and modifications of the Tiger and King Tiger.

Jentz has also written a two-volume work on armored forces titled *Panzertruppen: The Complete Guide to the Creation and Combat Employment of Germany's Tank Force*. This book is valuable because it draws on many other sources and participants in the development of the heavy tank battalions. It is especially helpful in tying together the doctrinal changes in the German Army with the technical development of the heavy tank and the Tiger program. This book contains heavy tank battalion combat reports that provide wartime recommendations for improving the doctrine, organization, and equipment associated with these units.

By far, the single most valuable work on this subject is yet another book by Jentz. *Germany's Tiger Tanks, Tiger I and II: Combat Tactics*, concentrates on the tactical application of Tigers and uses original accounts in the form of after-action reports. As he states in his introduction, "these original after-action reports are very valuable in obtaining a true picture of applied tactics. As written, they would have had to meet the tough test of peer acceptance."[7] Because they were written shortly after the events occurred, they also have the advantage of being recorded before memories became clouded by time. Most of the German reports appear to have been written with the motive of initiating improvements to the Tiger tanks themselves or of changing the tactics employed by heavy tank units. As useful as this book is in researching the heavy tank battalions, it still only provides a limited foundation to evaluate the units' performance and does not attempt to analyze combat effectiveness in a comprehensive manner. Finally, as the title of the book suggests, the primary focus is on the employment of units below battalion level, although there is some useful information on battalion tactics.

Looking at the heavy tanks from the opponent's view, David Fletcher's *Tiger! The Tiger Tank: A British View* provides excellent insight into the British perspective of the Tiger tank as a technical piece of equipment. More detail about the thoughts of British commanders during World War II regarding the heavy tank battalions, their doctrine, and effectiveness would have been useful, but may not have been available.

Overcoming Misperceptions

A thorough study of various battles and engagements from Allied unit histories and published historical accounts reveals strong biases within the Allied forces. Among the Allied armies, units continually reported that Tiger tanks were in their sector or that they had destroyed Tiger tanks. A casual reading of many Allied accounts during the battle of the Bulge, for example, would indicate that at least half of the German tanks employed there were Tigers. Actually, no more than 136 Tigers were involved, with the vast majority of

German tanks in the battle being Panthers and Panzer IVs.[8] The Soviet reports also have to be treated with the same skepticism in some instances. Soviet propaganda, for example, claimed that 700 Tigers were destroyed during the battle of Kursk. This number is five times more than the actual number engaged in the fighting.[9]

Generally, this phenomenon should be attributed to the formidable reputation of the Tiger among its adversaries, and sort of parallel to the insistence by many American infantrymen that they were being continuously shelled by "88s," when, in fact, they were almost always being bombarded by the 105mm and 150mm howitzers standard to a German divisional artillery regiment. Just as the deadly 88mm artillery piece was the most dreaded German gun, so also was the Tiger the most feared—and therefore, most often misidentified—German tank.

To obtain the most accurate picture possible, this study uses many different sources. Tank kills reported by the heavy tank battalions against the British and U.S. were verified in specific engagements from a variety of records, including unit histories, after-action reports, diaries and other personal accounts. Not surprisingly, Soviet tank losses were often omitted in their unit histories and in personal accounts, making an accurate count much more difficult to obtain. Several western sources provide some analysis of Soviet tank losses in several battles and were used to evaluate German claims.

A source of confusion in reporting tank losses and kills is the definition of what constitutes destruction of a tank. Tanks of World War II, especially the Tiger, were robust and resilient and could be repaired and put back into action if they were recovered and brought back to a maintenance unit. One side may have claimed the destruction of an enemy tank, but in reality, that tank was repaired and returned to service.

The German heavy tank battalions submitted regular reports on Tigers destroyed and also on the quantity that were operational. An unserviceable tank required the unit to make a report, identifying the chassis number, a survey of the damage, and an estimate of the time needed for the repairs.[10] A second report was made at a higher level, indicating the number of tanks in working order for the unit, and the number of tanks under repair.[11] In all cases, clarity and accuracy were required. This makes obtaining an accurate accounting of the number of German tanks destroyed easier with one notable exception. The records for the King Tiger equipped units, especially those fighting the Russians, are incomplete because the unit war diaries and other unit records were either destroyed or captured by the Soviets.[12]

The accuracy of German reporting, in terms of Tiger losses, can be verified literally almost down to the last vehicle against American and British forces. This is in part from the outstanding historical coverage by both the American and British military establishments at many different levels, from small unit journals to official army level reports. Included in these are a number of battle studies, including the "official histories," which received exhaustive coverage after the war, incorporating documents and sources from all sides. Another reason is that there were never more than three heavy tank battalions committed against American and British forces at any one time, thereby reducing the overall number of Tigers employed against them.[13] In other words, when American and British forces destroyed a Tiger, it was a noteworthy event.

The result is that, at least in the West, the German daily strength reports—and therefore losses—can be verified with a relatively high degree of accuracy. Usually, in cases where a conflict exists, records and a small amount of research will reveal the truth. For example, on 17 December 1944, in the Ardennes, a King Tiger of SS-Heavy Tank Battalion 501 was immobilized and subsequently abandoned as a result of a strike by P-47 "Thunderbolt" fighter bombers of IX Tactical Air Command.[14] Later, as German forces withdrew, the commander of an American Sherman from the 740th Tank Battalion reported destroying it. Although both forces justifiably claimed the King Tiger, the end result was still only one loss for the Germans.

Given the credibility of German reporting in the West, there is no reason to doubt the veracity of German Tiger losses in the east. Caution must be exercised, however, in assessing the number of tanks operational. As a member of the 1st Panzer Division stated:

> I must honestly confess that since 1942 we always reported we had 15–20 percent less than our actual combat-ready strength available to be put into action. . . . Any commanding general of any panzer division at that time was very happy if he could assemble 20 or 25 tanks. For that reason, as we well knew, if he reported we had 60 tanks, we were sure that on the next day, as we defended on our own front line 40 kilometers wide, we would have only 20 tanks because the high command would take them away to where the more critical points were.[15]

Due to extended frontages and heavy demand from higher echelons, it is logical and possible that some heavy tank battalions employed in the East also followed this unofficial practice of reporting fewer vehicles operational than were actually available. Unit commanders, however, wanted replacement vehicles as soon as possible and a replacement vehicle could only be requested if a vehicle was lost, not just inoperable, so it is highly likely that the heavy tank battalions would have been meticulously accurate in reporting the loss of any Tigers. The primary obstacle to overcome in researching engagements in the East against Soviet forces is confirming the kills made by Tigers.

While their accounts and reporting may indeed be accurate for the most part, German sources normally fail to provide a contextual background for the account, especially at the operational level of war. If an opponent's actions are included in the German account at all, it is usually cursory, superficial, focused at the tactical level, and does little to help explain the reasons behind German actions that resulted in failure or success.[16] German sources may simply state, for example, that a large number of Tigers were destroyed by their own crews to avoid capture after they had broken down. They fail to include in their account how or why those Tigers were threatened with capture and what action their opponents had taken to put those vehicles in an untenable position. Rather than being an impediment that cannot be overcome, however, the lack of context in German accounts simply reinforces the necessity of using sources from as many different perspectives as possible.

Measures of Effectiveness and Organization of Book

This book is organized into seven chapters. This first chapter provides an outline, an overview of the central theses, and a general background. Chapter 2 outlines the development of heavy tank battalions. This overview incorporates doctrine, organization, equipment, personnel, and tactics to assist the reader in understanding the doctrinal role of heavy tank battalions and the missions they were to be assigned.

Chapters 3 through 6 are historical examples and analyses of heavy tank battalions in combat. Chapter 3 examines the heavy tank battalions from their creation and initial combat actions in 1942 until the end of the Battle of Kursk. Chapter 4 continues to the summer of 1944. The Battle of Kursk in July 1943 marked a transitional turning point in the development and organizational composition of the heavy tank battalions. It was also the point after which the German Army was overwhelmingly engaged in the defensive at the operational level. Because heavy tank battalion employment in Italy is difficult to divide into distinct periods, this chapter also includes analysis of heavy tank battalions' combat in Italy throughout the war. Chapters 5 and 6 examine heavy tank battalion employment during the final year of the war.

Chapter 7 offers an assessment of the effectiveness of Tiger tanks in action.

German doctrine placed great emphasis upon the heavy tanks' destruction of opposing tanks in both the offense and the defense. Because of this emphasis, the heavy tank battalions' effectiveness is partly measured throughout this study as the tank kill/loss ratios they produced.

Because circumstances may have precluded a tank-to-tank battle, a simple ratio of kills to losses does not completely define effectiveness; therefore, a secondary measure of effectiveness used is that of mission accomplishment, or in other words, whether the battalions accomplished their assigned missions. Where possible, direct accounts from veterans or after-action reports are used to determine the unit mission. In many instances there is no written historical record, thus making it extremely difficult or impossible to know exactly the mission of an individual battalion. Using the larger operational and tactical environment and opposing forces, logical deductions are made about the probable unit mission.

The Levels of Warfare
and Heavy Tank Battalions

During WWII, convention divided military endeavor into three levels of war. They were the tactical, operational, and strategic. The tactical level involves battles and engagements. The operational level links those battles and engagements into campaigns designed to contribute to the accomplishment of strategic goals and objectives.[17] World War II in the European Theater contains many examples of operational-level maneuvers that linked small unit actions together to accomplish the larger strategic objective. In World War II, the operational level usually incorporated large groups of units in broad or extensive maneuvers. Finally, the strategic level is the level of war in which theater, or even national, policy is established; direction is given; and goals and objectives are pursued. This level, in both the military and civilian sectors, should include and address the overall resources available and those required to accomplish the strategic goals.

The levels of warfare are important in discussing heavy tank battalions for a number of reasons. Heavy tank battalions engaged enemy forces and destroyed enemy tanks or lost Tigers at the tactical level. This is also primarily where their mission accomplishment can be judged.

This mission accomplishment must however, be taken in context. This context can often be found by discerning the situation at the operational level. As will be seen, heavy tank battalions must not be judged on their tactical value alone.

Chapter 2

Heavy Tank Battalion Overview

It is vital to establish the basic purpose of the tank forces. Are they intended to storm fortresses and permanent defensive positions, or to carry out operational envelopments and turning movements in the open field; to act at the tactical level, making breakthroughs on our own account, and checking enemy breakthroughs and envelopments; or will they be no more than armored machine-gun carriers?[1]

Heinz Guderian, *Achtung-Panzer!* 1937

Heinz W. Guderian is widely viewed as the principle architect of Germany's armored forces during the Third Reich and the main intellectual author of the military theory for their use.[2] His writings greatly influenced the German Army and Hitler's enablement of Guderian's vision of armored warfare allowed Germany to enjoy great success during the initial years of World War II.

Doctrine

German doctrine during World War II is difficult to define precisely. German doctrine, like the doctrine of the Americans, British, French, and Soviets, did not precisely define the differences between light, medium, and heavy tanks. As well as generally following a vague weight classification, these tanks were also defined in discussions and publications of the period using doctrinal roles and missions. Although these roles overlapped to a certain degree and changed depending upon the time period and country discussed, they followed a general pattern. This common—although far from universal—classification categorized light, medium, and heavy tanks based on their differing doctrinal roles and missions.

Light tanks were intended to conduct reconnaissance missions that required great mobility, but little armor protection or offensive lethality. Medium tanks were intended to be used for exploitation or pursuit missions. Because these tanks might come into contact with fleeing forces, it required more balance in terms of mobility, armor, and armament. Speed is essential during exploitation and pursuit operations, however, so these tanks required a high degree of mobility, with an emphasis upon speed, range, and mechanical reliability. The last tank type, the heavy, was intended for overcoming prepared enemy defenses. These tanks, supporting or supported by infantry and artillery, were to penetrate enemy defenses to allow medium tanks to pass through and exploit that breakthrough.[3] Many theorists thought it necessary to require tanks to be able to conduct missions normally associated with vehicles in the next category, up or down. For instance, light tanks could also participate with medium tanks during an exploitation operation. Medium tanks could theoretically fulfill the roles of, or assist, both light and heavy tanks.[4] The multi-role use of heavy tanks was problematic, however. Because of their heavy armor and consequent weight, they were slower than both medium and light tanks. This meant that it was very difficult for them to participate in any exploitation operation that required high speed and/or combat radius (the distance that a vehicle can normally operate without refueling).[5]

German doctrine during World War II was drawn from numerous sources, but elements of its total form can be traced to three primary areas. The first source was the official German field service regulation, *Die Truppenführung* (Troop Guidance). Authored by General Ludwig Beck, the Chief of the General Staff, 1935–38, it was published in 1933 and remained the primary tactical manual of the German Army in World War II.[6] The second source of German doctrinal thought prior to World War II came from professional journals, the pre-eminent one being the *Militär-Wochenblatt*. The final source of doctrine, especially armor employment relating to that doctrine, came from Heinz W. Guderian's *Achtung-Panzer!*

Die Truppenführung provided the leaders in the German Army and *Waffen-SS* with a coherent foundation for thinking about future battle. Although primarily focused on incorporating the traditional branches of infantry and artillery, it did include the evolving concepts of armored warfare and air support. The manual addressed both the offense and the defense, and aimed at fighting mobile, decentralized battles likely to occur on the modern battlefield of the 1930s and 1940s. In addressing the use of tanks, the manual did not differentiate between light, medium, or heavy tanks.

In offensive operations, the manual stated that "the frontal attack is the most difficult of execution, yet it is the most frequent."[7] This statement was naturally based upon the German experience with static warfare during World War I and therefore the manual went into a great deal of depth in discussing the frontal attack. At the foundation of the discussion is the idea of conducting a breakthrough or a penetration of the enemy's defenses to subsequently exploit. This exploitation would be in the form of either a pursuit of a retreating enemy or an enveloping attack.

In providing doctrinal guidance on the employment of tanks during the breakthrough attack, *Die Truppenführung* states:

Tanks and infantry that work together ordinarily shall have the same objectives, the hostile artillery. As a rule, tanks are employed where the decisive action is desired.[8]

This emphasized the importance of the enemy's artillery and stressed that tanks should strive toward a decisive objective, seen in most theorists' eyes as the artillery supporting the defense.

The job of coordinating all arms during the attack was the responsibility of the senior commander. The only exception to this was when tanks were specifically given the mission of supporting the infantry "to break down the enemy."[9] In this case, the tanks were to be directly under the command of the infantry commander. In other words, integration of armor, infantry, and artillery was done at high levels or, on an exceptional basis, was something to be accomplished by the infantry commander solely.

Defeat of the enemy's antitank defenses was addressed, and emphasis was made to break through as rapidly as possible to continue the progress of the attack. This implied that total elimination of the enemy defenses was not as important as the continuation of forward progress in penetrating the entire defensive system.

As a rule the advance develops into numerous small attack groups that are composed of infantry and artillery, and, according to needs, of tanks. These must quickly break through or push back the enemy. If possible, we push past hostile advanced positions to avoid delaying the advance.[10]

Defeat of enemy tank counterattacks was to be accomplished by antitank guns that were to follow closely behind the leading elements.[11] Additionally, artillery was to support the attack by preventing "the intervention of hostile reserves."[12] Close air support was incorporated into the overall breakthrough. *Die Truppenführung* stated that "attack aviation supports the tanks by attacking hostile defense weapons, artillery, and reserves."[13] These assets were also to warn friendly tanks of a possible enemy tank counterattack.

In terms of the defense, *Die Truppenführung* advocated defending in depth, incorporating infantry, artillery, and antitank weapons into the main defensive positions.[14] In defeating tanks, it states that "advanced positions are to be especially provided with heavy machine guns, tank defense weapons, and light [artillery] batteries."[15]

If a breakthrough or penetration was made in the defensive positions, the manual prescribed the conduct of two different levels of counterattacks, namely local and general counterattacks. The force for the former type of counterattack consisted of "elements and supporting weapons which are in proximity of the penetration."[16] They were to "endeavor by immediate local counterattack to hurl back the enemy before he has opportunity to establish himself."[17] Should the local counterattack fail, or in the event of a very large enemy penetration, the "higher commander decides whether a general counterattack will be made to restore the position or whether the main battle position is to be taken up further to the rear."[18] The total guidance for tanks in the defense was:

> Tanks are employed offensively. They are a decisive reserve in the hands of the commander, especially suitable for general counterattacks or for the engagement of hostile tanks. Ordinarily their assembly position is far to the rear, out of effective hostile artillery range. Direct observation of the battlefield is desired. The various employment possibilities are reconnoitered. In general, tanks are employed on orders of the higher commander, who controls the time and objective of the attack and the cooperation of other arms.[19]

Prior to Guderian publishing his ideas on armored warfare, other theorists from England, France, the United States, and the Soviet Union developed their own ideas about the future of warfare. Guderian admits that the books and articles of J. F. C. Fuller and Basil Liddell Hart interested him and provided inspiration.[20] The Soviet Union produced some of the best military theorists in Mikhail Tukhachevsky, V. K. Triandafillov, and Aleksandr A. Svechin. They formed large mechanized units in the Red Army and it is likely that some of their writings and theories were published in German.[21] German theorists borrowed Soviet concepts, and their ideas are evident in the evolution of German military thought on the use of armored forces. In France, the then-obscure Colonel Charles DeGaulle published numerous works on the subject, and American officers wrote thoughtful—if unrealizable, due to Depression Era budget constraints—articles about combined arms mobility tactics in U.S. Army professional military forums such as the *Infantry Journal*, the *Cavalry Journal*, and *Military Review*.

In Germany, military leaders and theorists debated the use of armored forces, and armored doctrine continually evolved prior to World War II. In 1929, one German author published an article in the *Militär-Wochenblatt* (Military Weekly) that concluded that the tank had three different missions. The first was as an infantry battering ram during a tactical breakthrough. Next, they were required to suppress the enemy's artillery, and finally they were to penetrate deeply to block approaches, and to complete a strategic breakthrough.[22]

The German Army Chief of Staff, Ludwig Beck, published a modernization plan in 1935 that outlined two different requirements for tanks: frontally assaulting an evenly-matched opponent and exploiting beyond the front line toward deep objectives.[23] Guderian realized that tanks or infantry alone could not overcome a well-prepared enemy defensive sector and published an article in 1936 that focused on the combination of infantry, artillery, air support, and armor in offensive operations.[24]

A similar idea of most theorists during the inter-war period was the use of tanks in waves, first to overcome the enemy defensive line; then to engage the enemy artillery and defeat enemy counterattacks; and finally to exploit the penetration by seizing deep objectives.[25] The terms used and the number of waves of tanks varied with the different authors, but the ideas for overcoming enemy defenses remained similar. A constant theme was that tanks must be concentrated and that each wave must have a special, well-defined mission. The tasks associated with the first wave necessitated attacking under fire from artillery and antitank guns as well as being able to defeat enemy armored counterattacks. Heavy tanks were to comprise the first wave and follow on waves consisted of medium and light tanks.

In 1937, Guderian, in *Achtung-Panzer!,* detailed the tactics and concepts of the employment and use of tanks in a future war. It was based upon historical analysis of World War I employment and modern weapons capabilities, and was the product of a long evolution of thought that relied heavily on the work of previous armor theorists. Although it was not originally intended to serve as a tactical manual, it was widely read in the German Army and remained the primary and preeminent reference for employment of armored forces in the German military until the end of the war.[26]

In it, Guderian established the principles of concentration applicable to all tanks regardless of size or mission. These principles stated that tank forces must be concentrated and "deployed *en masse* in both breadth and depth."[27] He stated that "concentration of the available armored forces will always be more effective than dispersing them, irrespective of whether we are talking about a defensive or an offensive posture; a breakthrough or an envelopment; a pursuit or a counterattack."[28]

When discussing heavy tanks, Guderian was prophetic in writing that "there will never be many heavy tanks, and they will be used either independently or within the structure of the tank forces, according to the mission. They represent an extremely dangerous threat and are not to be underestimated."[29]

Guderian included a whole chapter in his book illustrating how he envisioned conducting a breakthrough of an enemy position with armored forces. He emphasized the incorporation of all arms throughout the breakthrough.

Of primary importance in assisting the heavy tanks were the engineers because they needed to locate and clear mines and other obstacles so that the tanks were not disabled or unduly delayed. The first adversaries that the heavy tanks had to defeat were the antitank guns in the defensive line. Guderian wrote that they could be defeated by direct fire; suppressed with artillery or machine gun fire; or blinded by smoke.[30]

The next goal of the heavy tank forces was the enemy's artillery, but Guderian theorized that the penetration of the infantry and antitank-gun defense would force the enemy to commit his own tanks.[31] In stressing the importance of the tank battle, Guderian wrote:

> The tank's most dangerous enemy is another tank. If we are unable to defeat the enemy armor, the breakthrough has as good as failed, for our infantry and artillery will be unable to make further progress. Everything comes down to delaying the intervention of the enemy antitank reserves and tanks, and getting in fast and deep into the zone of the hostile command centers and reserves with our own effective tank forces—and by "effective" we mean forces that are capable of waging a tank battle.[32]

The lead tanks that were tasked to complete this tactical breakthrough had to overcome a great deal of resistance, and Guderian theorized that the main weapon on the ground for this mission was the heavy tank. He stressed that the most important priority of the entire breakthrough battle was that of defeating the tank reserves.[33] Guderian wrote that "if we fail to beat down the enemy tank defenses and defeat the enemy tanks, the breakthrough has failed, even if we manage to wreak some destruction in the infantry battle zone."[34]

During the war, the German concepts behind this doctrine did not change drastically. Albert Kesselring, former supreme commander of Axis forces in Italy, and Max Simon, one-time commanding general of the 16th SS-Panzer-Grenadier Division and XIII SS-Corps, wrote in 1952 that tanks attacked in several waves, with the distance between waves dependent upon the terrain and enemy fire.[35] They stated:

> The heavy tanks form the core of the spearhead and their main objective is the enemy tanks and antitank guns that can be eliminated early by using the greater range and larger-caliber gun of the heavy tanks. The mission of the first wave is to penetrate into the enemy lines as deeply as possible while the second wave enlarges the penetration, never losing sight of the first wave in order to provide fire protection to that wave.[36]

In clearly defining the importance of penetrating to engage and defeat the enemy armor, they stated, "It is not the mission of the tanks to entirely eliminate enemy pockets of resistance. That is the mission of the panzergrenadiers."

(Panzergrenadiers could be motorized infantry, borne in trucks, or armored infantry, carried in armored halftracks, depending on the organization to which they belonged.)."[37]

German doctrine during this period focused almost exclusively on the offensive. The defensive implications evident from the examples of the breakthrough battle are that armor formations in the defense are to be held back to defeat any penetrations by enemy armored formations.

Albert Kesselring and Max Simon also wrote one paragraph in their manual on the employment of armored forces in the defense. They stated that armored units "are used for defensive purposes only in exceptional cases."[38] Their mission consisted of being at the disposal of the mobile reserve of the higher command level to smash enemy breakthroughs. These counterattacks were governed by the general attack principles. What those specific attack principles were, they did not specify. One can assume that one of the underlying principles they had in mind was the employment of tanks en masse, attacking quickly to defeat that breakthrough. They added that crews and vehicles must always be ready for action, that all counterattack routes must be reconnoitered, marked and maintained, and that the leaders of armored forces must be fully aware of the situation at the front.[39]

Organization

In a memo dated 24 November 1938, the Commander-in-Chief of the Army, General Walther von Brauchitsch, presented guidelines establishing a heavy tank company and assigning one to each panzer brigade.[40] Inexplicably, in February 1939 when the German Army General Staff outlined its plans for reorganization from light panzer divisions and panzer brigades to panzer divisions, it eliminated the heavy tank company authorization from the new panzer regiment organization.[41] In a special reorganization, the Army General Staff added a medium tank company to the panzer regiment organization in September 1939.[42] It was this panzer regiment and division organization that fought and won in Poland, France, and during the early stages in the Soviet Union.

Lacking a true heavy tank, the Germans used the Panzer IV with a low-velocity 75mm main gun to fulfill the heavy tank role within these medium tank companies through Poland, France, and during Operation BARBAROSSA in June 1941.[43] Until the German armored forces encountered Soviet heavy tanks, such as the KV I, KV II, and the T-34/76, the Panzer IV was sufficiently well armored and armed to meet the tactical demands of a heavy tank.[44] The appearance of the T-34/76 specifically, greatly influenced and decisively accelerated German heavy tank construction. The German Army needed a heavy tank with more armor and a larger main gun capable of penetrating the sloped armor of the T-34.

While the Army ordnance department was developing the heavy tank, the Army General Staff made plans to field heavy tank companies when production began. Initially, the plan for the heavy tank company included three platoons, each with three Tigers, for a company total of nine heavy tanks.[45] Until the spring of 1942, this plan included the heavy tank companies in the current panzer regiment organization within panzer divisions, although a formal change to the organization was not made.

After the automotive design office of the Army ordnance department finalized the Tiger and estimated production figures, the Army General Staff realized that the Tiger could never be produced in sufficient quantity to replace the Panzer IV on a one-for-one basis. The new tank also lacked the tactical mobility to be included in the panzer divisions.[46] It was difficult to find a suitable place for the Tiger in the panzer divisions, and as a scarce resource, the Army General Staff decided to consolidate the available Tigers in independent heavy tank battalions and employ them where they were needed most.[47] They thought that in so doing, they could be most economically employed directly under the command of an army or corps headquarters.[48]

On 16 February 1942, the Army General Staff created the first two heavy tank companies and subsequently assigned them to the Heavy Tank Battalion 501. The first three heavy tank battalions, Heavy Tank Battalions 501, 502, and 503, were created in May 1942.[49]

These units organized themselves based upon the contemporary wartime organizational table (in German, *die Kriegsstärkenachweisung,* or *K.St.N.*).[50] This table called for nine heavy tanks per company, consisting of three platoons with three tanks each. The heavy tank battalions received new guidance via an Army bulletin on 21 August 1942 to organize along the lines set forth in a new table of organization (T/O). The new heavy tank companies organized themselves in accordance with T/O 1176d, dated 15 August 1942.[51] This company organization was known as "Heavy Tank Company D" (hereafter referred to as the Company Organization D) (see figure 1). The primary difference between this organization and previous heavy tank companies was that this organization authorized a mix of heavy and light tanks, with Tigers and Panzer IIIs—which were then the standard German medium tank—being integrated within each platoon of the company.

This version of the heavy tank company lasted until the General Staff published a new T/O in May 1943. By that time, the German Army had equipped and fielded five heavy tank battalions, with Heavy Tank Battalions 504 and 505 being created in December 1942 and January 1943, respectively.[52]

The leaders of these battalions experimented and used almost every variation of Company Organization D. Some companies changed their

Figure 1. Heavy Tank Company, *K.St.N.* 1176d Dated 15 August 1942.
Source: Jentz, *Tiger I and II,* 25–26.

organization internally to form two light and two heavy platoons.[53] Sometimes, commanders organized their platoons so that each possessed a light section and a heavy section, while some had their sections within platoons integrated with a Panzer III and a Tiger.[54]

These internal reorganizations focused on finding the best combination and organization to accomplish the missions assigned. All echelons of command granted great latitude to experiment to find a combination of vehicles that worked best. Occasionally, some companies within the same battalion and some platoons within the same company were organized differently.

The purpose of mixing platoons and sections with Panzer IIIs and Tigers was for the medium tanks to provide the heavy tanks with close support against infantry and assist in destroying antitank guns threatening the Tigers.[55] The T/O did not specify which model of Panzer III was authorized for the heavy tank companies.

The heavy tank battalion was authorized three heavy tank companies, but because of a shortage of Tigers, no battalion ever fielded a third company of the Company Organization D in combat. A headquarters company and a maintenance company, along with the two heavy tank companies, completed the total organizational structure of the heavy tank battalion. The headquarters company was organized in accordance with T/O 1150d, dated 15 August 1942, thus keeping the "D" designation to the overall heavy tank battalion organization (see figure 2).[56]

The battalion "light platoon" was subordinated to the headquarters company, but presumably worked directly for the battalion commander during combat. The T/O for these platoons also failed to specify which model of Panzer III was authorized. This platoon could be used to reinforce the tank companies against infantry attacks or could be used to screen the battalion's flank.

The focus on finding a mixture of vehicles and an organization that worked best seems to have continued at the battalion level when using the light platoon. Three of the first four battalions fielded, namely Heavy Tank Battalions

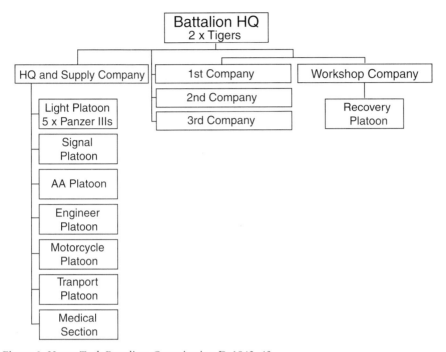

Figure 2. Heavy Tank Battalion, Organization D, 1942–43.
Sources: See Gudgin, *Tiger Tanks,* 92; Jentz, *Tiger I and II,* 24–25; Schneider, *Tigers in Combat I,* 79, 147, 228.
Note: According to Jentz, the T/O authorized only five Panzer IIIs in the light platoon; it appears, however, that the light platoons were issued ten Panzer IIIs in every one of the first three heavy tank battalions.

501, 502, and 504, retained the light platoon under the control of the battalion as it was originally intended.[57] Heavy Tank Battalion 503 formed a battalion light platoon consisting of five Panzer IIIs. The remainder of Heavy Tank Battalion 503's Panzer IIIs were allocated to the heavy tank companies, allowing each company to form a "heavy" platoon of three Tigers and one Panzer III, as well as a light platoon.[58]

The first five battalions created were fielded under the Battalion Organization D. These battalions fought in Tunisia against British and American forces, as well as in the Caucasus and in the vicinity of Leningrad against Soviet forces. These units' after-action reports indicated that the mix of medium and heavy tanks allowed these battalions a higher degree of flexibility. These reports also stated that the Panzer III did not have sufficient armor to conduct offensive missions against prepared defensive positions with the Tiger.

On 5 March 1943, the General Staff issued a new T/O for the heavy tank company and the heavy tank battalion. This new organization, T/O 1176e, formed a heavy tank company of 14 tanks, all Tigers (see figures 3 and 4). The new organizational structure reduced the number of platoons within each company from four to three, and maintained the number of tank companies authorized within the battalion at three.

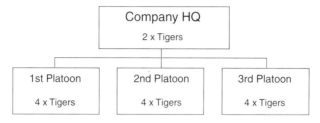

Figure 3. Heavy Tank Company, *K.St.N.* 1176e, Dated 5 March 1943. Source: Jentz, *Tiger I and II,* 26.

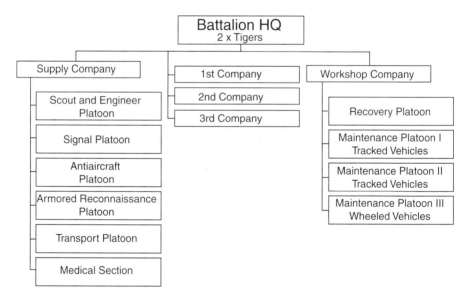

Figure 4. Heavy Tank Battalion, Organization E, 5 March 1943.
Note: There are several different versions of the battalion organization. This is probably due to the fact that when one of the sub-units changed its T/O, the overall battalion would change also. Numerous small changes were made to the elements of the battalion within the head-quarters company and the supply company, creating different battalion T/Os. This makes it extremely difficult to identify a single battalion organization. Also, different pieces of equipment were issued to different battalions as they became available. For example, Heavy Tank Battalion SS-Heavy Tank Battalion 501's AA Platoon was issued with the *Wirbelwind* ("Whirlwind") fully-tracked antiaircraft gun in lieu of the unarmored, half-tracked Sd.Kfz. 7/1. This was developed from Wolfgang Schneider's *Tigers in Combat 1,* Thomas L. Jentz's *Tiger I and II,* and Peter Gudgin's *The Tiger Tanks.*

The Army General Staff planned to field all three authorized tank companies, so the workshop and headquarters companies separated and increased in size. The workshop company increased to three maintenance platoons and a recovery platoon. The new battalion organization also did away with the light tank platoon within the battalion, but they gained an abundance of reconnaissance assets in return. This new organization added an armored reconnaissance platoon, as well as a scout and engineer platoon. Mounted in armored halftracks, the primary mission of the armored reconnaissance platoon was to reconnoiter to find the enemy or to provide Tiger companies with early warning of enemy attacks. The scout and engineer platoon assisted the armored reconnaissance platoon in the mission, but was primarily intended to contribute to the tank companies' mobility. This former platoon was divided into four scout sections, each equipped with wheeled and tracked motorcycles (an example of the latter is on page 143)), and three engineer sections mounted in halftracks. This platoon was capable of classifying and reinforcing bridges and was reponsible for clearing mines and other obstacles.

With three heavy tank companies and the battalion headquarters element, the new Battalion Organization E authorized 45 Tiger tanks for a heavy tank battalion. This was possible because of increased production of the Tiger. When the first battalions were fielded, the peak monthly output goal was set at ten, but this was not met until August 1942. By March 1943, when the new heavy tank battalion organization was published, the monthly output had increased to over 75 per month and the new goal was increased to 125, even though this would not be met until over a year later.[59]

This increased Tiger production allowed the German armed forces not only to field fully their existing heavy tank battalions, but also to field additional ones. On 8 May 1943, Heavy Tank Battalion 506 was created using the new heavy tank battalion organization. Three of the first five battalions created changed to the Organization E shortly after the new T/O was published. Two of these, Heavy Tank Battalion 503 and 505, were almost complete by the time they fought in Operation ZITADELLE in July 1943. The third battalion, Heavy Tank Battalion 502, changed to Organization E by the end of June 1943. In September 1943, three more heavy tank battalions, Heavy Tank Battalions 507, 508, and 509, respectively, were created using this new organization. Also, during September 1943, the German Army reestablished Heavy Tank Battalions 501 and 504 as Organization E battalions because they had been destroyed, captured, or seriously reduced by combat losses.[60]

In the spring of 1943, the German Army created a heavy tank battalion for the elite Panzer-Grenadier Division *Grossdeutschland*.[61] This battalion has the distinction of being the only heavy tank battalion assigned permanently to a division.[62] The battalion was designated as the 3d Battalion of the division's panzer regiment. This battalion was organized under the Battalion

Organization E and theoretically had 45 Tigers assigned to it, but because this unit was in almost continual combat from the day that it was organized, it never reached its full strength.[63] The last heavy tank battalion created on 6 June 1944 was Heavy Tank Battalion 510. This unit immediately deployed to and fought on the Eastern Front.[64]

In addition to increasing the number of army heavy tank battalions, the Germans began organizing similar units in the *Waffen-SS* as well. These heavy tank battalions were developed from the heavy tank companies that were already formed and fighting with units like the *Leibstandarte, Das Reich,* and *Totenkopf.* On 22 October 1943, SS Heavy Tank Battalions 101 and 102 were created, but they were not fully fielded and combat capable until April and May 1944, respectively.[65] The third and last SS heavy tank battalion, 103, was created on 1 November 1943. Tiger production did not meet the requirements of the German military, so the battalion never reached full strength and only fought in the last battles of the war.[66]

All of the SS heavy tank battalions eventually changed their designations to 501, 502, and 503. This led to some confusion that also caused the army to change the unit numbers for their first three heavy tank battalions. The primary difference between the SS heavy tank battalions and the army ones was the fact that the SS units were assigned directly and permanently to a corps. For instance, SS-Heavy Tank Battalion 501 was assigned to I SS-Panzer Corps.[67]

The final variation of the army heavy tank battalions was the inclusion of Heavy Tank Battalion 503 into the Panzer Corps "*Feldherrnhalle*" on 19 December 1944.[68] This was similar to the *Waffen-SS* heavy tank battalions because the unit was an integrated and permanent part of the corps. Officially, the battalion's name changed to Heavy Tank Battalion "*Feldherrnhalle*" or (*FHH*), but because the name implied close association with the Nazi party, the unit maintained the designation "503" throughout the war.[69]

When the first King Tiger was produced in November 1943, the General Staff issued a new T/O for both the headquarters element and the heavy tank company. The only change to the previous version of Organization E was that heavy tank companies and battalions were now authorized either the Tiger or the King Tiger tank.[70]

Ten heavy tank battalions received some King Tigers before the war ended.[71] Of these, only six received the full complement of 45 that were authorized.[72] These units continually rotated to different theaters and most often received only a handful of King Tigers at a time. This meant that only a few heavy tank battalions ever fielded the full complement of 45 King Tigers at the same time.

Throughout the war, heavy tank battalions were organized and equipped using either the D or E organizational structures. The majority of the Army battalions, as Army level units, were employed by *OKH*. The *Waffen-SS* and several of the special army battalions were treated differently and permanently assigned to particular headquarters, in most cases to a corps. Units produced successful results using both organizations. Even though Organization D allowed the heavy tank battalion to accomplish a wider variety of missions and gave it more flexibility, the Army General Staff implemented Organization E for all heavy tank battalions. This organization, with pure Tiger companies, was more suited for fighting the breakthrough battle.

Equipment

The first mention of a tank weighing more than 30 tons is included in a doctrinal report produced in October 1935 by General Liese, Chief of the Army Ordnance Department. He established the requirements for this vehicle as having armor protection up to 20 millimeters thick and for it to be armed with a 75mm main gun, making it capable of defeating the French Char 2C, 3C, and D heavy tanks.[73]

The first requirement in meeting the design of the 30-ton tank was to build an engine capable of powering it. This initiated a program to build a high-performance engine with adequate horsepower for a vehicle of that weight. In consultation with the engine designer Dr. Karl Maybach, the automotive design office of the Army Ordnance Department determined that a 700-horsepower engine was required.[74]

The required vehicle changed names frequently. This was probably due to the continuing doctrinal debate about how to employ armor and what types of tanks should be used for the different missions. In November 1936, the Army Ordnance Department requested that Krupp create a conceptual design of the 30-ton tank. This tank was called an "Escort Tank (strengthened)," implying that it would escort lighter tanks. On 12 March 1937, the Army Ordnance Department officially changed the name to "Infantry Tank," which implied that it was intended to support the infantry. On 28 April 1937, the name changed again to *Durchbruchswagen* ("breakthrough vehicle") or "*D.W.*"[75] This name implied that a new tactical role was envisioned for these heavy tanks, namely that of breaching enemy defenses, in a fashion similar to Guderian's "first-wave" tanks.

The *D.W.* underwent many name changes, but was finally called the *Panzerkampfwagen* ("armored combat vehicle") VI, or "Tiger." Throughout all of the name and designation changes that followed, the designation "*D.W.*" was retained.[76] The entire heavy tank program soon came to be known as the "Tiger Program," however, and was assigned a high priority by the Army and Hitler.

One of the main reasons that the tank went through so many different designations was that the Army Ordnance Department kept submitting new requirements for increasing the caliber of the main gun. These requirements were given the highest priority on 26 May 1941. On that day, a meeting took place at the Berghof in Berchtesgaden between Hitler, representatives of the armaments industry, and military experts.[77] During this meeting, Hitler discussed the need for developing and fielding a heavy tank. He said, "The main point is to create vehicles which, first, have greater penetrative capabilities against enemy tanks; second, which are more strongly armored than previously; and third, which have a speed which does not fall short of 40 kilometers per hour."[78]

Several months later, Hitler reduced the last requirement in favor of increased armor and issued more specific guidance. He praised the penetrative capabilities of the antiaircraft gun known as the 88mm *Flak* 41 L/74.[79] He recommended that it be improved to enable it to penetrate 100 millimeters of armor at a range of 1,400 to 1,500 meters and be adopted as a *Kampfwagen Kanone* (combat vehicle gun) or "*KwK*." Hitler also demanded that the frontal armor of future tanks be 100 millimeters thick and the sides 60 millimeters thick.[80]

Two firms, Henschel and Porsche, competed for the design and development of the future heavy tank.[81] These new requirements forced the firms' respective design teams to increase their weight projections of the new heavy tank. Initially, Henschel focused on accommodating the 75mm gun in their design and Porsche directed their efforts on installing the 88mm main gun in theirs. Ultimately, both companies armed their tanks with the 88mm weapon. Because weight projections for the tank increased to 45 tons, they became known as VK 45.01(H) and VK 45.01(P), for Henschel and Porsche respectively.

Despite all the changing requirements and guidance, development was given a high priority after the invasion of Russia.[82] Ultimately, the automotive design office of the Army Ordnance Department awarded Henschel the contract for the chassis and Krupp the contract for the turret; together, these made the Tiger (see table 1).[83]

The Tiger was a heavy tank in both weight and in doctrinal purpose. It weighed 57 tons and was armed with the 88mm *KwK* 36 L/56 gun, capable of penetrating 100 millimeters of armor at 1,000 meters using a *Panzergranate* 39 (*PzGr.* 39) projectile. This was a specially-designed armor-piercing round with a tungsten steel cap over an explosive filling. It also had phosphorus paint on the nose, making its ballistic track visible for adjusting subsequent shots (shells with this feature are called "tracers").[84] Although not widely available, another round, the *PzGr.* 40 armor-piercing projectile, with tungsten steel

Weight:	56,000 kilograms (early models); 57,000 kilograms (late models)
Crew:	5 men
Engine:	Maybach HL 210 P 45 - 12 cylinder / 600 horsepower (early models)
	Maybach HL 230 P 45 - 12 cylinder / 700 horsepower (late models)
Fuel Capacity:	540 liters (in four fuel tanks)
Speed:	Road: 38 kilometers/hour; Cross-Country 10–20 kilometers/hour
Combat Radius:	Road: 195 kilometers; Average Terrain: 110 kilometers
Armament:	One 88mm *KwK* 36 L/56 Main Gun
	2 x 7.92mm MG 34s (early models)
	3 x 7.92mm MG 34/42s (late models)
Ammo:	88mm: 92 rounds; 7.92 mm: 4,500–5,700 rounds
Armor:	25mm–40mm (Top)
	80mm (Side and Rear)
	100mm–120mm (Front)

Table 1. *Panzerkampfwagen VI Type E* (Tiger) Specifications.
Source: Jentz and Doyle, *Tiger Tanks, D. W. to Tiger I*, 177–81.

core with tracer, could penetrate 110 millimeters of armor at 2,000 meters.[85] The Tiger's primary opponent at the time that it was fielded, the T-34/76, only had 45mm of frontal armor.[86] The KV-1, however, an infrequent but more formidable battlefield opponent, had over 75mm of frontal armor. Although the Tiger's main gun could penetrate both at ranges at which the Soviet tanks' 76mm weapons could not penetrate the Tiger's frontal armor, the performance of the L/56 with the commonly-available *PzGr.* 39 round still fell well short of Hitler's stated requirement.[87]

Even so, the 88mm *KwK* 36 L/56, combined with the armor of the Tiger, maintained a standoff advantage over virtually all of their opponents throughout the war. This meant that for Allied tanks' guns to penetrate a Tiger's armor, they had to maneuver to a range that was well within the ability of the Tiger's main gun to penetrate. This normally required movement—often, much of it devoid of cover or concealment, over hundreds of meters of terrain, during which the Allied vehicles were completely vulnerable to the Tigers' main armament.

Development of the King Tiger was a continuation of the heavy tank program. The King Tiger was developed because of the constant emphasis on armor penetration capabilities and the desire to mount the 88mm *Flak* 41 L/74 gun or something similar in a tank turret. Ultimately, Krupp developed the 88mm *Kwk* 43 L/71 gun that had similar penetrative capabilities to the 88mm *Flak* 41 L/74 gun.[88] This gun was mounted on a chassis developed by Henschel, and when mated together, produced the King Tiger (see tables 2 and

3). Various departments and companies throughout Germany designated and called the King Tiger tank many different things. Officially, the Army Ordnance department either called it the Tiger II or the *Panzerkampfwagen Tiger Ausführung* (Type) *B*, although a number of other titles were used by the Ordnance Department and other agencies throughout the war.[89]

Using a *PzGr.* 39-1 round, the King Tiger's 88mm gun could penetrate 148 millimeters of armor at a range of 1,500 meters (see table 3). Using the rare *PzGr.* 40/43 round, it was capable of penetrating 170 millimeters of armor at

Weight:	69,800 kilograms
Crew:	5 men
Engine:	Maybach HL 230 P 30 / 12-cylinder / 700 horsepower
Speed:	Road: 38 kilometers/hour; Cross-Country: 15–20 kilometers/hour
Range:	Road: 170 kilometers; Cross-Country: 120 kilometers
Fuel Capacity:	860 liters
Armament:	88mm *KwK* 43 L/71 and 3 x 7.92mm MG 34/42s; (1 x MG - hull); (1 x MG - coaxial); (1 x MG - cupola)
Ammo:	88mm: 84 rounds (68 stowed, 16 loose on turret floor); 7.92mm: 5,850 rounds
Armor:	40mm (Top); 80mm (Side and Rear); 150mm–180mm (Front)

Table 2. *Panzerkampfwagen VI Type B* (King Tiger) Specifications.
Source: Jentz and Doyle, *Tiger Tanks, VK45.02 to Tiger II,* 152–65.

	Tiger I: 88mm *KwK* 36 L/56			Tiger II: 88mm *KwK* 43 L/71	
Ammunition Type	*PzGr.*39	*PzGr.*40	Gr.39HL	*PzGr.*39/43	*PzGr.*40/43
Shell Weight (Kilograms)	10.2	7.3	7.65	10.2	7.3
Initial Velocity (meters/second)	773	930	600	1,000	1,130
Penetration Capability (millimeters)					
Range	*PzGr.*39	*PzGr.*40	Gr.39HL	*PzGr.*39/43	*PzGr.*40/43
100 meters	120	170	90	202	237
500 meters	110	155	90	185	217
1,000 meters	100	138	90	165	197
1,500 meters	91	122	90	148	170
2,000 meters	84	110	90	132	152

Table 3. Tiger and King Tiger Main Gun Comparison.
Source: Jentz, *Tiger I and II: Combat Tactics,* 9.
Note: Penetration capability was measured in millimeters of rolled homogeneous steel plates at a 30-degree angle of impact.

that same range.[90] This far exceeded the original requirement put forth by Hitler of penetrating one hundred millimeters of armor at a range of 1,400 to 1,500 meters.

The King Tiger incorporated design and material elements, such as the engine, from the Panther tank.[91] At almost 70 tons, the King Tiger was the heaviest tank of the war. (Although its tank destroyer variant, the *Jagdtiger,* or "Hunting Tiger," was, and remains today, the heaviest armored fighting vehicle to ever see action, at 79 tons.) The designs of the Tiger and King Tiger made them formidable battlefield opponents. From the published histories of both Allied and Axis forces, very few Allied tankers willingly engaged in direct combat with a Tiger or King Tiger. If there were other options, such as bypassing their positions or employing artillery or tactical aircraft against the Tigers, these options were used first.[92]

The Tiger and King Tiger also had a few weaknesses that became evident in the defensive withdrawals after 1943. The complexity of the designs required extensive maintenance to keep a Tiger or King Tiger operational. Their short radius of action was also a problem. These two weaknesses caused severe logistical and maintenance challenges which were particularly burdensome for Germany in the latter stages of the war.

Given Germany's strategic situation and its chronic and worsening petroleum shortages, the fuel required for the Tiger and King Tiger was a major design weakness. This is clearly evident when one considers that the Tiger had a maximum combat radius of 195 kilometers, but used 540 liters of fuel in the process. The King Tiger could manage only 170 kilometers on one 860-liter tank of gasoline. By comparison, a T-34/76 could travel 455 kilometers using only 480 liters of fuel.[93]

If a vehicle did break down, was damaged in combat, or became stuck, its weight and the absence of an adequate armored recovery vehicle created a challenge in maintaining a high operational rate. Generally, recovering a Tiger in the forward areas required towing it with at least one other Tiger, although this was officially forbidden. The workshop company did have 18-ton half-track tractors, but two of these were required to tow one Tiger.[94] Additionally, if being towed over hilly terrain, a trail vehicle at least as large as a Panzer III was required to stabilize the Tiger so it did not become unmanageable.[95] Beginning in 1944, heavy tank battalions started to receive some armored recovery vehicles, the *Bergepanther,* in addition to keeping the 18-ton half-track tractors. The difficulties in recovering a damaged Tiger in combat usually resulted in it being abandoned and destroyed by its crew. Ultimately, this was a devastating flaw that vastly reduced the number of Tigers available to the German armed forces.

Given that the Tiger battalions were assets of operational, if not strategic, value, they were shuffled from place to place—and even front to front—as a sort of "fire brigade." Long road marches inflicted serious mechanical problems, and caused the Tigers to devour huge quantities of precious gasoline. Thus, the preferred method of movement across any great distance was rail.

As the war went on, however, the German rail net was increasingly disrupted by Allied strategic and even tactical air attack. Rail movement of Tigers, however, involved even more difficulty, because special cars were required to transport Tigers.[96] This limited the Germans' ability to transfer heavy tank battalions from one sector to another without a great deal of lead time and careful coordination. Even with the special rail cars, Tigers and King Tigers had to remove their combat tracks and replace them with special, smaller ones to avoid excessive overhang when in transit. Beyond the great additional effort by the crewmen that it undoubtedly required, such a changeout process took even more time away from the Tiger's combat role. Also, it imparted a heavy logistical burden on the units, as they had to essentially maintain two sets of track for every vehicle to enable rail movement.

Another major weakness of both vehicles was the production costs in terms of labor, time, and material. A Tiger cost 800,000 *Reichsmarks* and required 300,000 man-hours to produce.[97] In an attempt to make those numbers more personal to the Tiger crewmen, the *Tiger Handbook,* a handbook produced by the Inspector of Panzer Troops, stated that it required one week of hard work from 6,000 people to produce one Tiger.[98] It also stated that the 800,000 *Reichsmarks* was equivalent to the weekly wages for 30,000 people.[99]

Because Germany essentially controlled or had access to almost the entire continent of Europe, these high resource costs probably were not detrimental in 1942 when Tiger production first began. The time required to produce a Tiger was an input that the Germans could not overcome, regardless of material resource availability. In the end, the combination of dwindling resources and a very labor-intensive tank, made mass production difficult. This meant that Germany produced only 1,348 Tigers and fewer than 500 King Tigers throughout World War II.[100]

Personnel

The personnel of the heavy tank battalions came from many sources. One of the primary sources was from experienced units that had fought in Poland, France, and Russia. Another source was from Heavy Panzer Replacement and Training Battalion 500, established at Paderborn, Germany in early 1942.[101] From the creation of Heavy Tank Battalion 503 on, some of the personnel required for these units came from remnants of tank units destroyed in combat or tank units that had rotated back to Germany or France to reequip.

In some instances, an existing battalion was ordered to convert itself into a heavy tank battalion. The 3d Battalion of Panzer Regiment 33, 9th Panzer Division, for example, became Heavy Tank Battalion 506 on 20 July 1943. This unit had been in combat in France and in Russia since the beginning of that campaign. Similarly, veteran elements of Panzer Regiment 4 from the 13th Panzer Division became Heavy Tank Battalion 507. The 1st Battalion, Panzer Regiment 29 from the 12th Panzer Division became Heavy Tank Battalion 508.[102] It had served in Russia since the summer of 1941.

Because of a shortage of Tigers, training was conducted mainly on Panzer IV tanks at Paderborn. The recruits assigned as replacements for heavy tank battalions were almost exclusively volunteers between 17 and 18 years old.[103]

The heavy tank battalions benefited from receiving veteran personnel, although replacements later in the war were young and inexperienced. The practice of converting entire combat-experienced units to new heavy tank battalions must have increased their morale, *esprit de corps,* and cohesion. Also, because the Tiger and King Tiger were very survivable vehicles, these battalions benefited by retaining those experienced crews, even in instances where the tank was lost.

Tactics

The first three heavy tank battalions received little guidance on how to accomplish their missions. They were given a copy of memorandum Number 87/42 from the *General der Schnellen Truppen* (General of "Fast," or Armored and Motorized Troops) dated 10 February 1942. This memorandum provided only general statements on capabilities, and did not provide details of tactical employment.

The Organization D companies and battalions, which integrated Panzer IIIs and Tigers into the same units, adhered to the following general tactical employment:

> In the attack, the role of the Tiger is that of supporting the lighter tanks by fire; the latter leads, followed by the heavier Tigers, and, when contact with the enemy armor is made, the screen of lighter tanks deploys outward to the flanks, leaving the Tigers to engage frontally. In defense, the Tiger is usually sited in a covered and defiladed position. The lighter tanks watch the flanks of positions occupied by the Tigers.[104]

The first battalions were generally left to experiment and report back to the Army General Staff to develop further doctrine. By 20 May 1943, the German Army published tactical manuals for the employment of the heavy tank company and the heavy tank battalion.[105] The manual for the training and employment of the heavy tank company established four primary capabilities or missions. They were: (1) to attack in the first wave against strong defenses, (2) to destroy heavy enemy tanks and other armored targets at long ranges, (3) to decisively defeat the enemy defenses, and (4) to break through positions reinforced by defensive works.[106]

The first half of the company manual contained sections on the organization of the heavy tank company, as well as basic gunnery principles of the Tiger tank. The second half contained sections on the platoon and company that established basic tactical guidance and outlined combat formations for both the platoon and the company. The four formations available to the platoon were the column, line, double column (or box), and wedge. The manual stated that the wedge formation was preferred during the attack.[107] The four formations available to the company were the column (with the three platoons in column abreast), the double column (with the platoons in two columns), wedge (with one platoon forward and two platoons following), and the broad wedge (with two platoons forward and one platoon following).[108] The manual stated that the broad wedge was the most useful attack formation and when the company deployed in this formation, it occupied an area 700 meters wide and 400 meters deep.[109]

The manual provided guidance to overcome the large fuel consumption of the Tiger by stating that "after leaving the assembly area it is often necessary to take a short halt within our own lines to again refuel to be able to totally exploit the small radius of action in enemy territory."[110]

The company manual placed emphasis on tank-versus-tank combat by including an entire subsection addressing it. It stated that "the most important task of the heavy tank company is the engagement of enemy tanks. It always has priority over every other assignment."[111] Emphasis on the offensive was evident by noting that the only reference that could even remotely be considered defensive in nature is the last sentence of the manual, which stated "knocked-out or immobilized enemy tanks are to be blown up during retreats."[112]

The manual for the heavy tank battalion was much shorter than the one for the heavy tank company. It contained only two sections covering (1) purposes, tasks, and organization; and (2) employment. Portions of the first section included doctrinal and tactical guidance such as:

The weapons and armor in combination with the high maneuverability make the Tiger the strongest combat weapon of the *Panzerwaffe* (Tank/

Armor branch). The Tiger battalion is therefore a powerful, decisive point weapon in the hands of the troop commander. Its strength lies in concentrated, ruthlessly-conducted attacks. Each dispersion reduces its striking power. Basic preparations for employment at decisive locations guarantee great success. Tiger battalions are Army Troops. They will be attached to other armored units in the decisive point battle to force a decision. They may not be used up too early from being employed for secondary tasks. They are especially suited for fighting against heavy enemy tank forces and must seek this battle. The destruction of enemy tanks creates the prerequisite for the successful accomplishment of the tasks assigned to our own lighter tanks. It is forbidden to assign the Tigers missions that can be accomplished by the lighter tanks or assault guns. In the same way, they are not to be entrusted with reconnaissance or security missions.[113]

The focus was on defeating enemy tanks, and the guidance was fairly clear that the heavy tank battalions should not be assigned missions that did not involve the destruction of enemy tank formations.

The entire heavy tank battalion manual was surprisingly general and did not focus solely on offensive missions like the heavy tank company manual did. Instead of purely offensive words like "breakthrough," the manual used terms like "decisive point" and "decisive action." An interesting comment, considering the Tiger's extremely limited radius of action, mechanical unreliability, and lack of mobility, was that "the Tiger is especially suitable for pursuit."[114] It continued by stating that "preplanned scouting and early stockpiling of fuel and ammunition are the prerequisites for this."[115]

Worthy of note for its absence was the lack of any section in the heavy tank battalion manual regarding formations for tactical movement of the entire battalion together. There were several paragraphs that discussed the employment of some of the separate platoons of the battalion. These statements were very general and did little to provide real guidance to the battalion commander; for example, "the armored reconnaissance platoon is to be sent in by the battalion commander for combat reconnaissance" was the total amount of guidance for employment of that platoon.[116] Similarly vague and obvious guidance of "timely deployment . . . and close cooperation with these (the engineer platoon) to determine and clear mines and obstacles are necessary" was included for the engineer platoon.[117]

The General Inspector of Armored Troops published an instruction pamphlet for army- and corps-level commanders to guide them in the correct employment of the heavy tank battalion. The pamphlet, organized into 25 points, stated vaguely that all guidance was based upon the characteristics of the Tiger and the purpose for which it was created. Optimistically, the pamphlet went on to say that "operations with this outstanding special weapon promise success if the following 25 points are observed."[118] Because the Tiger had a limited radius of action and required a great deal of maintenance, the pamphlet included the following guidance:

1. Close liaison of Tiger commander with the operationally-responsible command headquarters [is necessary].

Reason: Long-range disposition is indispensable to the Tiger units. All pre-operation preparations (reconnaissance and supply) require more time than with other weapons.

2. Issue orders for movement or action to Tiger commanders as early as possible.

Reason: As in 1.[119]

This pamphlet emphasized the importance of this unit in the breakthrough and it provided guidance to keep the heavy tank battalion informed of its mission. The pamphlet also discussed the concept of breakthrough by the heavy tank battalion and exploitation by lighter, faster forces in the following waves.

3. As a general principle, issue orders to the Tiger commanders first.

Reason: The Tiger is the carrier of the breakthrough. They are to be incorporated in the first strike at the point of main effort.

4. Never place a Tiger unit under the command of an infantry division in an attack.

Reason: In difficult situations contact breaks down between division and battalion. The infantry division lacks troops which, on the basis of their equipment and experience, can fight with and keep pace with the Tigers. In most cases the Tigers' success cannot be exploited by the infantry and the conquered territory cannot be held.

11. As a general principle, employ the Tiger unit in coordination with other weapons.

Reason: Following the penetration, it is the Tiger's task to push through to the enemy artillery and smash it. All other weapons must support them toward reaching this objective. Simultaneously, light tanks and assault guns are to smash the enemy's heavy infantry weapons and antitank guns. Our own artillery suppresses the enemy artillery and covers the flanks. Panzergrenadiers follow mounted on the tanks and occupy the conquered territory. They protect the Tigers against close-in attack by enemy infantry. Light tanks exploit the success and expand the tactical penetration into a strategic breakthrough.[120]

In keeping with the German Army's concept for the employment of tanks formulated by Guderian, the pamphlet discussed the need to concentrate the battalion to achieve its mission.

10. The Tiger unit must be the commander's main weapon for the decisive action.

Reason: Concentrated employment of the Tiger unit at the point of main effort forces the success. Any dispersal of forces places it in question.[121]

The authors of the pamphlet realized the Tiger's deficiencies and weaknesses, including its weight, which limited the bridges it could use; and its high-maintenance requirements. Because of these weaknesses, regarding movement, the pamphlet stated:

5. As much as possible allow the Tigers to move alone.

Reason: The stress on the automotive parts of the Tiger are least when it is given the opportunity to drive quickly without changing gears, braking, and restarting. The Tiger also disturbs the movement of other units. Bottlenecks, bridges, and fords often present surprises for the Tigers through which traffic can become completely blocked.

7. Do not request forced marches.

Reason: The result will be high wear on the engine, transmission, and running gear. The Tiger's combat capability will thus be used up on the road and not in action. *The average speed for a Tiger unit is ten kilometers per hour by day and seven kilometers per hour by night.* [Italics by the editor]

8. Have tanks travel as little as possible.

Reason: During movements the great weight of the Tiger results in considerable material wear.

24. Following prolonged action, allow the Tiger battalion two to three weeks to restore its fighting power.

Reason: Otherwise the percentage of technical breakdowns will climb increasingly in subsequent operations.[122]

As with other doctrinal guidance, this pamphlet focused on offensive operations, but did provide some guidance relevant to defensive operations. The focus of the pamphlet was on the concentration of all tanks in the decisive action. This could be adapted to offensive breakthroughs or to mobile counterattacks conducted while in an overall defensive posture.

The sections on movement and maintenance are important when considering using the heavy tank battalion as a mobile reserve in the defense. With the high maintenance requirements of the heavy tank battalion, positioning it as a mobile reserve was very important so it could counter enemy penetrations of the defensive line with the least amount of movement. This was especially true across the vast distances of the Eastern Front.

Summary

Based on the published German doctrine and the Tiger program guidance, the heavy tank battalion was formed with the primary focus of killing tanks. German doctrine envisioned a decisive tank battle once a penetration of the initial defensive line had been made. The heavy tank battalion was developed and fielded to fight that decisive tank battle. Originally, it was intended to fight that battle on the offensive during breakthrough operations, but it was also capable of fighting in a defensive posture by counterattacking enemy armor penetrations as a mobile reserve. However, it was fully recognized that Tiger battalions' mobility was extremely limited; its mobility was barely 50 percent greater than a foot-borne infantry battalion by day, and about the same as an infantry battalion by night. Attempts to move faster than this—or to move a great deal, at any speed—were sure to cause serious maintenance problems. These were indeed harbingers of things to come when Tiger battalions were committed to battle against mobile and agile foes. . . .

Chapter 3

Growing Pains and Adaptation

The enemy doesn't have anything to oppose us of equal value to the Tiger. Not more than four Tigers were in operation at the same time. In open terrain these few Tigers totally dominated the battlefield.[1]

Report by Headquarters, German 18th Army, 2 April 1943

From May 1942 until the Battle of Kursk in July 1943, the German Army created and fielded five heavy tank battalions.[2] The initial combat actions involved Heavy Tank Battalion 502 in August 1942. They attacked as part of Army Group North in the vicinity of Leningrad.

One company of Heavy Tank Battalion 504 and all of Heavy Tank Battalion 501 fought in Tunisia from November 1942 until the surrender of German forces in May 1943. The deteriorating tactical situation for the Germans in both theaters caused these battalions to be introduced piecemeal into battle as their platoons and companies arrived.

Heavy Tank Battalion 503 participated as part of Army Group Don in attempting to stop the Soviet advance following the encirclement of the German 6th Army around Stalingrad.[3]

During Operation ZITADELLE (the German offensive near Kursk in the summer of 1943), OKH committed the only two fully-operational heavy tank battalions. These were Heavy Tank Battalions 503 and 505, which were the only heavy tank battalions remaining (Heavy Tank Battalions 501 and 504 had been destroyed or captured in Tunisia and Sicily and were being rebuilt in Germany).

At the same time, Heavy Tank Battalion 502 had only one understrength company serving with Army Group North.[4] Until Operation ZITADELLE, the German Army only employed Tigers in small numbers. These were usually cross-attached with other units equipped with other tank types and other arms. Prior to Kursk, moreover, they were never employed for the specific purpose of creating a breakthrough to facilitate operational-level exploitation by other units.

Heavy Tank Battalion 502 with Army Group North

In the summer of 1942, Hitler ordered the first company of Heavy Tank Battalion 502, assigned to Army Group North, to support the attack on Leningrad. This company, along with elements of the workshop company and battalion headquarters, conducted combat operations in the vicinity of Leningrad starting at the end of September 1942. The 2d Company of this battalion wasn't formed until later, and in an attempt to stabilize the front after the Soviet encirclement of Stalingrad, *OKH* attached them to Army Group Don in early 1943.[5] The 1st Company of Heavy Tank Battalion 502 fought in the vicinity of Leningrad with Army Group North until the battalion was reunited in the summer of 1943 after having been refitted in accordance with Organization E.[6]

A vast amount of literature exists concerning the initial employment of Tigers in the vicinity of Leningrad. In this literature, there are many different versions of the events, dates, and combat venues of Heavy Tank Battalion 502. A common theme in all accounts, however, is a degree of criticism about the employment of heavy tanks in swampy terrain that did not allow much off-road movement. Guderian summarized the lessons learned from the employment of this company with Army Group North in *Panzer Leader*:

> He [Hitler] was consumed by his desire to try his new weapon. He therefore ordered that the Tigers be committed in a quite secondary operation, in a limited attack carried out in terrain that was utterly unsuitable, for in the swampy forest near Leningrad heavy tanks could only move in single file along the forest tracks, which, of course, was exactly where the enemy antitank guns were posted, waiting for them. The results were not only heavy, unnecessary casualties, but also the loss of secrecy and of the element of surprise for future operations.[7]

During this initial attack, all of the Tigers received some damage, and the Soviets captured one Tiger. Even though the Tiger was superior to any Soviet tank at that time, several subsequent attacks achieved similar results because the Soviets positioned antitank guns in depth along the few roads in the area.

The capture of the single Tiger had some long-term and detrimental consequences for the Germans. The Soviets evaluated the Tiger, determining its strengths and weaknesses, and took steps to develop vehicles to counter the design. The testing and evaluation of the Tiger, and the consequent development and fielding of new Soviet vehicles was accomplished in an amazingly short time, although these new vehicles did not see service in great numbers until the Battle of Kursk in the summer of 1943.

During the next year, the Soviets launched several major attacks that forced the Germans onto the defensive in this sector. The swampy terrain that restricted heavy vehicle movement enabled this company to provide excellent defensive support throughout the sector. The Soviets did not possess a tank or armored vehicle capable of defeating the Tigers, except at close range, so the Tigers dominated the battlefield in this environment.[8] From 12 January to 31 March 1943, this company destroyed 160 Soviet tanks while losing only six Tigers, establishing a kill ratio of 26.7 to 1.[9]

As with most similar units, Heavy Tank Battalion 502 suffered from inadequate recovery assets and a low operational-readiness rate among its Tigers. During this entire two-and-one-half-month period, the unit never had more than four operational Tigers out of an on-hand strength that changed continually with losses and replacements. The highest number of Tigers on hand was thirteen on 20 February 1943 and the lowest number on hand was two on 31 January 1943.[10] Three of the six Tigers lost were destroyed by their own crews; two of them after they had become stuck in a "peat-bog" and one because of mechanical failure.[11] This may have been a result of the poor terrain, but adequate recovery assets might have compensated for some of the losses. The unit's diary is filled with entries about pulling out "bogged" Tigers and there is one instance where the recovery took three days.[12]

Heavy Tank Battalions in Tunisia

After the British victory at El Alamein in the autumn of 1942 and the Allied Operation TORCH landings during that same period, *Panzerarmee Afrika* was forced onto the defensive and withdrew toward ports in Tunisia. As a result of the emphasis placed upon this theater by Hitler, *OKH* ordered Heavy Tank Battalion 501 to North Africa. The first elements landed in Bizerte, Tunisia, on 23 November 1942. Because of Allied pressure on the ports and airfields in Tunisia, elements of the battalion formed part of an ad hoc Combat Group immediately upon disembarkation, fighting their first action on 1 December 1942.[13] Heavy Tank Battalion 501 engaged in minor counterattacks until 17 March 1943. This unit fought in many small actions and some large scale attacks such as Operations *EILBOTE* (COURIER) *I*, *FRÜHLINGSWIND* (SPRING WIND), AND *OCHSENKOPF* (OX HEAD).[14] Combat actions usually involved elements of the battalion no larger than a company. One of the largest consolidated actions of the battalion occurred during Operation *EILBOTE I*, when the battalion fielded 13 Tigers, although they were attached to two separate units.[15] Another large-scale employment of the entire battalion occurred during Operation OCHSENKOPF when the battalion fielded 14 Tigers as part of the 10th Panzer Division's Panzer Regiment 7, during its attack toward Beja.[16]

Heavy Tank Battalion 501's first engagement was around Tebourba in early December 1942. Generalfeldmarschall Kesselring directed General der Panzertruppen Walther Nehring, commanding the German forces defending Tunis, to enlarge the German lodgment in Tunisia.[17] The most immediate threat came from forces in the Tebourba area, which were a little more than 48 kilometers from the primary German port of Bizerte and fewer than 32 kilometers from Tunis. Nehring, directed to seize the Tebourba Gap area, placed the operation under Generalleutnant Wolfgang Fischer, who commanded the 10th Panzer Division. Elements of this division, along with Heavy Tank Battalion 501, were only beginning to arrive in theater. (see map 1)

Drawing on a wide variety of units, Fisher divided his force into four separate combat groups.[18] The operation called for attacks from three different directions using these four different forces. Combat Group Koch's mission was to fix Allied forces from the south by attacking El Bathan. Tanks from Heavy Tank Battalion 501 were divided between Combat Groups Lüder and Djedeida. Combat Group Lüder, named after the commander of Heavy Tank Battalion 501, Major Lüder, was given the mission of attacking to the south to destroy the American armored force at Chouigui, effectively blocking the road through Chouigui Pass. After completing that task and in conjunction with Combat Group Hudel, it was to maneuver south to attack Tebourba from the west. The soldiers of Combat Group Djedeida were to wait and pursue Allied forces if they pulled back during the operations north of Tebourba.

Early on 1 December 1942, Combat Groups Lüder and Hudel combined in their attack and successfully forced American forces south. During Combat Group Lüder's attack south of Chouigui, a counterattack by tanks of the British 17th/21st Lancers was defeated by the "longer-ranged guns" of the German tanks.[19] Five Crusader tanks were lost, although it is uncertain whether any of these were destroyed by elements of Heavy Tank Battalion 501.[20] This attack was stopped just north of the main road, between the Tebourba Gap and Tebourba, by concentrated artillery fire.

Later that day Combat Group Djedeida attacked the Allied defenses on the ridge west of Djedeida. These were the closest Allied units to Tunis at the time and would be the closest the Allies would come to Tunis for several months. According to a German after-action report:

> The attack was carried forward against enemy tanks in the olive groves five kilometers west of Djedeida. The field of view and the field of fire were very limited in the thick olive groves. Enemy tanks could only be fought at close range. . . . The Tigers were hit by General Lee tanks firing

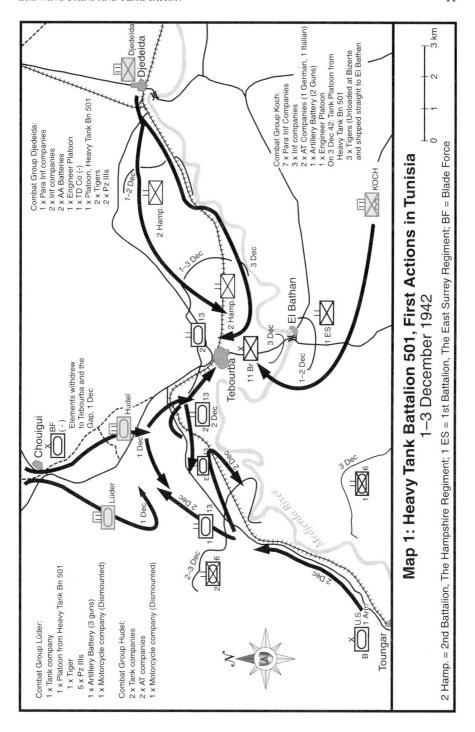

**Map 1: Heavy Tank Battalion 501, First Actions in Tunisia
1–3 December 1942**

2 Hamp. = 2nd Battalion, The Hampshire Regiment; 1 ES = 1st Battalion, The East Surrey Regiment; BF = Blade Force

Combat Group Lüder:
1 x Tank company
1 x Platoon from Heavy Tank Bn 501
  1 x Tiger
  5 x Pz IIIs
1 x Artillery Battery (3 guns)
1 x Motorcycle company (Dismounted)

Combat Group Hudel:
2 x Tank companies
2 x AT companies
1 x Motorcycle company (Dismounted)

Combat Group Djedeida:
1 x Para Inf companies
2 x Inf companies
2 x AA Batteries
1 x Engineer Platoon
1 x TD Co (–)
1 x Platoon, Heavy Tank Bn 501
  2 x Tigers
  2 x Pz IIIs

Combat Group Koch:
7 x Para Inf Companies
3 x Inf companies
2 x AT Companies (1 German, 1 Italian)
1 x Artillery Battery (2 Guns)
1 x Engineer Platoon
On 3 Dec 42: Tank Platoon from
Heavy Tank Bn 501
3 x Tigers (Unloaded at Bizerte
  and shipped straight to El Bathan

at a range of 80 to 100 meters. This resulted in deep penetrations, but the last ten millimeters of the side armor held. This proved that the armor was excellent. . . . Two General Lee tanks were knocked out at a range of 150 meters.[21]

The report went on to state that other Allied tanks were destroyed by 88mm antiaircraft guns, and that the remaining Allied vehicles pulled back. It is clear from reading U.S. and British sources, however, that the 2d Battalion, The Hampshire Regiment held the key terrain in the area at the end of the day and that the Germans made little progress in the east during 1 December 1942.

The attack in the east continued with Combat Group Djedeida on 2 December 1942. The 2d Hampshires continued to hold against this force, but was forced to withdraw to a new line of defense three kilometers to the west. During this day's action, only one Tiger and three Panzer IIIs were operational in Combat Group Djedeida because one Tiger suffered engine failure on the previous day. Indicative of the ferocity of the day's fighting, all three Panzer IIIs were destroyed.[22]

The U.S. 1st Armored Division's 1st Battalion, 13th Armored Regiment launched a strong counterattack using 30 Stuart light tanks and a company of M4 Sherman mediums against the combined forces of Combat Groups Hudel and Lüder.[23] Most of the vehicles of this American force were destroyed during the attack, with the elements of Heavy Tank Battalion 501 claiming to kill six of the very thin-skinned Stuarts. This ill-fated American attack did, however, produce the benefit of denying the German combat groups in the west the opportunity of continuing their attack toward either Tebourba or the Tebourba Gap.

By 3 December, the Germans finally forced the withdrawal of Allied forces around Tebourba. The single remaining operational Tiger of Combat Group Djedeida, along with two Panzer IIIs, assisted in eliminating stubborn British defenses on Hill 186. According to British sources, this single Tiger was apparently hit by a British 17-pounder (76mm) antitank gun; although only damaged and not destroyed, it was sent back to the rear area for repairs. The remaining two Panzer IIIs from Heavy Tank Battalion 501 continued to support the attack throughout the day. After dark that evening, the remaining Allied forces began to withdraw to the west. A key avenue of retreat was sealed off when Combat Group Koch, possibly supported by several Tigers that had just arrived from the port, captured the key town and bridge at El Bathan.[24]

Throughout three days of fighting, Allied forces lost a total of 55 tanks. Of these, elements of Heavy Tank Battalion 501 claimed the destruction of at least 15.[25] Although Heavy Tank Battalion 501 contributed ten or fewer tanks to the overall effort of all four combat groups, they destroyed 27 percent of the total achieved.[26] This was an exceptional achievement, although 9 of the 15 destroyed enemy tanks were very poorly armed (37mm main gun) and armored Stuarts.

On 10 December 1942, Generalleutnant Fischer ordered elements of Panzer Regiment 7, supported by a contingent of Heavy Tank Battalion 501's Tigers, to seize the town of Medjez el Bab. This force, consisting of about 30 tanks, was part of a general attack aimed at expanding the German bridgehead in Tunisia, and was in its fifth and final day. This attack was an envelopment intended to seize Medjez el Bab, effectively trapping Allied forces between Medjez el Bab and the Tebourba Gap. (see map 2)

There was a heavy rain the previous night so vehicular operations were restricted primarily to the roads. Supported by three Tigers from Heavy Tank Battalion 501, the envelopment was led by two of them, with the third in reserve near the rear of the column.[27] This attack met with initial success, destroying ten Stuart light tanks and half-tracks of the U.S. 1st Armored Division's 1st Battalion, 1st Armored Regiment, forcing the remainder of the unit to withdraw to the west.[28] It was ultimately stopped by obstacles and heavy artillery fire from Free French forces three kilometers from Medjez el Bab.[29]

Combat Command B of the 1st Armored Division tried to relieve pressure on Medjez el Bab by using elements of the 1st Battalion, 13th Armored Regiment, and Company C, 701st Tank Destroyer Battalion in a flank attack from the north.[30] The Germans, along with at least two Tigers and several Panzer IIIs from Heavy Tank Battalion 501, turned back to meet this new threat. Being composed primarily of Stuart light tanks, the American force was no match against the Tigers. The official U.S. Army history states:

> The American light tanks were outgunned by the enemy and mired when they maneuvered off the road; 19 were lost. The tank destroyers claimed ten German medium tanks knocked out before being put out of action themselves.[31]

In a single day's combat, an attack led by a small element of Heavy Tank Battalion 501 destroyed 36 tanks, four armored reconnaissance vehicles, two antitank guns, and other miscellaneous equipment.[32] The three Tigers alone claimed 14 of the tanks destroyed, 38 percent of the total, during the day and led the attacks throughout the operation. Although the attack did not capture the town of Medjez el Bab, because of severe losses during the day, the American commander withdrew all forces to the west of the town during the night. It must be remembered, however, that the Tigers were primarily facing the least well-armed and armored tank in the U.S. Army's inventory.

For the next month, Heavy Tank Battalion 501 acted primarily as the reserve for Generaloberst Hans-Jürgen von Arnim's 5th Panzer Army, but did participate in some operations with small elements of the battalion. The 2d

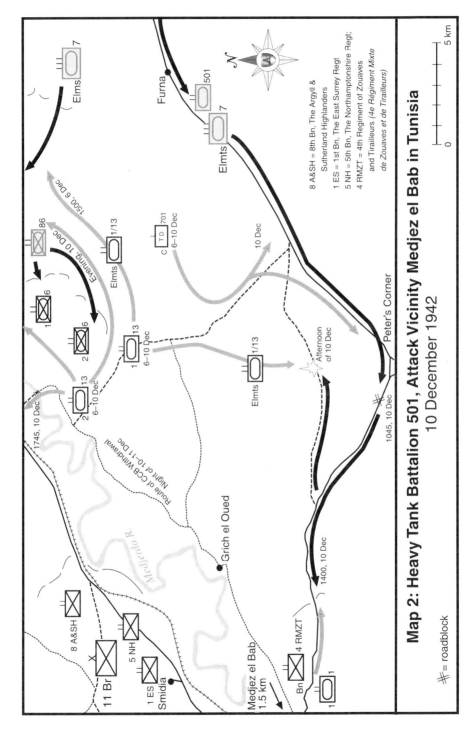

Map 2: Heavy Tank Battalion 501, Attack Vicinity Medjez el Bab in Tunisia
10 December 1942

8 A&SH = 8th Bn, The Argyll &
 Sutherland Highlanders
1 ES = 1st Bn, The East Surrey Regt
5 NH = 5th Bn, The Northamptonshire Regt;
4 RMZT = 4th Regiment of Zouaves
 and Tirailleurs (*4e Régiment Mixte
 de Zouaves et de Tirailleurs*)

= roadblock

Company finally arrived in Tunisia in early January 1943, just in time to participate in Operation *EILBOTE I* in the middle of that month.[33] This operation was the first time that most of the battalion participated in a single operation.[34] Operation *EILBOTE I* was conceived of as a limited attack, meant to protect the lines of communication from Tunis and Bizerte to Rommel's headquarters. Its objective was to push back Allied forces threatening that line of communication between Enfidaville and Sousse.[35] (see map 3)

Generalmajor Friedrich Weber, Commanding General of the 334th Infantry Division, was given command of the main effort of the operation. He organized his force in three combat groups. The first two were tasked with conducting breakthroughs of the enemy positions for exploitation by the third group. The third group was to exploit the breakthrough by advancing to the west to complete the destruction of Allied units on the Eastern Dorsal hills.[36] Elements of the 2d Company, Heavy Tank Battalion 501 were ordered to support Corps Group Weber in its attack to seize the high ground by the Kebir Reservoir (467) and the high point known as the Djebel Mansour (675).[37] Combat Group Lüder, with the 1st Company and the Engineer Platoon of Heavy Tank Battalion 501, was to push up the Kebir valley to the road intersection at the southwest end of the reservoir, then swing south for about 20 kilometers to the Hir Moussa crossroads. After that, it was to turn east toward the Karachoum Gap. If possible, this group was also to secure the Kairouan-Ousseltia road that ran through the gap between Djebel Halfa (572) and Djebel Ousselat (887).[38]

Combat Group Weber broke through the defending French forces, opening the way into the Kebir valley for Combat Group Lüder on 18 January 1943. During this attack, the Tigers led both prongs of the attack and encountered a device for which they never really developed an effective countermeasure throughout the war—the land mine. As the unit after-action review stated:

> At 5:30 A.M., in close cooperation with 2d Battalion, Mountain Infantry Regiment 756, the *Panzer-Kampftruppe* [small, mobile, combined arms units] started engaging antitank guns and gun positions as well as bunkers that were very cleverly built into the mountain slopes. Toward 11:00 A.M., the left-hand *Kampftrupp* came to a halt because a further advance on the main road was prevented by a mine barrier watched over by heavy supporting fire. It was cleared after employing an additional three Tigers and three Panzer IIIs as well as the armored engineer platoon. . . . Losses were: one Tiger from destruction of the suspension components and damage to the transmission caused by hits, one Tiger by a hung-up transmission, and two Panzer IIIs due to hits on the suspension and driving onto mines.[39]

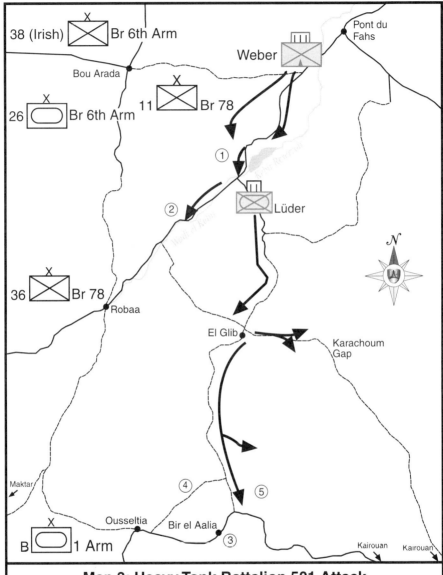

Map 3: Heavy Tank Battalion 501 Attack
During Operation EILBOTE, Tunisia, January 1943

1. 18 Jan 43: One Tiger disabled and subsequently scrapped after hitting a mine.
2. 20 Jan 43: 2d Company, Heavy Tank Battalion 501 employed along the main road to Robaa.
   Two Pz VI (Tigers) destroyed.
3. 21Jan 43: U.S. Tank Company counterattack repelled by 2nd Platoon, 1st Company,
   Heavy Tank Battalion 501, 3 of 12 attacking American tanks destroyed.
4. 22 Jan 43: Battalion light platoon assists in repelling American flank attack, loses 1 Pz III.
5. 22 Jan 43: One Tiger burns out after fuel leak caused by direct
   artillery hit catches fire.

0   5   10 km

The report stated that the engineer platoon cleared over 100 mines throughout the day and that this was accomplished only through "the closest coordination and continuous personal exchange of ideas with the infantry battalion commanders."[40]

Combat Group Lüder continued the attack that same day, starting around 2100 hours. Against heavy resistance, and led by Tigers, this force reached its objective of the road bend southwest of the Kebir Reservoir around midnight.[41] On 19 January, Combat Group Lüder continued its attack to the south, capturing the key crossroads in the vicinity of El Glib. This attack was delayed by effective and extensive use of land mines, along with artillery and antitank fire, but the German force managed to seize its objective for the day.

> The attack flowed smoothly forward after opening a narrows that had been blocked by antitank guns and mines. The surprised opponent found no time for a serious attempt to effectively block the road. Resistance first increased in the afternoon. Two Tigers were immobilized by mines at a mine barrier guarded by antitank guns. About 25 guns (antitank and artillery) and 100 motor vehicles of all types were destroyed or were ready for capture by following elements and about 100 prisoners brought in.[42]

There were no recorded instances of the hull being penetrated, but the German combat report stated that "the effect of the mines on the Tigers is more or less heavy damage to the suspension, based on the type of mine."[43]

On 20 January, Combat Group Lüder completed its initial mission by attacking toward the Karachoum Gap, ultimately linking up with Italian forces attacking from the east.[44] After regrouping, the attack resumed to the south around 1700 hours, continuing with the help of a full moon until around 0300 the next morning.[45] Allied forces were adapting to the Tigers and taking into account their own weaknesses in armor and strengths in terms of artillery and mines. According to the Germans:

> The opponent very cleverly pulled back from ridge to ridge while laying numerous mine barriers that he guarded with antitank guns and artillery. Often the last elements of the motorized mine layers were captured. The following combat methods were employed: Two advance Tigers followed the armored engineer platoon, followed by the rest of the tanks. If the first tank hit a mine barrier, all of the rest of the tanks immediately drove right and left to build straight platoon fire fronts and suppressed the antitank guns and artillery by suddenly opening fire. Under this protective fire, the engineers cleared the barrier while halted on the road; the panzer-grenadier battalion provided flank security by firing from the vehicles.[46]

Amazingly, using the Tigers as mine detectors to locate the leading edge of minefields seems to have been the preferred technique because the mines "did not cause any substantial damage" but rather immobilized the Tigers, "even if only for a short time."[47] The lesson, therefore, was that "the more Tigers, the better the advance flows" when facing extensive minefields.[48]

On 21 and 22 January 1943, Combat Command B of the American 1st Armored Division conducted cautious counterattacks against Combat Group Lüder, which defended the Kairouan-Ousseltia road. Throughout these two days, Allied forces used extensive artillery and air support. One of the casualties from the heavy artillery was a Tiger that caught fire returning to the rear.

Operation EILBOTE I was a costly success for the Germans. It succeeded in accomplishing all of its objectives and even continued on, accomplishing the follow-on mission of attacking and seizing the Kairouan-Ousseltia road. The Tigers of Heavy Tank Battalion 501 led the attacks throughout the operation, but paid a heavy price for it. For its efforts, Heavy Tank Battalion 501 claimed the destruction of only seven tanks and more than 30 guns, for the loss of four Tigers and at least two Panzer IIIs.[49] The after-action report indicated that the battalion's leadership was aware of the impact of mines and terrain on the Tigers:

> On average three Tigers and eight to ten Panzer IIIs were operational each day during this period. The stress of the previous marches through the mountains and the damage caused by mines started to become noticeable in the tanks. . . . The fact that only one Tiger out of nine was still fully operational and two or three others were conditionally operational at the end of the operation should not be disregarded.[50]

The maintenance problem was exacerbated by the fact that the battalion's maintenance company and supply element still had not arrived in Tunisia.

The 5th Panzer Army's attack against Sidi Bou Zid, designated Operation FRÜHLINGSWIND, was placed under the direct command of General von Arnim's chief of staff, Generalleutnant Heinz Ziegler.[51] This attack, conducted primarily by the 10th Panzer Division, was supported by the 1st Company of Heavy Tank Battalion 501. The attacking forces were organized into three combat groups. (see maps 4 and 5)

Combat Groups Gerhardt and Reimann broke through the Faid Pass by 0600 on 14 February 1943, destroying Company G of the American 1st Armored Regiment in the process. After traveling generally along the main road to Sbeitla, Combat Group Gerhardt moved to the north and encircled the high ground near Djebel Lessouda, on which the Americans had constructed a strongpoint. At the same time, Combat Group Reimann, led by Tigers, attacked along the main road.

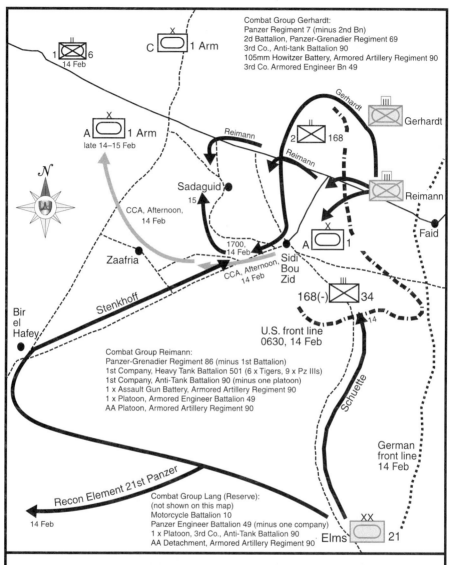

Combat Group Gerhardt:
Panzer Regiment 7 (minus 2nd Bn)
2d Battalion, Panzer-Grenadier Regiment 69
3rd Co., Anti-tank Battalion 90
105mm Howitzer Battery, Armored Artillery Regiment 90
3rd Co. Armored Engineer Bn 49

Combat Group Reimann:
Panzer-Grenadier Regiment 86 (minus 1st Battalion)
1st Company, Heavy Tank Battalion 501 (6 x Tigers, 9 x Pz IIIs)
1st Company, Anti-Tank Battalion 90 (minus one platoon)
1 x Assault Gun Battery, Armored Artillery Regiment 90
1 x Platoon, Armored Engineer Battalion 49
AA Platoon, Armored Artillery Regiment 90

Combat Group Lang (Reserve):
(not shown on this map)
Motorcycle Battalion 10
Panzer Engineer Battalion 49 (minus one company)
1 x Platoon, 3rd Co., Anti-Tank Battalion 90
AA Detachment, Armored Artillery Regiment 90

Map 4: Heavy Tank Battalion 501, Attack in the Vicinity of Sidi Bou Zid, Tunisia, Operation *FRÜHLINGSWIND*
14–15 February 1943

14 Feb 43: Attacks as part of CG Reimann. Defeats two counterattacks by CCA,
    1st Armored Division, claims the destruction of 20 Shermans while suffering no losses.
15 Feb 43: Withdrawn to reserve during the envelopment of the counterattacking
    2d Battalion, 1st Armored Regiment, 1st Armored Division
    (Combat Command C)

0   5   10 km

Map 5: Heavy Tank Battalion 501, Attack Vicinity Sidi Bou Zid, Tunisia During Operation *FRÜHLINGSWIND*, 14–15 February 1943

1. 140630 Feb 43: Company G. 1st Armored Regiment destroyed defending the Faid Pass.
2. Morning (0630–0900) 14 Feb 43: U.S. forces counterattack from vicinity of Sidi Bou Zid. Combat Group Reimann, supported by the 1st Company of Heavy Tank Battalion 501, forces U.S. forces to withdraw with losses.
3. 140900 Feb 43: Combat Group Reimann links up with Combat Group Gerhardt, which had maneuvered around the north side of Djebel Lessouda. Company H, 1st Armored Regiment counterattacks German forces on the west side of Djebel Lessouda from the south. This attack is also forced to withdraw with losses. After this, U.S. forces withdraw to the west where possible, while German forces consolidate, seize the town of Sidi Bou Zid, and reduce U.S. forces that have been encircled. During the day, the six Tigers claim 20 Shermans.

Uncertain of the situation, Combat Command A of the 1st Armored Division sent two companies from the 1st Armored Regiment and a company from the 701st Tank Destroyer Battalion "to clear up the situation."[52] This force traveled up the road from Sidi Bou Zid to the road junction called Poste Lessouda. At some point they were warned by American forces on the Djebel Lessouda that the Germans were in the vicinity of Poste Lessouda. A few minutes later, they came within sight and range of the enemy and began to take losses from what was believed to be 88mm guns, perhaps from Tiger tanks.[53]

Combat Group Reimann, supported by six Tigers of the 1st Company, Heavy Tank Battalion 501, forced the American tanks and tank destroyers to withdraw. Later in the day, only one of the American companies was available to conduct another "counterattack by fire and maneuver" to delay the Germans.[54] This counterattack was also turned back with the assistance of the Tigers. According to the American official history, "American losses were heavy, and, in the last hour of the morning, the unequal contest ended in a withdrawal southwestward." The remainder of the day was spent completing the encirclement of American forces on their mountaintop strongpoints, to be followed by their eventual reduction and elimination.

The accomplishments of the handful of Tigers operating with Combat Group Reimann—in the space of about six hours, just prior to daybreak until around noon—was remarkable. They assisted in breaking through their opponents' forward defenses, destroying a tank company in the process. They continued the attack and assisted in defeating two counterattacks, destroying a total of 20 Shermans throughout the day.[55]

The next day, 15 February 1943, the 1st Company of Heavy Tank Battalion 501 was held in reserve during the envelopment of the ill-fated counterattack of the 2d Battalion, 1st Armored Regiment.[56]

During the remainder of the operation that ultimately came to be called the "Kasserine Pass" battles, the 1st Company of Heavy Tank Battalion 501 was held in reserve and engaged in supporting operations 65 kilometers north of Sidi Bou Zid. There were no Tigers lost throughout the nine days of the German offensive.

On 26 February, Heavy Tank Battalion 501 became the 3d Battalion of the 10th Panzer Division's Panzer Regiment 7.[57] This was the same day that they began an ultimately-unsuccessful attack as part of the large-scale operation known as Operation OCHSENKOPF (OX HEAD). This offensive took place along the entire Fifth Panzer Army front and was designed to gain a further extension of their bridgehead.[58] The main effort, which involved all of Fifth Panzer Army's available armor, was directed at Sidi Nsir, with Beja as its ultimate objective.[59] (see map 6)

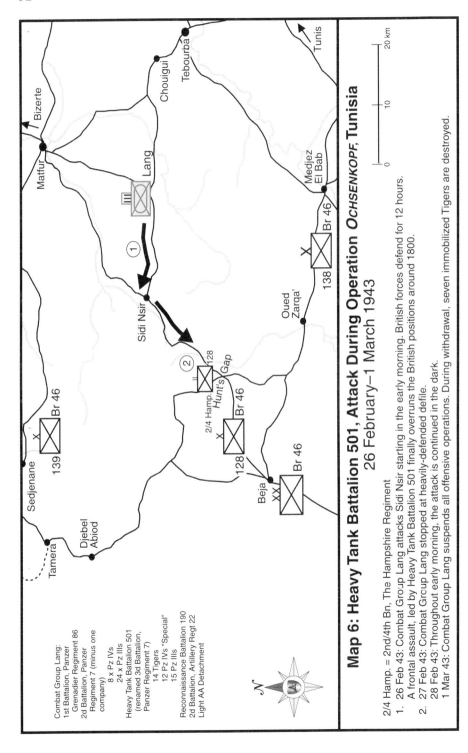

Map 6: Heavy Tank Battalion 501, Attack During Operation OCHSENKOPF, Tunisia
26 February–1 March 1943

Combat Group Lang:
1st Battalion, Panzer Grenadier Regiment 86
2d Battalion, Panzer Regiment 7 (minus one company)
  8 x Pz IVs
  24 x Pz IIIs
Heavy Tank Battalion 501 (renamed 3d Battalion, Panzer Regiment 7)
  14 Tigers
  12 Pz IVs "Special"
  15 Pz IIIs
Reconnaissance Battalion 190
2d Battalion, Artillery Regt 22
Light AA Detachment

2/4 Hamp. = 2nd/4th Bn, The Hampshire Regiment

1. 26 Feb 43: Combat Group Lang attacks Sidi Nsir starting in the early morning. British forces defend for 12 hours. A frontal assault, led by Heavy Tank Battalion 501 finally overruns the British positions around 1800.

2. 27 Feb 43: Combat Grcup Lang stopped at heavily-defended defile.
   28 Feb 43: Throughout early morning, the attack is continued in the dark.
   1 Mar 43: Combat Group Lang suspends all offensive operations. During withdrawal, seven immobilized Tigers are destroyed.

The force conducting this mission, Combat Group Lang, commenced its attack on Sidi Nsir on 26 February 1943. Led by Tigers, Combat Group Lang attacked along the main road and ran into the defenses of the 128th Infantry Brigade of the British 46th Division.[60] This force constituted only a combat outpost, but managed to delay the German attack for 12 hours.[61] The British position was seized only after the Germans outflanked and suppressed the defenders from both flanks and then frontally assaulted the defenders, with the Tigers leading the assault.[62]

The main British defensive positions were located 20 kilometers southwest of Sidi Nsir, in a key defile known as Hunt's Gap. Combat Group Lang continued their attack along the main road to Beja the next day. Muddy ground conditions and hilly terrain confined the attack primarily to the main road.[63] The attackers were stopped at Hunt's Gap by a well-placed defensive position consisting of mines and antitank guns with excellent observation and fields of fire, supported by five batteries of field artillery. A well-timed appearance by the Royal Air Force also assisted in halting the attack.

The attack was continued throughout the night, but by 28 February, seven Tigers were immobilized in the British minefield. Of the 14 Tigers that started the operation two days previously, only two Tigers were still operational.[64] According to the U.S. Army history:

> The leading section could not turn around, could not leave the road, could not back out. Some of the vehicles, abandoned during what appeared to be a panic, were demolished by British engineers after dark.[65]

According to the British Army's official history:

> Lang's defeat was caused mainly by the excellent British artillery fire, by the rain-soaked ground on which his tanks could not manoeuvre, and by the well-staged infantry attacks during which the Sappers destroyed damaged tanks which the enemy might have pulled out of harm's way.[66]

All hopes of continuing the attack were gone by 1 March 1943 and German forces ultimately withdrew to defensive positions in the vicinity of Sidi Nsir. After four days of fighting, none of Heavy Tank Battalion 501's 14 Tigers were operational.[67] Seven Tigers were lost, along with four Panzer IVs and eight Panzer IIIs.[68] A report from Heavy Tank Battalion 501 provided the following reasons for the loss of the Tigers:

> Bottomless terrain that had been softened by violent rain storms operating on a narrow front. Enemy minefields hindered further attack. Enemy artillery fire of all calibers and antitank gunfire then hit the Tiger attack, which was immobilized in the mud and on mines. Strong enemy

counterattacks didn't let our own infantry attacks advance far enough to recover the damaged Tigers. Five Tigers had tracks damaged by mines (one of these Tigers was also hit by an antitank gun), one Tiger took a direct hit from an artillery shell, and one Tiger became stuck in the mud.[69]

Other than assisting in breaking through what amounted to a weakly-held forward defensive position, Operation OCHSENKOPF was a complete failure for Heavy Tank Battalion 501. The area around Hunt's Gap, just north of Beja, came to known as the "Tiger Graveyard" by Allied forces.[70]

Interestingly, this was the first and only occasion during the campaign in North Africa that Heavy Tank Battalion 501 was employed as a concentrated and combined battalion under more or less a single command. One of the reasons for the generally piecemeal employment of the battalion was the fact that the individual vehicles arrived over a six-week period from late November to early January.[71] German forces employed combat vehicles as soon as they were available in response to continual Allied pressure. Another reason for the piecemeal employment was that the heavy tanks of the battalion were needed in many places to stop the penetrations of the American and British forces and to support numerous German attacks attempting to expand their bridgehead.

The final reason for employment in a fragmented fashion was that this unit was plagued by a low operational rate of Tigers during its time in North Africa. Of the 22 Tigers assigned to Heavy Tank Battalion 501 throughout this period, the highest number operational at the same time was 14 Tigers, on 14 and 26 February 1943.[72] Although the battalion managed to achieve an overall 62-percent operational average for Tigers throughout its time in Tunisia, this is misleading by itself; on many occasions, the battalion only had a handful of tanks on hand.[73]

This low rate was due in part because the Tiger was a new weapon that had design flaws requiring modifications. The combat elements of the battalion, possibly because they were given a higher priority in shipment to Tunisia than the support units, arrived in Tunisia before any support units of the battalion. This forced the heavy tank companies to operate for an extended period of time without dedicated maintenance support. The first maintenance platoon from the workshop company did not arrive until 25 December 1942.[74] This absence of support severely hindered the battalion's ability to not only maintain its vehicles, but also to recover and tow them back from the front to be repaired. Additionally, because the Allies often interdicted the Axis supply lines in the Mediterranean, there was always a shortage of repair parts. In fairness, of course, the Germans' supplies had far less distance to travel than those of the Allies.

Heavy Tank Battalion 501 improvised as best it could to maintain its tanks, but it was especially challenged because they were the only unit in North Africa equipped with the Tiger. On 18 January 1943, a Tiger that had hit a land mine was officially scrapped because the battalion lacked the replacement idler wheel to fix it.[75] This Tiger was cannibalized to establish a reserve of necessary repair parts for the other damaged Tigers.

An additional problem created by the dispersal of the battalion was that the maintenance elements were also necessarily dispersed. Because the maintenance elements were spread out, the battalion's 18-ton recovery vehicles found it difficult to provide support to all areas. Also, the 18-ton recovery vehicles did not have armor protection, so they could only recover and tow a Tiger in a secure area.

The lack of an armored recovery vehicle and of towing vehicles in general forced the battalion to destroy some disabled Tigers that may have otherwise been recovered. The battalion again improvised as best it could and in one instance, a single Panzer III towed a disabled Tiger out of the effective range of the enemy antitank guns and infantry weapons.[76]

Whatever the reason for piecemeal employment of the battalion, it violated the principle of concentrated employment of the battalion that was necessary to achieve decisive results. Given the results of the one time that the battalion was concentrated, perhaps the principle of concentration was not always applicable, either. The author of final after-action review of the battalion's operations in Tunisia blames the inability to employ the bulk of the battalion at the same time to mountainous terrain which forced the attacks to largely follow the roads in their zones.[77]

It is interesting to note that this report only mentions the devastating effect of mines once and then only to confirm that Tigers must lead attacks once contact has been made because they are "not as susceptible to mines."[78] Presumably, the solution to breaking through a minefield still lay in having enough Tigers. This is extraordinary, considering that the United States, the British, and the Soviets were all experimenting and fielding a wide variety of mine-breaching equipment attached to tanks.[79] The Germans, however, seemed to be content with using—and abusing—their most expensive, most valuable tanks as mine detectors and breaching vehicles.

The doctrinally-correct method, as inferred from published German reports, was for the Germans to overwatch an obstacle with Tigers and other direct- and indirect-fire systems, while engineers breached the obstacle. Until the end of the war, this required dismounting personnel to either physically remove the mines or obstacle or to emplace explosive charges to blow a breach through the minefield. Obviously, this required exposing skilled personnel to great hazards.

Although non-doctrinal, an accepted and supposedly preferred method in many instances was to "bull through" the minefield with Tigers. This saved personnel from having to expose themselves, but was costly in terms of maintaining a high operational rate for Tigers. This is apparently the method that was chosen during Operation OCHSENKOPF. How else could five Tigers have become immobilized in the minefield on a single road? When the leading Tiger was immobilized by the leading edge of the minefield, it must have been apparent to all following that there was a minefield to their front. The only way for four more Tigers to become damaged by mines was to move forward beyond those already disabled Tigers. The problem of overcoming mines was one that heavy tank battalion leaders never solved during the course of the war.

Heavy Tank Battalion 501 destroyed more than 150 Allied tanks in North Africa while losing only 11 Tigers.[80] This amounts to a kill ratio of 13.6 enemy tanks destroyed for every Tiger lost. Most sources do not differentiate the kills of the Panzer IIIs from those of the Tigers, but the unit diary is filled with specific entries that indicate the kills of the day were by the Tigers. There are few entries that specifically mention the Panzer IIIs destroying an enemy tank.[81] Regardless of vehicle type, the high kill ratio is a testament to the unit's effectiveness in spite of its infrequent deployment in accordance with doctrinal precepts. Another indication of the effectiveness of the vehicles, if not necessarily the unit, is the fact that of the 11 Tigers lost, only three were destroyed by enemy fire.[82]

Even though the primary tank killer of the heavy tank battalion was the Tiger, the reports continually emphasized the necessity of incorporating the Panzer IIIs within the battalion. The battalion commander stressed that the battalion "constantly needs light panzers for maintaining contact with other units, reconnaissance, and other similar duties (that is, scouting, guarding, bringing repair parts, or retrieving wounded under fire) for which you can't use Tigers."[83]

Even with only a few Tigers, Heavy Tank Battalion 501 helped the units it supported to accomplish many of their missions. German reports indicate that the Allied forces recognized the superiority of the Tiger and did not attempt to engage it frontally, if at all. On the attack toward Medjerda, the battalion reported that "the objective was reached without encountering any enemy activity," but that "fleeing enemy columns and tanks were observed as soon as the Tigers appeared."[84] Evidently in an attempt to counter this and destroy more enemy tanks before they could escape, the battalion commander issued the guidance that "Tigers may not open fire too early against enemy tanks, in order to keep retreating enemy tanks within the effective range of our weapons as long as possible."[85]

The Allied forces did not have a tank that could counter the Tiger, so they resorted to the tactic of pulling back from ridge to ridge while laying minefields that were protected by antitank guns. Artillery bombardments were also fired on the Tigers when they were slowed by the minefields.[86] As has been shown, this tactic was very effective.

On 17 March 1943, Heavy Tank Battalion 504 took possession of Heavy Tank Battalion 501's 11 remaining Tigers; it later surrendered on 12 May 1943.[87] During this time, they encountered many of the same problems as their predecessors, although German forces were primarily on the defensive during the two months Heavy Tank Battalion 504 fought in North Africa. They assisted in stopping the breakthrough of the American 1st Armored Division in the vicinity of Maknassy during the end of March 1943.[88] They also helped temporarily stop the British offensive in the vicinity of Medjez el Bab, as well as numerous other smaller defensive engagements.[89] This battalion did not engage in any large-scale offensive operations. It performed defensive missions to defeat enemy penetrations of the front line. The battalion also counterattacked several times, as part of a larger German force, to reestablish front line positions.

The battalion was only able to maintain an operational readiness rate of about 50 percent for their Tigers, and the largest number of Tigers that were operational at one time was 17 on 4 April 1943.[90] Heavy Tank Battalion 504 lost a total of eight Tiger tanks between 17 March and 12 May 1943, and destroyed the remaining 14 to prevent their capture before the unit surrendered to Allied forces.[91]

During the two months that they operated in Tunisia, Heavy Tank Battalion 504 destroyed more than 150 enemy tanks.[92] Prior to destroying the 14 remaining Tigers, the battalion achieved a tank kill ratio of 18.8 enemy tanks for every Tiger lost; because the entire battalion was ultimately lost, however, the kill ratio measured against all 22 Tigers committed was still a respectable 6.8 enemy tanks destroyed for every Tiger.

This battalion's counteroffensive actions were effective in delaying the Allied forces in Tunisia. They could have been even more cost effective had the Germans been able to evacuate the remaining Tigers of the battalion to Sicily or Italy.

This battalion, like Heavy Tank Battalion 501, also suffered from inadequate recovery assets during its retrograde actions. Of the eight Tigers lost prior to surrendering, only four were lost as a result of direct enemy contact.[93] Of these four, the battalion destroyed two because they were unable to recover them. That meant that enemy fire completely destroyed only two Tigers, one from concentrated antitank and artillery fire, and the other from a direct hit by an artillery round.[94]

This testifies to the survivability of the Tiger tank, but it also highlights its weaknesses. As the Germans were discovering, the Tiger was a very maintenance-intensive combat vehicle that had a limited radius of action because of the high fuel consumption and maintenance requirements. These weaknesses were exacerbated when the Germans withdrew following the Allied offenses in Tunisia.

Although the actions of Heavy Tank Battalion 504 indicate that Tigers were effective in destroying enemy tanks, if the German Army had devoted some resources to developing an armored recovery vehicle, they may have been able to reduce the number of Tigers destroyed by their own crews. Only two Tigers were total and complete losses on the battlefield as a result of enemy direct fire. For the loss of these two Tigers, the battalion destroyed over 150 Allied tanks, which equals a kill ratio of 75 to 1 in tank versus tank combat. Fortunately for the Allies, there was more than one way to kill a Tiger. Unfortunately for the Germans, the solutions to the twin problems of recovering such massive machines when damaged on the battlefield and conducting the maintenance required to keep such complex vehicles running would prove elusive.

Heavy Tank Battalion 503 with Army Group Don in Southern Russia

On 27 December 1942, *OKH* sent Heavy Tank Battalion 503 to Army Group Don to assist in stabilizing the front.[95] This unit was needed to help protect Rostov so that the 1st and 4th Panzer Armies and other German units in the Caucasus could withdraw across the Don River to the Donets River, where the high command planned a new defensive line.[96]

This battalion arrived at the beginning of 1943 and Army Group Don immediately assigned it the mission of securing bridges across the Manytch River for use by withdrawing forces.[97] By this time there was not a continuous front in the area. German forces defended a series of blocking positions and strongpoints in an attempt to stop the Soviet advance. These were located at key points at road or railroad junctions and major river crossings.[98] The fighting was characterized by rearguard actions, while the main body of troops took up new positions farther back.

Heavy Tank Battalion 503 participated in this fighting from 1 to 17 January 1943, primarily securing important river crossing sites. Due to the fluid nature of the battlefield, however, they were sent from one important area to another, and in one instance covered 65 kilometers in one day.[99] (see map 7)

Probably the battalion's largest single employment occurred on 6 January 1943 when the battalion, supported by 2d Battalion, Panzer-Grenadier

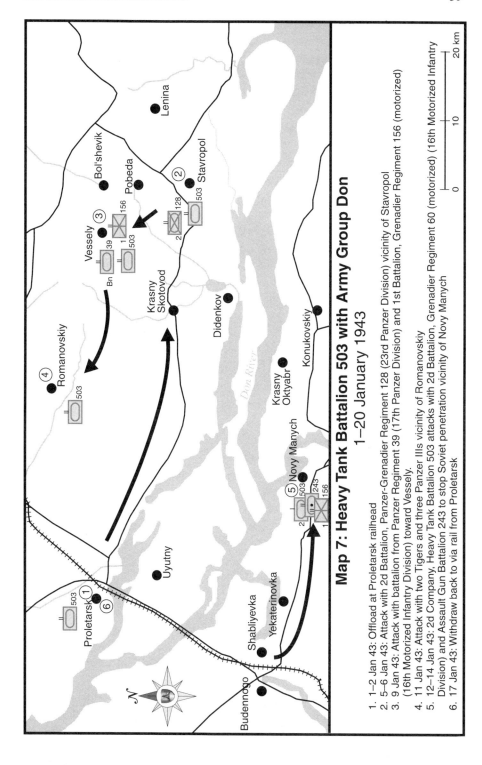

Map 7: Heavy Tank Battalion 503 with Army Group Don
1–20 January 1943

1. 1–2 Jan 43: Offload at Proletarsk railhead
2. 5–6 Jan 43: Attack with 2d Battalion, Panzer-Grenadier Regiment 128 (23rd Panzer Division) vicinity of Stavropol
3. 9 Jan 43: Attack with battalion from Panzer Regiment 39 (17th Panzer Division) and 1st Battalion, Grenadier Regiment 156 (motorized) (16th Motorized Infantry Division) toward Vessely.
4. 11 Jan 43: Attack with two Tigers and three Panzer IIIs vicinity of Romanovskiy
5. 12–14 Jan 43: 2d Company, Heavy Tank Battalion 503 attacks with 2d Battalion, Grenadier Regiment 60 (motorized) (16th Motorized Infantry Division) and Assault Gun Battalion 243 to stop Soviet penetration vicinity of Novy Manych
6. 17 Jan 43: Withdraw back to via rail from Proletarsk

Regiment 128, attacked towards Stavropol. The 1st Company attacked frontally with the battalion of panzergrenadiers, while the 2d Company attacked from the left flank.[100] Altogether, the battalion fielded 17 operational Tigers out of 20 assigned and 20 Panzer IIIs out of 31.[101] During the engagement, the Tigers knocked out 18 Soviet tanks and destroyed an armored car and five antitank guns.[102] The enemy retreated, and during the pursuit the battalion lost its first vehicle during the entire engagement, a Panzer III, to artillery fire.[103]

Possibly the most important mission given this battalion was its attack to reduce a Soviet penetration at Vessely. The battalion fielded 11 Tigers and 12 Panzer IIIs and was again supported by the 2d Battalion of Panzer-Grenadier Regiment 128, as well as by a battery of light howitzers.[104] The attack began in the early morning of 9 January 1943. German forces made three attempts to achieve their objective during the day, but the Soviets repulsed all attacks.[105]

The battalion managed to destroy eight T-34s during the attack, but also lost two Tigers and one Panzer III to enemy fire.[106] In addition, the nine other Tigers were so badly damaged that the battalion had only one operational Tiger at the end of the day. Two of these Tigers were sent back to Germany for general repairs.[107] In the space of six hours, one of these received 227 hits from antitank rifles and was struck 14 times by 57mm and 11 times by 76mm antitank rounds. It is a testament to the vehicle's durability that despite this damage, the Tiger still traveled back 60 kilometers under its own power.[108]

On 14 January 1943, the 2d Company, Heavy Tank Battalion 502 was attached to Heavy Tank Battalion 503.[109] This became the only instance where three Organization D companies were combined under the control of a single battalion. This arrangement lasted only eight days because of losses to the battalion, however; on 22 January 1943, the battalion disbanded the 2d Company.[110] The battalion integrated the remnants of this company into the 3d Company, and continued to operate with only two Organization D companies.[111]

After partially rebuilding its strength, Army Group Don assigned the battalion missions that involved securing the important railroad centers around Rostov. The battalion participated in many minor local counterattacks that forced it to operate in company- and platoon-sized units. These elements operated with a wide variety of other units, usually in a subordinate role. In accomplishing these missions, the battalion demonstrated excellent flexibility in command and control and in company and platoon organizations, repeatedly changing command relationships and composition to accomplish the mission. (see map 8)

During this fighting, the battalion integrated Tigers and Panzer IIIs in many different ways. On two occasions the battalion formed a light company

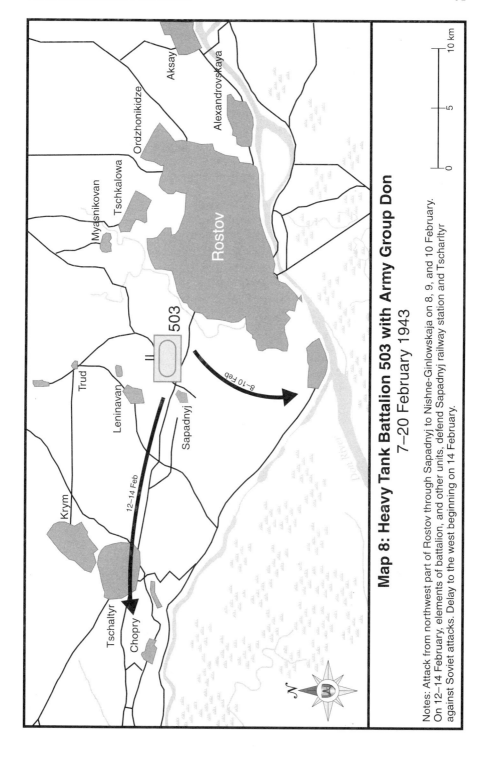

**Map 8: Heavy Tank Battalion 503 with Army Group Don
7–20 February 1943**

Notes: Attack from northwest part of Rostov through Sapadnyj to Nishne-Ginlowskaja on 8, 9, and 10 February. On 12–14 February, elements of battalion, and other units, defend Sapadnyj railway station and Tscharltyr against Soviet attacks. Delay to the west beginning on 14 February.

consisting of a company's worth of Panzer IIIs and a heavy company equipped with Tigers and the remainder of the Panzer IIIs. This light company primarily covered other units' withdrawals, but did participate in an attack of 8 February 1943 in the northwestern sector of Rostov, where it destroyed 12 enemy tanks and three antitank guns.[112] The battalion commander employed this light company because of the difficult terrain, consisting of many ditches, across which the attacks were carried out.

From 19 February to 22 February 1943, the light company, starting with eight Panzer IIIs and two Tigers, conducted local counterattacks and occupied covering positions in the vicinity of Rostov. During this four-day period, the company destroyed 23 T-34s and 11 antitank guns while losing one Tiger and one Panzer III.[113] After an engagement on 22 February 1943, the battalion had only two Tigers and five Panzer IIIs operational and withdrew to an area near Taganrog to refit.[114] This battalion was not employed again until Operation ZITADELLE in July 1943.

During the almost two months of combat with Army Group Don, Heavy Tank Battalion 503 destroyed more than 71 enemy tanks and 55 antitank guns.[115] In so doing, they lost around 13 Panzer IIIs and had three Tigers knocked out due to enemy actions.[116] Another Tiger was destroyed while waiting at the Budenny rail station for transport back to Germany for factory repair when the battalion was forced to retreat to Rostov.[117] A total of four Tigers were so badly damaged in combat that they were transported back to Germany.[118] This means that this battalion destroyed 23.6 enemy tanks for the loss of each Tiger, or 4.4 enemy tanks for the loss of any type tank, Panzer III and Tiger.

Heavy Tank Battalion 503 was much more effective than the units around Leningrad and in North Africa in recovering disabled Tigers. During combat that always involved retrograde movements, its soldiers destroyed only one Tiger to avoid capture. Additionally, this Tiger had already been recovered and loaded on a rail car for transport back to Germany. This battalion's leadership was very reluctant to destroy its own vehicles and did everything possible to recover Tigers. In one instance, three Tigers broke down in a withdrawal; instead of destroying them, the crews stayed with the vehicles until they could be recovered, which was over 30 hours later.[119] Diary entries are filled with examples of operational vehicles towing damaged vehicles back to the maintenance platoon to be repaired. In another instance, while the rest of the unit withdrew, six 18-ton recovery vehicles and two other Tigers recovered a Tiger that broke through the ice of a stream.[120]

Despite the great efforts of the recovery elements, this battalion still suffered from a low operational readiness rate of its Tigers. On average, the battalion only maintained around 35 percent of its Tigers in operational condition.[121] Probably one of the main reasons for Tigers being in need of repair was from damage due to enemy fire. Another reason may have been the great distances that the unit had to traverse. In one instance, the 2d Company conducted a 107-kilometer roadmarch in ten and a half hours.[122] This unit did not lose any vehicles to maintenance breakdowns during the roadmarch, however, probably because the company commander ordered a maintenance halt every 20 kilometers.[123]

Overall, Heavy Tank Battalion 503 was very successful in its operations around Rostov. This unit played a large part in protecting the key road and rail networks that allowed the 1st Panzer Army to retreat. Some historians attribute the actions of this battalion to preventing the Soviets in breaking through to Rostov and cutting the road and rail lines.[124]

Changes Before Operation ZITADELLE

A measure of the effectiveness of the heavy tank battalions fighting the Soviets can be ascertained by looking at the number of actions that the Soviets took in response to this threat. They did not have time to develop a tank to counter the Tiger before Operation ZITADELLE, but they did begin planning for vehicles such as the T-34/85 and the KV-85 heavy tank.

In the interim, the Soviets developed and fielded a heavy self-propelled gun, the SU-152, which was armed with a 152mm gun designed to defeat the German heavy tanks.[125] Additionally, the Soviets continued to field the SU-76 and the SU-122, which were armed with 76mm and 122mm guns, respectively. All of these vehicles were grouped by type into regiments of 21 vehicles (four batteries of five vehicles each and one for the commander) By the time Operation ZITADELLE began, 21 such regiments were at the front, mainly concentrated in the vicinity of Kursk, with three in reserve and 17 still in training.[126]

Also in response to the Tigers, the Soviets formed antitank battalions and assigned them to tank and mechanized corps. Some of these were armed 85mm antiaircraft guns on special mounts with crews trained as antitank gunners. Many, although not all, of the tank and mechanized corps at Kursk had been reinforced with the 85mm antitank battalions prior to the German attack.[127]

Another Soviet response to the appearance of the Tiger was the formation of heavy tank regiments. Production of the KV-85, armed with an 85mm main gun, did not begin until August 1943, after the German offensive at Kursk.[128] So the Soviets gathered all available KV1s and KV2s, armed with a 76mm and 152mm guns, respectively, and formed five heavy tank regiments before the

German offensive began.[129] None of the new tank regiments took part in the Battle of Kursk, but their availability was an indication of the concern to bolster the defense against the German Tigers and the heavy tank battalions.[130]

The Russians realized that the Tiger had a powerful long-range 88mm main gun and thick frontal armor, making it superior to their tanks with 76mm guns and less armor protection. They believed that they could "only be fought effectively in close combat, where the T-34 could use its greater maneuverability and direct its fire at the sides of the heavy German tanks."[131] This tactic resulted in the Soviet tanks "charging" at the German Tigers in an attempt to close the range as quickly as possible so the T-34/76 could have a chance of destroying the Tigers.

The Germans, for their part, were also busy reorganizing the heavy tank battalions into Organization E battalions, doing away with all the Panzer IIIs in the battalion. The deletion of the Panzer IIIs from the organization is contrary to almost all of the recommendations in the available heavy tank battalion after-action reports.[132]

The sole exception to the call for Panzer IIIs in the after-action reviews was a recommendation from the heavy company of the Panzer-Grenadier Division *Grossdeutschland.* At this time, this unit fielded only a heavy company as part of the divisional panzer regiment, but this was soon increased to an entire heavy tank battalion. This report stated:

> The previous combat actions have shown that the Panzer III, originally intended to be a security vehicle for each Tiger, has not evolved to withstand hits from enemy weapons. The opponent's defensive weapons take it under fire in preference to firing at the Tiger. In addition, it would aid in improving the number of operational Panzers by having a pure company made up of only one type of Panzer. A very inefficient and complicated repair staff for the Tiger Company is necessary only because of transportation of Panzer III repair parts in addition to the difficulties with Tiger repair parts. In this case, it is appropriate to reduce Tiger units to only one type of Panzer—the *Panzerkampfwagen VI* (Tiger).[133]

This report was probably more insightful, in retrospect, than the others that advocated retention of the Panzer IIIs. The majority of the recommendations argued for the continued inclusion of the Panzer IIIs so that they could accomplish missions other than those for which they were originally intended, namely scouting, liaison, evacuation of wounded, and resupply of Tigers. General Guderian, as Inspector of Armored Troops, rejected the majority of the recommendations that advocated continued inclusion of Panzer IIIs and argued for the concentration of Tigers in Organization E.[134] He did, however, see the need for an improved scouting and liaison capability, and requested the creation of a reconnaissance platoon, mounted on armored half-tracks, that became part of Organization E.[135]

Another report from Panzer-Grenadier Division *Grossdeutschland* suggested incorporating a heavy tank platoon into every panzer battalion.[136] Others recommended incorporating a heavy tank company into the panzer regiment of every panzer division. Guderian rejected this, saying "dispersing them [Tigers] . . . is an idiotic squandering of this valuable equipment."[137]

The report by the heavy tank company of the Panzer-Grenadier Division *Grossdeutschland* indicated that the unit was constantly employed as the lead element. This initiated responses from the Chief of the Army General Staff, as well as from Guderian, which contradicted the established doctrine for the heavy tank battalions. The armor representative to the German Chief of the Army General Staff wrote:

> Employing Tigers as the lead units is not self-evidently correct. Situations will occur where this is necessary or useful. The controlling factors are the tasks and the number of operational Tigers. If there are [only a few Tigers], their assignment to the point means that the Tigers will not be available when they are needed to attack enemy tanks. Losses will frequently occur due to mines and bridge failure, plus getting hung up in uncrossable terrain. In order to maintain the high operational and production value of the Tigers, it is necessary to concentrate the Tigers in units so that concentrated purposeful employment, maintenance, and care can be achieved.[138]

This message was followed shortly by another from Guderian who took a similar position that seemed to argue against the use of the heavy tank battalion as the lead element in the attack. He wrote:

> The Tiger unit is the most valuable and strongest weapon in a Panzer unit. If it is used as the point unit, it will quickly bring localized success because of its high combat power. However, they will have insufficient force at the start of a decisive battle that could mean destruction of the opponent in the depths of his position because the Tigers will suffer heavy breakdowns due to mines, hits, and terrain obstacles. Therefore, they will enter the decisive phase of the battle already greatly depleted. Fundamentally, point units have increased fuel consumption. Because the Tiger already has a limited radius of action, when it is used as a lead vehicle it will sometimes be short of fuel at the start of the decisive phase of the battle.[139]

Despite these views, there is no record of any new doctrinal guidance being formally published. In any case, one aspect of the doctrine that clearly did not change was the emphasis upon concentration of the heavy tank battalion instead of dispersing it.

Operation ZITADELLE: The Battle of Kursk

Two heavy tank battalions participated in the Battle of Kursk, and both were intended to play major, if not decisive, roles. Heavy Tank Battalion 503 was still in southern Russia as part of Army Group South. It was attached to III Panzer Corps, part of Army Detachment Kempf, during Operation ZITADELLE as part of the southern thrust against the Kursk salient.[140] The other heavy tank battalion involved in this operation was Heavy Tank Battalion 505, attached to Army Group Center.[141]

Both of these battalions received orders to change from Organization D to Organization E in the spring of 1943. Heavy Tank Battalion 503 had completed this transition and fielded 45 Tigers in three companies for the operation.[142] Heavy Tank Battalion 505 was still in the process of making the transition to the Organization E as the offensive began. It completed the formation of two Organization E heavy tank companies, but the third company did not arrive until 8 July 1943, after the start of the offensive.[143] In an attempt to compensate for this, *Funklenk* (Wireless Radio) Company 312 was attached to it.[144] This unit fielded remote controlled Borgward B IV vehicles, carrying 500 kilograms of TNT each. These vehicles were remotely maneuvered into position and then exploded to destroy antitank positions and other emplacements.[145] This company's mission was to detect minefields and assist in clearing lanes through them, as well as assisting in destroying enemy defensive strongpoints such as fortified antitank guns as well as heavy tanks.[146]

This battalion was also unique because of the way in which they used the Panzer IIIs that were still present at the time of the battle. They converted these obsolescent tanks into bridging material carriers by removing their turrets and placing planks, beams, and other bridging material on top.[147] Although the battalion was ordered to repair these vehicles, they had not repaired or turned them in prior to the start of the offensive.[148]

The two heavy tank battalions involved in Operation ZITADELLE were not only organized differently, but were also employed in dissimilar fashions. In the North, Army Group Center attached Heavy Tank Battalion 505 to the 6th Infantry Division of the XLVII Panzer Corps. This corps consisted of three panzer divisions and one infantry division, and was assigned as the main breakthrough force in the North.[149] This was a mission fully in keeping with the doctrinal role for which Tiger battalions had been created. On the other side of the Kursk Salient, Army Group South attached Heavy Tank Battalion 503 to III Panzer Corps, which also consisted of three panzer divisions and one infantry division. This corps was part of the larger *ad hoc* organization known as Army Detachment Kempf and initially had the mission of guarding the flank of II SS-Panzer Corps. It was also tasked with destroying enemy counterattack forces expected to arrive from the east and the north.[150] In spite of Guderian's guidance that Tigers be employed in a concentrated heavy tank battalion and against the strong advice of the battalion commander, the commander of III Panzer Corps initially attached one heavy tank company to each of the corps' panzer divisions.

The units comprising the southern pincer of the German attack consisted mainly of armored units, but there was a shortage of infantry for the tasks at hand. The commanders of 4th Panzer Army and Army Detachment Kempf thus decided to use their tanks in the initial assault on the first day.[151] III Panzer Corps' zone of attack took its units across a level flood plain crisscrossed with small tributaries of the Northern Donets and Razumnoe Rivers. These made excellent obstacles for defense by the Soviets. The defenders reinforced these with mines and other obstacles to vehicular movement, severely restricting German armored units' mobility.[152] (see map 9)

Records concerning Heavy Tank Battalion 503 are filled with accounts of Tigers being halted by minefields; tank ditches; and streams and rivers. On the first day of the attack, the 2d Company had 13 of its 14 Tigers disabled by mines in a single minefield.[153] After attempting but failing to ford the Donets River at 0230 on the first day of the attack, the 3d Company was finally able to cross early in the afternoon, using a bridge erected by combat engineers.[154] During the first three days of the attack, the battalion's Tiger companies supported the three Panzer divisions of III Panzer Corps. During this time, the corps managed to break through the first and second defensive lines, but was still only about 20 kilometers from their line of departure, with another 100 kilometers to go to reach Kursk.[155]

By 7 July 1943, the Soviets were focusing their attention primarily on the success of II SS-Panzer Corps to the west. Tasked to protect the flank of II SS-Panzer Corps, but still well to the south, this success presented a problem for III Panzer Corps. On 7 July 1943, III Panzer Corps consolidated Heavy Tank Battalion 503 and subordinated it to Panzer Regiment 11 of the 6th Panzer Division.[156] The commander of III Panzer Corps gave 6th Panzer Division the mission of spearheading the attack to link up with II SS-Panzer Corps.[157] To complete this link up, the corps had to cross the Donets River again further upstream.[158] Supported by Heavy Tank Battalion 503, the 6th Panzer Division fought through Soviet defenses to Rzhavets across the Donets River, before being detached from III Panzer Corps.[159]

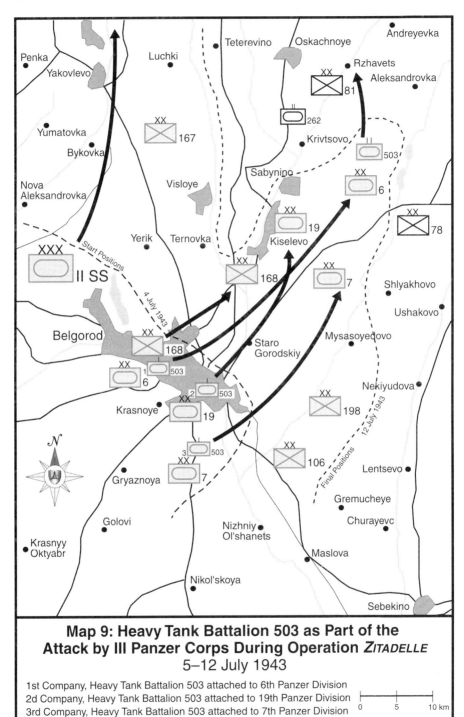

Map 9: Heavy Tank Battalion 503 as Part of the Attack by III Panzer Corps During Operation ZITADELLE
5–12 July 1943

1st Company, Heavy Tank Battalion 503 attached to 6th Panzer Division
2d Company, Heavy Tank Battalion 503 attached to 19th Panzer Division
3rd Company, Heavy Tank Battalion 503 attached to 7th Panzer Division

0   5   10 km

The highlight of this attack was a bold infiltration of Soviet defenses on the night of 11–12 July 1943 by Panzer Regiment 11 and Heavy Tank Battalion 503. This attack, led by Major Franz Bäke under cover of darkness, successfully moved through Soviet defenses and then infiltrated Soviet armor columns as they attempted to reposition in preparation for the next day's operations. To assist in the delicate and risky action, Bäke used two captured T-34s to lead the column, along with two tank commanders who spoke fluent Russian. He also gave orders for the infantry riding on the tanks to smoke and act relaxed. The German column was finally discovered on the outskirts of the town of Rzhavets. This allowed Soviet engineers to blow up the bridges across the Donets before the Germans could capture them. German infantry and engineers used a small bridge to cross over and establish a bridgehead, but it was several days before a much larger bridge capable of carrying the Tigers across was built. As a result, III Panzer Corps did not link up with II SS-Panzer Corps before the tanks from the Soviet 5th Guards Tank Army attacked on 12 July 1943.

Heavy Tank Battalion 503 destroyed approximately 72 Soviet tanks from the beginning of the offensive until the battalion was taken from III Panzer Corps on 14 July 1943.[160] During this time, they lost four Tigers in combat and no Tigers had to be destroyed to avoid capture.[161] This was primarily due to the fact that the battalion was on the offensive and its maintenance and recovery elements could evacuate and repair damaged and disabled Tigers on the battlefield, instead of having to abandon them as in previous battles involving retreats. Overall, the battalion achieved a kill ratio of 18.0 to 1.

In a little over ten days of almost continuous combat, the battalion was able to maintain 57 percent of its Tigers operational, with the highest number available at one time being 42 at the beginning of the operation and the lowest number being six, on 14 July 1943.[162]

In the north, 9th Army had fewer tanks than the southern pincer attack and thus, its commander chose to attack primarily with infantry forces on the first day. The plan was for the infantry to break through the Soviet defenses, allowing panzer units to exploit that breakthrough. The exception to this was the main effort in the north, the XLVII Panzer Corps. This corps attacked on the first day with the 20th Panzer Division and the 6th Infantry Division.[163] Despite the official guidance against attaching a heavy tank battalion to an infantry division, Heavy Tank Battalion 505 was attached to the 6th Infantry Division as part of the XLVII Panzer Corps. (see map 10)

On the first day of the attack, after crossing the river Oka and seizing the village of Novy-Chutor, the commander of the 6th Infantry Division ordered Heavy Tank Battalion 505 to attack at 0930 hours.[164] With its two companies and the attached *Funklenk* Company 312, the battalion easily destroyed

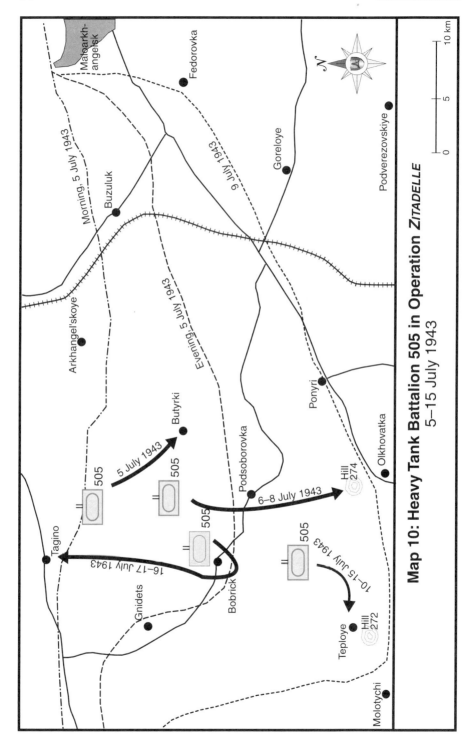

Map 10: Heavy Tank Battalion 505 in Operation ZITADELLE
5–15 July 1943

dug-in enemy tanks to their front and penetrated the defenses on the 15th Rifle Division's right wing. This battalion attack allowed German forces to secure the important village of Butyrki and threatened the Soviet first echelon divisions with encirclement. Heavy Tank Battalion 505 had advanced farther and faster than Model had ever anticipated, but because the plan called for the commitment of the panzer divisions on the second day, these units were not in position to exploit the breakthrough. German accounts mention an opportunity lost by not positioning armored forces to exploit the tactical breakthrough of the Soviet defenses by Heavy Tank Battalion 505. The Commanding General of the 6th Infantry Division stated:

> We could observe movements by the Russians. If the tanks had rolled through then, we could perhaps have reached the objective of Kursk because the enemy was completely surprised and still weak. Valuable time was lost, which the enemy used to rush in his reserves.[165]

The unit history of Heavy Tank Battalion 505 tells more of the potential opportunity lost:

> 5 July 1943: The battalion's penetration to Butyrki leads to the complete collapse of the Soviet 15th Infantry Division, causing a major crisis on the right wing of the 70th Army. The employment of the 2d Panzer Division at that time, not as scheduled on the following day, would have destroyed the whole front![166]

The success of the battalion's attack is reemphasized by the fact that the Central Front commander, General Rokossovsky, quickly reinforced the 13th Army with 350 aircraft and control of the 13th and 1st Antitank Brigades, an artillery brigade, and the 21st Separate Mortar Brigade from the Central Front Reserve.[167] In an immediate attempt to stabilize the front, the 13th Army commander, General Pukhov, committed his reserve 27th Guards Tank Regiment and combat engineer units from all parts of the 13th Army.[168]

The next day, 6 July 1943, Heavy Tank Battalion 505 continued its attack, this time supporting the 2d and 9th Panzer Divisions.[169] This attack caused the front and army commanders to commit further armored reserves to defeat the German penetration and reestablish the first defensive belt.[170] The Soviets committed the 16th Tank Corps consisting of two tank brigades.[171] The lead tank brigade unexpectedly encountered Heavy Tank Battalion 505 and in a matter of a few minutes, the Germans destroyed 46 of the brigade's 50 tanks.[172] The supporting tank brigade was also heavily damaged, losing a further 23 tanks.[173]

For the next three days, the battalion continued to attack, along with the 2d and the 9th Panzer Divisions, in an attempt to secure the strategically important town of Ol'khovatka.[174] In addition to determined resistance from Soviet infantry, the Soviets continued to commit their armored reserves into the battle and the Germans never took the town.

On 9 July 1943, 9th Army ordered Heavy Tank Battalion 505 to withdraw from the battle to act as corps reserve for XLVII Panzer Corps.[175] From 10 to 11 July 1943, Heavy Tank Battalion 505 supported attacks toward Toploye.[176] The battalion went over to the defense and from 15 to 17 July 1943, it withdrew to its original start line.[177]

Heavy Tank Battalion 505 was successful in destroying a large number of enemy tanks during their breakthrough attempt on the first day and were again successful in destroying a large group of enemy tanks during the Soviet counterattack on the second day. They were, however, unable to overcome the repeated counterattacks and the well-established, deep Soviet defenses, to assist in breaking through on an operational level.

Heavy Tank Battalion 505 destroyed 42 Soviet tanks on the opening day of Operational ZITADELLE on 5 July 1943 and another 67 the next day.[178] During fighting in the next few days, the attached *Funklenk* Company 312 destroyed an additional T-34.[179] After the German offensive in the north stalled, the battalion assisted in repulsing Soviet armored counterattacks on 15 and 17 July 1943, destroying another 22 and 32 enemy tanks respectively.[180] During the period of employment when the Germans were on the offensive, Heavy Tank Battalion 505 destroyed a total of 110 enemy tanks, and a further 54 tanks after going over to the defense.[181]

During the same time, this unit lost a total of only five Tigers to enemy fire.[182] Three of these were lost during offensive operations and two were lost during defensive operations after 16 July 1943. As with Heavy Tank Battalion 503 in the south, this battalion was on the offensive and could more easily recover its damaged and broken vehicles. The result was that there were no Tigers destroyed by their own crews. Even though this battalion was unable to penetrate through the entire Soviet defenses and accomplish its mission, it was able to achieve a 36.6-to-1 kill ratio during offensive operations against an enemy that was in well-prepared, deeply echeloned defenses and a 27.0-to-1 kill ratio when on the defensive.

This battalion suffered from a low operational rate during Operation ZITADELLE, maintaining an average of only 45.7 percent operational from 4 to 20 July 1943.[183] At the start of the battle it fielded 26 Tigers, but by the end of the second day of fighting, it only had six operational Tigers remaining.[184] After its 3d company arrived on 8 July 1943, the battalion fielded 29 Tigers, the highest total that it was able to achieve throughout Operation ZITADELLE.[185]

Unit diaries and other histories do not indicate exact numbers, but they make it clear that a major portion of the vehicles from both heavy tank battalions involved in Operation *ZITADELLE* were damaged by mines. This is very surprising considering that both battalions were augmented or supported by additional engineer troops during some or all of the operation. Also, German sources do not mention it, but Soviet sources credit the Tiger tank with being mounted with a mine roller capable of detecting the forward edge of a minefield.

> Under pressure of our powerful artillery fire, the Germans cleared mines and obstacles with the help of tanks, together with the work of sappers. For this purpose the enemy used Tiger tanks in front of which were attached 6 to 7 meter rods with a wooden roller set up on them. When the roller came up against a mine, the mine exploded, while the tank remained unharmed. In this manner the enemy easily detected the forward edge of the minefield, which was cleared with the help of sapper units.[186]

The heavy tank battalions did, however, receive considerable damage from mines and when they encountered a minefield they were slowed or stopped until sappers could clear a path.

Regardless of whether these mine rollers were actually used, it appears that the preferred method of mine clearing was by manual means, exposing personnel outside of an armored vehicle. When enemy fire was too heavy, it seems that the secondary method of mine breaching was to drive through the minefield with Tigers. This resulted in damage to the vehicles, but saved personnel. Minefields probably had a great deal to do with the dramatic decline in operational rates within both battalions after the first day or two of combat.

Summary

From the initial employment until the Battle of Kursk, the heavy tank battalions evolved from Organization D, which integrated Tigers with Panzer IIIs, to the Tiger pure Organization E. This change was made based upon experience gained in combat in North Africa and throughout Russia, and was made possible by increased Tiger production. The inclusion of Panzer IIIs provided the heavy tank battalion with a high degree of flexibility in tailoring the force required to accomplish the missions assigned. However, the Panzer IIIs were not sufficiently well armored to survive long in combat as part of a heavy tank battalion.

With a few notable exceptions, the heavy tank battalions were not employed in accordance with the doctrine established for them. Specifically, their employment violated the concept of concentration. This was largely due to the tactical requirements of each situation. At Kursk, when they were concentrated, they did not meet the high expectations throughout the German Army for these units, although they did achieve respectable results in terms of sheer numbers of enemy tanks destroyed.

During this period, guidance for the employment of heavy tank battalions changed slightly based upon after-action analyses. Originally, doctrine advocated using the battalion as a point element. After evaluating several reports from heavy tank companies and battalions, Guderian and other influential leaders cautioned restraint in employing it in the lead in all cases. They felt that the unit would achieve initial results as the vanguard of the attack, but might not be available to fight the decisive battle. This did not deter the leaders at Kursk from employing the heavy tank battalions as the leading units in the attack. Guderian's fears were realized during Operation ZITADELLE when both heavy tank battalions involved were reduced to low numbers of operational Tigers within a few days.

The Tiger proved to be an excellent tank that could withstand many hits from large-caliber shells and still continue its mission. The low number of Tigers destroyed by direct enemy action is proof of its resilience. It was, however, a very maintenance-intensive vehicle. On many occasions, this forced heavy tank battalions to operate with only a fraction of the vehicles authorized.

The low operational rate may have, paradoxically, contributed to the low number of Tigers destroyed in combat. There were only a few Tigers operational during the various campaigns, therefore, there were also only a few Tigers available to be destroyed in battle. The handful of operational vehicles proved many times, especially in the defense, however, that they were capable of locally wreaking havoc on enemy armored units. The defense, a mission for which heavy tank battalions were not originally intended, became the primary focus of German units after the Battle of Kursk.

Chapter 4

On the Strategic Defensive

An A.F.H.Q [Armored Force Headquarters] training instruction states that the size and weight of the *Pz Kw VI* [Tiger] present many problems. PW [Prisoner of War] indicated that extensive reconnaissance of terrain, bridges, etc., was necessary before operations with this tank could be undertaken. Bridges had to be reinforced in many cases, and it was necessary for the "going" to be good for the effective employment of the *Pz Kw VI.*[1]

> British interrogation report of captured
> German prisoner, April 1943

Tiger production greatly increased after the Battle of Kursk. The three heavy tank battalions that were largely destroyed by the summer of 1943 were reconstituted and all new heavy tank battalions fielded were equipped and organized in accordance with Organization E. By the beginning of summer 1944, Germany fielded 12 heavy tank battalions and was in the process of equipping the last Army heavy tank battalion, Heavy Tank Battalion 510. Throughout this 12-month period, most of these heavy tank battalions were employed against Soviet forces in the east. Only two heavy tank battalions fought against American and British forces during this year, both in Italy.

As the expected Allied invasion of France neared however, the Germans positioned several heavy tank battalions in the West to counter the anticipated landings. Two of these were newly-fielded *Waffen-SS* battalions, with SS-Heavy Tank Battalion 501 being stationed in Belgium and SS-Heavy Tank Battalion 502 being stationed in the Netherlands. The third heavy tank battalion was the very combat-experienced Heavy Tank Battalion 503, which was reconstituted in Germany.

In spite of the fact that the German military was forced into a defensive posture at the strategic and operational levels, doctrine for the employment of heavy tank battalions did not change. Expectations were high for heavy tank battalions and they were continually given extremely difficult missions. As a result, heavy tank battalions suffered from heavy losses of Tigers and experienced sharp declines in the number of operational Tigers when committed. Additionally, the Tiger's mechanical unreliability continued to plague the heavy tank battalions and stress their recovery and maintenance assets, especially during rapid and extended movements.

Fighting on the Russian Front

The failed German offensive at Kursk was followed by a series of Soviet counteroffensives that pushed the Germans back 240 kilometers across a front of 1050 kilometers.[2] In addition to the two heavy tank battalions that participated in Operation ZITADELLE, OKH committed four more heavy tank battalions to Army Groups Center and South by the end of 1943 in an attempt to stop the Soviet offensives.[3] The Soviet threat was focused in the south, so three heavy tank battalions joined Heavy Tank Battalion 503 in Army Group South's sector. These three battalions, the 3d Battalion of Panzer Regiment Grossdeutschland, and Heavy Tank Battalions 506 and 509 arrived on the Eastern Front in August, September, and November, respectively.[4]

All of the battalions that took part in the retreat in the latter half of 1943 encountered many difficult situations. These heavy tank battalions defended across extended frontages, often without any infantry support. They also had to overcome obstacles such as recovery of damaged and broken-down vehicles during retrograde operations involving river crossings. Another common experience among these battalions was that of piecemeal employment as elements of the battalions arrived at the front at different times.[5]

One of the most extensive and candid after-action reviews from a unit during this time came from the commander of Heavy Tank Battalion 506, Major Withing. It exhaustively detailed the losses that the Tigers suffered and the transportation problems encountered, as well as the problems of maintenance; command and control; and coordination with supporting units, especially infantry. The nature of the problems this battalion encountered are probably indicative of the problems encountered by all of the heavy tank battalions with Army Groups South and Center at this time.

During its deployment in September 1943, it took four days for the trains carrying the battalion's vehicles and equipment to arrive and be downloaded at a single station.[6] It was attached to the 9th Panzer Division of the XL Panzer Corps, which had the mission of containing the Soviets in the Zaporozhe bridgehead. Withing's report was very critical of the supporting infantry, and placed the blame for their poor performance on low morale resulting from long retreats and substandard training.

The battalion was in continuous combat from the moment they arrived at the front and because of the repeated Russian attacks, XL Panzer Corps transferred them back and forth across the front to the most threatened sectors.

This did not allow much time for maintenance of the Tigers and the report states that they barely had time to refuel and load available ammunition between engagements.[7]

This type of employment, without adequate maintenance periods, caused extreme difficulties. Within seven days, the battalion was reduced from 45 new, operational Tigers to zero ready for combat.[8] Only six of these Tigers were totally destroyed, however, all from hits by direct-fire weapons. The unit after-action report did contain a complete accounting of the damage to the other Tigers of the battalion. This report made it clear that there were many other Tigers that were very badly damaged from combat.

An interesting aspect of the damages is the fact that even small deficiencies like the destruction of the driver's vision block severely degraded the Tiger's operation. The Soviets found it difficult to penetrate the Tiger; consequently, the battalion commander wrote that "the Russians fired all of their weapons at the running gear, gun, and vision slits."[9] This effectively immobilized a large number of Tigers or rendered them combat ineffective. Another deficiency on many Tigers was the failure of the vehicle's internal communication system. The report stated that "the driver could no longer be directed by the commander, which made command extraordinarily difficult because the Tiger had to halt and the engine switched off each time the commander needed to redirect the driver."[10]

Withing made it clear in his report that he believed that the battalion was not being employed correctly. He complained that other units and his higher headquarters had such high expectations for his unit that the battalion was given impossible missions, without proper support from the other branches of the Army. A common theme throughout this report is that this battalion was a victim of the propaganda concerning the Tiger tank. The battalion commander wrote:

> The extensive propaganda in the newspapers touts the Tiger as being invulnerable and pure life insurance, so the higher command as well as the simple infantry soldier believes that they can continuously accomplish everything with this fortress.[11]

Major Withing was killed in action less than a month after he wrote the report, but his successor was equally critical of the employment of Heavy Tank Battalion 506.[12] After many difficult months of continual employment across wide frontages, usually in the foremost defensive positions and often with little or no infantry support, the battalion commander sought to clarify the doctrinal role of his battalion. He wrote:

> Our understanding still remains the same as a year ago, that the Tiger is a battering ram in the attack and a bumpstop to be used as the

Schwerpunkt [decisive point, or main effort] on defense. It is to stand ready in sufficient numbers for the higher command to use at the decisive moment. However, this can occur only if, in between the main battles, time is given for care and maintenance instead of being continuously employed as mobile bunkers.[13]

His real criticism was on the performance of the infantry whom he stated lacked the training and morale to remain in defensive positions without the direct support of Tigers. As a positive example, he cited the conduct of the panzergrenadiers of the 13th Panzer Division as exemplary because they remained alone in their forward positions, allowing tanks to consolidate and counterattack from assembly areas in the rear. In other units he stated, "as soon as the tanks pull back, the infantry immediately follow, as if drawn magnetically."[14]

Encirclement: The Cherkassy Pocket

On 3 January 1944 Heavy Tank Battalion 503 received a full complement of 45 new Tiger tanks.[15] The replacement vehicles arrived just in time to take part in the fighting around Cherkassy.

On 11 January 1944, III Panzer Corps incorporated at least 35 Tigers of Heavy Tank Battalion 503 with the 2d Battalion of Panzer Regiment 23 and several support units to form Heavy Panzer Regiment Bäke, named for its commander, Oberstleutnant Franz Bäke.[16] This regiment's employment around Cherkassy can be viewed in three phases. The unit's initial mission was to relieve pressure on the two German corps defending further east, at Cherkassy, by attacking north into the encircling Soviet formations around Medwin.[17] Soviet forces had not yet completed their encirclement of German forces around Cherkassy and this attack was intended to intercept and destroy Soviet armored forces before they could complete their task.[18] The second and third phases involved the regiment spearheading attacks attempting to break through the encircling Soviet forces to allow German forces to escape.

This improvised combat group began its initial attack toward Oratoff at 0600 hours on 24 January 1944.[19] Over the next five days of fluid fighting, the group destroyed 267 enemy tanks while losing only three Tigers and four Panthers.[20] Furthermore, one of the Tigers was reportedly destroyed by a mistaken shot by a Panther, not from enemy fire.[21]

During this attack, the battalion was plagued by resupply problems. These problems stemmed from two sources: a lack of supply vehicles and strong partisan forces and other mobile Soviet formations that operated along the battalion's supply route. Extensive and continual combat employment, in addition to experiencing difficulties in maintaining Tigers, caused this battalion to have trouble maintaining its wheeled and tracked support vehicles that were necessary for it to function effectively.

At one point in the operation, only 68 out of Heavy Tank Battalion 503's 111 cross-country vehicles were operational. This meant that the battalion could carry only 119 tons out of the total 234 tons of supplies required.[22] This led to severe logistical problems since there were no paved roads in the area of operations and supplies, especially fuel, had to be transported long distances over muddy ground when temperatures rose above freezing.

The already-overburdened supply and maintenance sections had to deal with the constant threat of Soviet attacks along their main supply routes. The 1st Company's entire maintenance section was killed by partisan forces around Oratov.[23] In fact, when the battalion was ordered to reposition further south to begin attempts to break through to encircled German forces, they found Soviet forces occupying the railhead from which they were to depart.[24] After a short battle, involving the destruction of 46 Soviet tanks, Heavy Panzer Regiment Bäke loaded their vehicles onto railcars. This unit was lucky to depart when it did because it narrowly escaped yet another Soviet attack on the railhead.

After the Soviets completed the encirclement of German forces in Cherkassy on 28 January 1944, the 1st Panzer Army commander ordered the III Panzer Corps and Heavy Panzer Regiment Bäke to move south and prepare for an attack to the northeast, toward the town of Medvin. This was the shortest distance between German forces outside of the Soviet encirclement and German forces in the pocket and as such, was anticipated by Soviet commanders. This attack, known as Operation WANDA, was spearheaded by Heavy Panzer Regiment Bäke.[25] Following behind this unit were the two panzer divisions in the corps, the 16th Panzer Division on the left and the 17th Panzer Division on the right.[26] Heavy Tank Battalion 503 often led the attack of Heavy Panzer Regiment Bäke throughout the operation.[27]

This attack began at 0600 hours on 4 February 1944 and was preceded by a strong artillery bombardment on the Soviet positions. Despite the fact that the Soviets expected a German attack in this area, the German attack progressed very well on its first day. Fighting over muddy road conditions because of an unusually early thaw, German units still managed to penetrate over 30 kilometers into the Soviet defensive positions.[28] This may have been due to the fact that on the first day the Germans were opposed by only one Soviet rifle corps, which possessed no tanks.[29] The next day, however, Soviet defenses were reinforced by 130 tanks from the 5th Mechanized Corps and the 5th Guards Tank Corps.[30]

On 5 February 1944, the two trailing panzer divisions lost contact with each other because of the strong Soviet defenses. The corps commander ordered Heavy Panzer Regiment Bäke to close the gap. During this operation, commencing early in the morning, the regiment encountered a Soviet tank force, reinforced by antitank guns, defending between two ravines. Oberstleutnant Bäke used a tactic that he employed several times during the existence of the heavy panzer regiment. The Tigers of Heavy Tank Battalion 503 fixed the Soviet forces frontally, probably through long-range direct fire, while at the same time the Panthers of 2d Battalion, Panzer Regiment 23 maneuvered around the flank of the Soviet defensive position. Carefully coordinating the two units, the regimental commander described his plan:

> The attack began at 0600 hours. . . . At daylight, the Panther battalion advanced in a large arc around the right-hand *balka* [ravine] until it was possible to cross over in the enemy's rear. At about 0830 hours, the Panther battalion attacked in the rear of the completely-surprised enemy.[31]

In conjunction with the attack from the rear, Oberstleutnant Bäke also ordered the Tigers, supported by the reconnaissance battalion from the 16th Panzer Division, to attack the Soviet forces frontally. This tactic was applied without the loss of a single Tiger or Panther and resulted in the rapid destruction of 31 of the 40 Soviet tanks defending the ravines. It also resulted in a quick penetration of Soviet defenses.[32]

The German attack continued until the evening of 7 February 1944, but failed to achieve the desired link-up with the encircled German forces. This failure can be attributed to several factors. First, the mud and poor terrain conditions severely restricted vehicular movement. This caused resupply problems for the forward elements in terms of both ammunition and fuel. As Oberstleutnant Bäke wrote later:

> The movement, especially of tracked vehicles, was especially hindered by the completely muddied roads. As an example of the strength-robbing nature of the men against the mud, many Grenadiers took off their boots and walked barefoot through the morass, as this was easier than taking several steps, each time having to stop to dig one's boots out of the mud.[33]

Although the weather and terrain were theoretically neutral, in that they did not favor one side over the other: the Soviets were able to transfer the 5th Guards Tank Corps as well as remnants of the 3d and 16th Tank Corps to the threatened sector.[34]

An indication of the ability of Soviet armored forces to continue to operate and the difficulties that the German forces had at the same time is seen in Heavy Panzer Regiment Bäke's operations on 6 February 1944. On this day, some elements were tasked with providing protection for supply convoys, with Tiger tanks being used to pull supply vehicles through the mud, since nothing else seemed to work.[35] Some Tigers did stay in front-line positions and consequently suffered from a lack of supplies. As one tank commander wrote:

> For days, neither rations nor other supplies had made it to us, since the perpetual rain had turned every path into a sea of mud. Again and again, Russian tanks and infantry were shot to pieces in various attacks. Our basic load had been reduced to a few rounds. A fourth tank brought us 15 rounds for the three Tigers.[36]

Heavy Tank Battalion 503's capability to assist in further attacks after 5 February 1944 was also limited by the destruction a key bridge in the area: the only span across the Gniloy Tikich River capable of bearing the weight of a Tiger was blown up as they neared it.[37]

Finally, on the evening of 7 February 1944, the 1st Panzer Army called off further attacks because the German forces in the pocket had moved further to the east, away from the German spearheads attacking to link up with them.[38] This was due in part from increasing Soviet pressure, but the German commander inside the pocket also wanted to shorten his defensive lines.[39]

Heavy Panzer Regiment Bäke continued to defend for several more days until moving further to the south to prepare for yet another relief attempt. Army Group South ordered the 1st Panzer Army to move III Panzer Corps south to attack in an easterly direction toward the town of Lysyanka, where they were to link up with German forces in the pocket.[40] By 9 July 1944, most of Heavy Tank Battalion 503 returned to the original starting position from which they had attacked on 4 February 1944.

By this time, the battalion was in very poor condition. At best, they probably had only 20 mission-capable Tigers.[41] In terms of personnel, the battalion was in even worse shape. Out of the 17 officers authorized in the battalion, only three were available for duty.[42] One of these was the battalion surgeon, and another was a logistics support specialist. The sole combat officer was Oberleutnant Walter Scherf, the Commander of the 3d Company, who took over as battalion commander. He dissolved the tank companies and reorganized the "battalion" into four platoons.[43]

This battalion's shortage of operational Tigers was in part made up by the attachment of Heavy Tank Battalion 506 to Heavy Panzer Regiment Bäke, although it appears that they were reassigned to the 16th or 17th Panzer Divisions after the first day of operations.[44] This battalion possessed 27 Tigers, although it is doubtful whether even half of them were operational.[45] The attack began early in the morning on 11 February 1944 and continued until 16 February 1944 when elements inside the pocket began their breakout. (see map 11)

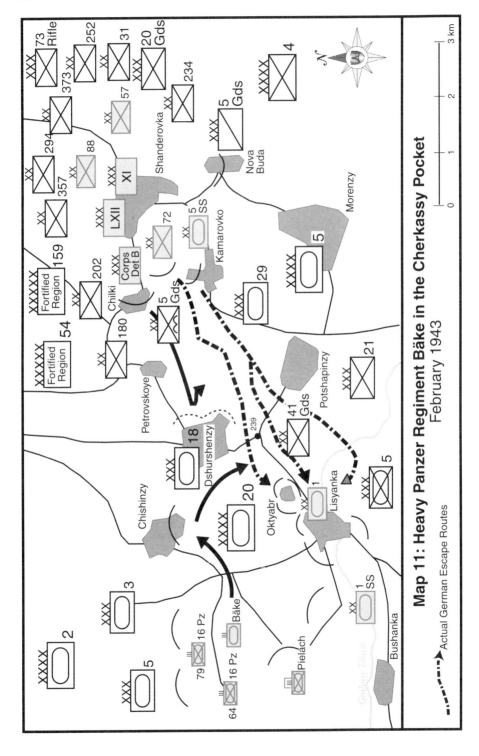

Map 11: Heavy Panzer Regiment Bäke in the Cherkassy Pocket
February 1943

Actual German Escape Routes

Just as with their attack during the previous week, Heavy Panzer Regiment Bäke met with great initial success on the first day, overcoming three Soviet defensive belts and penetrating to a depth of 15 kilometers.[46] During this first day's attack, the Tigers of both heavy tank battalions assisted in capturing a bridge over the Gniloy Tikich River. Even though great care and effort was made in capturing this bridge intact, they found that it was not strong enough for the Tigers to use. The Panthers and other German elements, therefore, continued the attack on the north side of the river, leaving the Tigers behind. Later in the day, reconnaissance efforts successfully located a ford site and the Tigers moved to the north side of the river near the town of Frankovka. They were short of fuel so they formed an assembly area and waited for the supply trains to catch up.

Soviet forces countered the German attack on 12 February 1944 by positioning elements of the 5th Guards Tank Corps and the 20th Tank Corps in a strong defensive position north of Frankovka. This force consisted of approximately 80 tanks and 50 antitank guns that effectively blocked the advance of German units toward their objective. Integrating Stuka dive bombers with the attack, Oberstleutnant Bäke employed the same tactic that worked so well for his unit during their last attack. After being refueled, the Tigers of Heavy Tank Battalion 503 fixed the Soviet forces frontally while the Panthers maneuvered around the right flank. This attack was also supported by elements of the 16th Panzer Division, which enveloped the left flank. Altogether, the German attack destroyed 70 of the 80 Soviet tanks as well as 40 of the 50 antitank guns.[47] Of these, Heavy Tank Battalion 503 claimed to have destroyed between 20 and 25 of the Soviet tanks.[48] German losses in Heavy Panzer Regiment Bäke were four Tigers and four Panthers.[49]

The regiment continued their attack on 13 February 1944, reaching the Medwin-Lisyanka road. There, they defeated several Soviet armored counterattacks. By this time, Heavy Tank Battalion 503 had only 12 Tigers operational. They managed to destroy six out of seven Soviet tanks attacking down the road from Medwin.[50] Later in the day, they destroyed 10 of 15 Soviet tanks attacking from the town of Chishinzy.[51]

By 14 February 1944 Heavy Tank Battalion 503 was reduced to only nine operational Tigers.[52] While follow-on forces secured the towns on either flank, they continued to defend against Soviet counterattacks in the general area of the Medwin-Lisyanka road. As one of the tank commanders described later:

> We remained in our positions on the road to Dzhurshenzy and had to ward off at least four attacks by groups of five to seven Russian tanks, each attack thus approximating a weak tank company. At least 20 tanks were knocked out in the process. Increasingly, we also had to fight off infantry. In the meantime, our own infantry closed up and we were a bit

more secure against hunter/killer teams. Snow squalls and fog dampened the noise of the fighting; due to poor visibility enemy tanks did not emerge into sight until they were extremely close.[53]

The first part of 15 February 1944 was spent conducting an attack northeast toward Dzhurshenzy in an attempt to break through to the pocket. Unfortunately for Heavy Tank Battalion 503, the Soviets were continually concentrating forces, probably from the 20th Tank Corps, in that very area. The Tigers in the battalion succeeded in destroying 14 Soviet tanks, but in the process, lost one Tiger completely and had three others damaged.[54] Despite their losses, the Soviets held back the German attack.

Sometime during the day, III Panzer Corps ordered Heavy Panzer Regiment Bäke, minus the Panther battalion, to move to support an attack to seize the key terrain feature known as Hill 239. They linked up with Combat Group Frank of the 1st Panzer Division later in the day and succeeded in capturing a section of the town of Oktyabr. They ended the day extremely low on supplies, including fuel, and with only seven operational Tigers in Heavy Tank Battalion 503.[55]

Early in the morning on 16 February 1944, Ju-52 transports parachuted steel drums of gasoline and crates of tank ammunition to the German forces preparing to attack Hill 239.[56] After refueling and stowing ammunition inside their tanks, they attacked and seized the remainder of the town of Oktyabr. From here, they prepared for the final assault on Hill 239, only two kilometers away. Between the attacking German forces and the ones trapped inside the pocket were an increasing quantity of Soviet forces. In addition to the 20th Tank Corps, elements of the 3d Tank Corps were now in the area. These were reinforced by two rifle divisions and an antitank brigade. Although many of these units were understrength, they were able to achieve an average density of between eight to ten tanks reinforced by 30 to 36 artillery and mortar tubes per kilometer of front.[57]

Maintenance efforts actually increased Heavy Tank Battalion 503's strength to eight Tigers ready for the attack. Supported by nine Panthers and 12 half-tracks carrying infantry, these Tigers attacked Hill 239 and succeeded in reaching the road intersection near its crest.[58] Once there, however, they came under intense counterattacks and direct fire from tanks in the town of Dzhurshenzy and from woods around the hill. Initially, because of their vulnerability, the half-tracks withdrew, but eventually the Tigers also withdrew from the intersection. During this brief attack, Heavy Tank Battalion 503's Tigers destroyed 20 Soviet tanks while losing one Tiger.[59] Although the Germans developed plans to retake the hill, the attack on 16 February 1944 was the furthest that the relief attack came to the German forces inside the pocket before they began their breakout.

At some point prior to 17 February 1944, Oberstleutnant Bäke assumed command of a combat group in the 1st Panzer Division. The acting commander of Heavy Tank Battalion 503, Oberleutnant Walter Scherff, took over Heavy Panzer Regiment Bäke. A few months before, he had been a mere platoon leader in the 3d Company of Heavy Tank Battalion 503; now he was commanding a regiment, albeit in name, not in size.

German forces inside the pocket were unaware that the linkup site of Hill 239 was not controlled by relieving forces. When they began their breakout at 1100 hours on 16 February 1944, therefore, they moved toward that point as planned. The first elements breaking out managed to infiltrate past Soviet forces in the dark and made contact with the Tigers of Heavy Tank Battalion 503, just a few hundred meters southwest of Hill 239, around 0410 hours on 17 February.[60] After Soviet forces became aware of the breakout attempt, German units were forced to move to the south to attempt a link up with German forces around Lisyanka.

By 1100 hours, Oberstleutnant Bäke realized that German forces breaking out were having great difficulty in crossing over the Gniloy Tikich River three kilometers east of Lisyanka. In addition, Soviet forces were freely roaming throughout the countryside searching for German units attempting to breakout. As Leon Degrelle, commander of SS Assault Brigade "Wallonia," one of the units breaking out of the pocket, wrote:

> We were scarcely starting up the slope when, turning back, we saw hundreds of cavalry racing down a hill to the southwest. We thought at first that it was German Uhlans [Lancers. Ed.]. Looking through my binoculars, I could clearly make out the uniform of the cavalry. They were Cossacks. I recognized their nervous little brown horses. They were rushing up behind us, swarming in every direction. We were stupefied. The Soviet infantry was machine-gunning us. The Soviet tanks were following us. And now the Cossacks were storming in for the kill.[61]

Bäke ordered Heavy Tank Battalion 503 to seize Hill 239 and attack toward the town of Pochapintsy. This was intended to relieve the pressure on the troops breaking out of the pocket as well as shortening their route to friendly lines.

In command of eight Tigers, Oberleutnant Scherff attacked and seized Hill 239 against little opposition by 1130 hours. Ordered by Bäke to continue the attack, Scherff's unit was relieved on Hill 239 by several Panthers. By 1230 hours the eight Tigers reached the outskirts of Pochapintsy and quickly defeated several Soviet counterattacks.[62] After several groups of German troops linked up with the Tigers, intense artillery fire forced Scherff and his men to withdraw to Hill 239. Artillery fire continued on the hill as the Soviets launched a series of attacks, supported by armor. At 1545 hours, low on ammunition and fuel, Scherff withdrew to German lines at Oktyabr.

By the evening of 17 February 1944, Heavy Panzer Regiment Bäke only had eight operational Tigers and six Panthers.[63] Other German units relieved it on 19 February and Heavy Panzer Regiment Bäke disbanded six days later.[64]

Reports do not differentiate between the tank kills of Heavy Tank Battalion 503 and of the Panthers of the 2d Battalion, Panzer Regiment 23. These two battalions of Heavy Panzer Regiment Bäke are credited with the destruction of 329 Soviet tanks during almost two months of fighting around Cherkassy.[65] During that time, Heavy Tank Battalion 503 lost 22 Tigers, six of which were destroyed by their own crews because of failed recovery attempts.

Even though the battalion was unable to break through the encirclement, they did penetrate far enough to allow German forces in the pocket to link up with relieving forces. They were continually given the most difficult missions as the spearhead of the German attacks. The seemingly impossible was often asked of them, and they usually accomplished it. As the lead unit throughout most of the operation, their participation must be viewed as successful. The battalion played a major role in the attacks to relieve the 56,000 German soldiers trapped inside the pocket, and much of the credit for the extrication of more than 30,000 of these German soldiers must be awarded to this unit.[66]

Because the number of enemy tank kills cannot be directly attributed to Heavy Tank Battalion 503, a precise kill ratio comparison cannot be made. Attributing even a conservative number of the 329 Soviet tank kills to the battalion establishes this as a very successful operation.[67] The low number of Tigers destroyed by their own crews is also notable, although the battalion was attacking most of the time, making it easier to recover damaged and disabled vehicles.

Italy

The employment of the heavy tank battalions in Italy highlighted their deficiencies in recovery vehicles and the high maintenance requirements of Tiger tanks. Two heavy tank battalions, Heavy Tank Battalion 508 and 504, saw action in Italy. The first to be committed, Heavy Tank Battalion 508, arrived at the Anzio front in the middle of February 1944.[68] Army Group C committed this battalion in various locations in Italy during the next year until they turned over their remaining 15 Tigers to Heavy Tank Battalion 504 on 12 February 1945.[69] That battalion was first employed in Italy on 20 June 1944 and surrendered to American and British forces in Italy at the end of the war without any operational tanks.[70]

After the Allied landings at Anzio on 22 January 1944, *OKH* ordered Heavy Tank Battalion 508 to assist in eliminating the beachhead.[71] Due to Allied air superiority and the problems in transportation created by aerial interdiction of German lines of communication, the battalion was unloaded at a railhead 200 kilometers from its destination of Anzio. The Tigers' mechanical deficiencies were highlighted during this roadmarch. About 60 percent of the Tigers broke down because of problems in negotiating the narrow, sharply-twisting mountain roads and one Tiger even caught fire and exploded.[72] Instead of a single powerful force of 45 Tigers, the battalion arrived at the Anzio front piecemeal.[73]

The battalion's first attack was on 16 February 1944, but because of the swampy terrain, the Tigers were forced to stay on the few roads in the area, and they did not achieve their objective.[74] This battalion participated in several more unsuccessful attacks that attempted to reduce the Allied bridgehead from the north. Operating out of the area known as "The Factory," small elements of the battalion supported attacks against the American forces defending along Dead End Road and then along the Lateral Road. Because of the swampy terrain, the Tigers stayed on the primary roads and supported attacks along the road from The Factory to Anzio and the road called "The Bowling Alley." Its crews and their vehicles also helped to contain the bridgehead, destroying three Shermans that penetrated the front lines on 21 February 1944.[75] (see map 12)

The German forces launched their last attempt to eliminate the bridgehead on 29 February 1944. It was doomed to failure because of the restrictive terrain, forcing the attack to proceed along the main roads. (see maps 13 and 14)

Even though the Germans supported this attack with a strong smoke screen to mask their movement, the attack suffered losses from an overwhelming and accurate barrage of naval gunfire; from well-placed mines, and from antitank fire from the American 601st Tank Destroyer Battalion. As a Tiger crewman remembers:

> Our artillery began firing at 0500 hours. At 0700 hours we moved out of the assembly area, single file on a muddy road past Cisterna in the direction of Isola Bella. . . . The lead tank, commanded by Oberfähnrich Harder, ran over a mine. While the tank track withstood the shock, the leading road wheel's torsion bar was broken. The tank had to be towed away. The entire column came to a halt since none of the other vehicles could pass in that marshy area. What to do? Engineers were called up to clear the mines, but for the time being we had to wait. And then it began. The enemy artillery began ranging in on us.[76]

Another crewmember takes up the story:

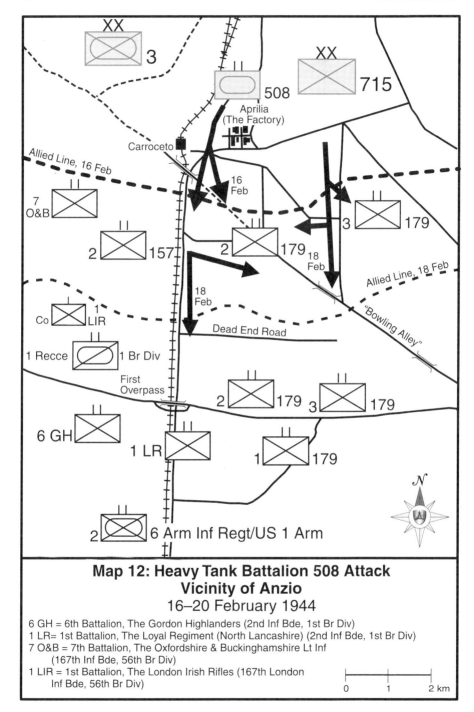

Map 12: Heavy Tank Battalion 508 Attack
Vicinity of Anzio
16–20 February 1944

6 GH = 6th Battalion, The Gordon Highlanders (2nd Inf Bde, 1st Br Div)
1 LR= 1st Battalion, The Loyal Regiment (North Lancashire) (2nd Inf Bde, 1st Br Div)
7 O&B = 7th Battalion, The Oxfordshire & Buckinghamshire Lt Inf
     (167th Inf Bde, 56th Br Div)
1 LIR = 1st Battalion, The London Irish Rifles (167th London
     Inf Bde, 56th Br Div)

0   1   2 km

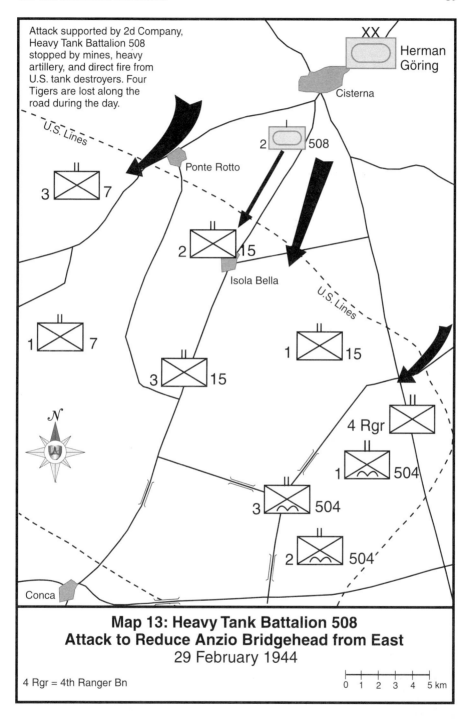

Attack supported by 2d Company, Heavy Tank Battalion 508 stopped by mines, heavy artillery, and direct fire from U.S. tank destroyers. Four Tigers are lost along the road during the day.

Herman Göring

Cisterna

U.S. Lines

2 508

3 7

Ponte Rotto

2 15

Isola Bella

U.S. Lines

1 7

1 15

3 15

𝒩

4 Rgr

1 504

3 504

2 504

Conca

Map 13: Heavy Tank Battalion 508
Attack to Reduce Anzio Bridgehead from East
29 February 1944

4 Rgr = 4th Ranger Bn

0 1 2 3 4 5 km

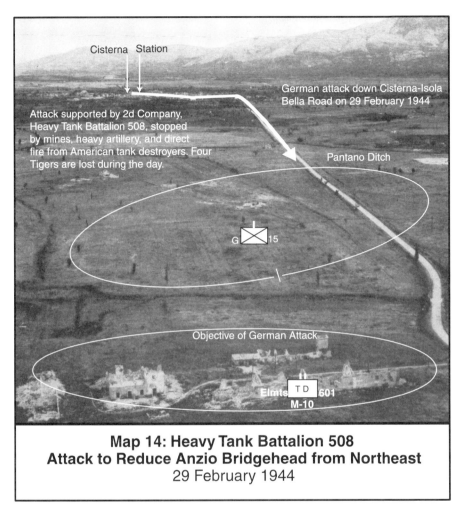

Cisterna Station

German attack down Cisterna-Isola
Bella Road on 29 February 1944

Attack supported by 2d Company,
Heavy Tank Battalion 508, stopped
by mines, heavy artillery, and direct
fire from American tank destroyers. Four
Tigers are lost during the day.

Pantano Ditch

G ⊠ 15

Objective of German Attack

Elmts TD 601
M-10

**Map 14: Heavy Tank Battalion 508
Attack to Reduce Anzio Bridgehead from Northeast
29 February 1944**

The artillery fire became heavier by the minute. The rounds were burst-
ing quite close to us. Shrapnel struck our vehicle. One burst shredded
two road wheels on the right side, and a fragment pierced the storage box
on the back of the turret. By that time it was noon. A suspicious house
about 1,500 meters in front of us was peppered with high-explosive
rounds. Enemy infantry ran away.

1400 hours: The enemy fire was unbroken. Then, suddenly, we were hit
twice on rear of the turret; four or five hits more followed. Two Sherman
tanks were firing at us from the right. We immediately returned fire; one
Sherman began to burn; the other ran for it.[77]

This tank was ultimately disabled when its fuel, leaking from hits by artillery fire, was ignited by white phosphorus rounds fired by American artillery. The crew was forced to abandon the Tiger and retreat to their original start positions.

The first crewman's story reinforces the impotence of the German armored column in dealing with the American minefield without being able to maneuver off the road.

> Enemy artillery gave us no rest. The [U.S.] artillery spotter directed the salvoes closer and closer to us. Then my commander decided to change position. We pulled off the road past the trail vehicle. Bang! Another mine exploded and blew off a torsion bar. The vehicle was disabled. A dreadful feeling to be sitting in a minefield like that. It was obvious that we were not going to reach our objective. We would have to wait for night before we could have the damaged vehicles towed away for repairs. The remaining serviceable vehicles withdrew toward the outskirts of Cisterna, from where they could cover the disabled vehicles. Luckily, at that point, the enemy artillery abated.[78]

In the course of this abortive attack, eight tanks were damaged by mines, artillery fragments and direct fire.[79] During the next five days, the battalion recovered all of the disabled Tigers, usually at night and under constant artillery fire. Four Tigers were so badly damaged that they were beyond repair. All of the disabled Tigers were under direct observation from Allied forces, so the unarmored German recovery vehicles were useless, and only Tigers were used to tow the disabled vehicles.[80]

The battalion's recovery problems were partially offset by the acquisition of two Shermans. Sometime around the end of February, the commander of the 3d Company succeeded in capturing these two vehicles during a night engagement. The German company commander, Oberleutnant Stein, "moved his Tiger between the two, climbed out, pounded on the enemy tanks and convinced their crews to surrender."[81] After having their turrets removed, these Shermans were used to recover disabled Tigers. These decapitated American tanks were found to be excellent recovery vehicles because of their mechanical reliability. Further,

> These enemy tanks were equipped with an escape hatch in the bottom of the hull. We saw this as advantageous to us. In many cases, the tracks of disabled tanks had to be cut off with a welding torch. During recovery, this work naturally drew enemy fire. It seemed a good idea to install welding gear in the Shermans. We could drive right up to the track of a disabled Tiger, run the hoses through the floor hatch and cut off the track in safety.[82]

After a short time in Rome, where the battalion consolidated and prepared for further combat operations, it was employed along the front in small groups, down to individual tanks. On 11 April 1944, the unit's log recorded an entry that became familiar with Tiger units in Italy; "several tanks are employed in an artillery role."[83] This was probably because of the acknowledged inadequacies of the terrain for conducting armored attacks and because the Germans were primarily on the defensive.

In an attempt to stop the Allied offensive to link the Anzio beachhead with other Allied forces breaking through from the south, the battalion was given the mission of counterattacking American forces in the vicinity of Cisterna.[84] (see map 15) This was the last accomplishment before the battalion lost many Tigers during their retreat north. During this attack, one Tiger was lost to enemy fire. It was the first of 22 Tigers lost over a three-day period. The 3d Company, starting the operation as an overstrength company with 16 Tigers (instead of the 14 authorized), experienced most of the trouble. Its problems are indicative of the problems experienced by the entire battalion. As a German after-action report described the action:

> The 3d Company formed up behind the railway embankment between the Mussolini Canal and the level crossing, and engaged troop concentrations with high-explosive fragmentation shells. It then crossed the embankment. Three Tigers broke down in the attempt (one with transmission trouble and two with tracks riding over the sprocket teeth). The remaining 13 crews all had to stop on open ground because their guns had dug into the ground when the Tigers descended the steep embankment, and needed to be cleaned out.... The first loss sustained in action was a Tiger that had one radiator destroyed by an artillery round and had to limp back toward Cori in stages. Twelve Tigers were thus left in action during the night of 23/24 May 1944.[85]

Though costly, this attack across the Cisterna-Littoria railway embankment managed to destroy 15 Shermans and drive American forces back three kilometers in this local sector.

On the morning of 24 May 1944, Army Group C ordered a withdrawal in the face of the Allied breakthrough between Cisterna and the Mussolini Canal.[86] Maintenance failures and recovery problems during the withdrawal resulted in the destruction of every 3d Company Tiger save one. The following relates the details of the calamity experienced by this company in this operation:

> Eleven Tigers withdrew to the embankment and the 3d Company commander ordered five Tigers to continue to hold the enemy while six were used to tow away the three Tigers that originally had failed to cross. Four

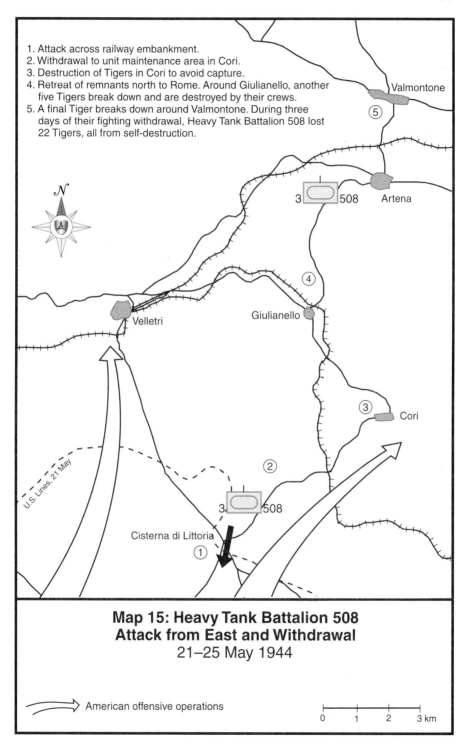

1. Attack across railway embankment.
2. Withdrawal to unit maintenance area in Cori.
3. Destruction of Tigers in Cori to avoid capture.
4. Retreat of remnants north to Rome. Around Giulianello, another five Tigers break down and are destroyed by their crews.
5. A final Tiger breaks down around Valmontone. During three days of their fighting withdrawal, Heavy Tank Battalion 508 lost 22 Tigers, all from self-destruction.

Valmontone

⑤

3 508 Artena

④

Velletri

Giulianello

③ Cori

②

U.S. Lines, 21 May

3 508

Cisterna di Littoria

①

**Map 15: Heavy Tank Battalion 508
Attack from East and Withdrawal
21–25 May 1944**

American offensive operations

0   1   2   3 km

of the six towing Tigers experienced transmission trouble, and the commander then ordered the three towed Tigers to be destroyed. Two of the five operational Tigers assisted in towing away the new breakdowns. These eight Tigers got back to an assembly point near Cori, leaving only four Tigers in fighting order. Of these four, one was hit by antitank fire and two more experienced transmission trouble (all three were blown up), so that only one operational Tiger was left. Two converted Sherman tanks came down from Rome during the night of 24/25 May 1944 and extricated the last operational Tiger, which had also broken down in the meantime, by towing it in tandem along the railway track. By 24 May 1944 [the author possibly means 25 May?], the situation had deteriorated so much that it was manifestly impossible to get towing vehicles through, and the 3d Company commander ordered that the nine Tigers which had reached the assembly area be blown up.[87]

Remnants of the battalion continued their retreat north to Rome throughout 25 May 1944. Around Giulianello, another five Tigers broke down and were destroyed by their crews. A final Tiger broke down near Valmontone and was also destroyed by its crew to avoid capture.

During the three-day period from 23 to 25 May 1944, Heavy Tank Battalion 508 lost 22 Tigers.[88] Every one of these was destroyed by its own crew and only a handful were damaged in combat prior to their destruction. Of those damaged in combat, none were damaged beyond repair, but because they were under enemy fire and recovery was impossible, the crews were forced to destroy them.

On 25 May 1944, the battalion commander reported to Hitler's Headquarters, as ordered.[89] The battalion's losses were considered so high that the battalion commander was relieved that evening, presumably on Hitler's orders.[90] The battalion lacked a suitable recover vehicle and the Tiger had a tendency to break down in hilly, rugged terrain, however, so the battalion commander's performance cannot be the sole reason, if he can be blamed at all, for the high Tiger losses.

Immediately following the German withdrawal, the Allies conducted a study of the destroyed Tigers in this area to "find out what weapon or what tactics had been responsible, so that the dose might be repeated on other occasions."[91] This report concluded that:

> The Tiger is not yet sufficiently developed to be considered a reliable vehicle for long marches. It suffers from frequent suspension defects and probably also gearbox trouble. When pushed, as in a retreat, these troubles are too frequent and serious for the German maintenance and recovery organization to deal with.[92]

This assessment was very astute. Tiger units were severely challenged when confronted with difficult terrain or the requirement to move long distances by road march. These flaws did much to offset the otherwise tremendous tactical advantages possessed by Tiger battalions.

This battalion was not alone in its problems of maintaining and recovering Tigers. Heavy Tank Battalion 504 was first employed in Italy on 20 June 1944, just in time to take part in the great withdrawal north of Rome.[93] During the ten days from 22 June to 1 July 1944, the battalion lost 28 of its 45 Tigers and is a classic example of destruction from rapid maneuver.[94] (see map 16)

The battalion lost most of its Tigers while withdrawing along Highway 439 north from Massa Marittima to Pomarance while attempting to delay American forces. On 22 June 1944, the 1st Armored Division attacked as part of a larger offensive drive to Route 68.[95] As the official Division history notes, the straight-line distance of this attack was only 65 kilometers, but because of the winding nature of the roads over the mountainous terrain, the attack had to cover 190 kilometers over narrow, winding, secondary routes.

Initially, the 1st Armored Division attacked with two combat commands, each one attacking up on the right and left of the division zone. Combat Command B, in the west, attacked along the best road in the zone, Highway 439. Tigers from the 1st Company, Heavy Tank Battalion 504 initially stopped this attack, destroying 11 Shermans and forcing the abandonment of 12 more. The 1st Armored Division committed a third force, Task Force Howze, along a trail that ran between and paralleled Combat Command A and B's routes. This force made better progress that the other two Combat Commands and the Germans withdrew to the north.

The Tigers of Heavy Tank Battalion 504 attempted to delay U.S. forces primarily along the best of the three routes, defending against Combat Command B, although a few Tigers were reported defending in the center against Task Force Howze. The terrain throughout this area was extremely hilly and ill-suited to armor operations. As the battle history of the 1st Armored Division stated:

> There were no first-class roads, few second-rate roads, and a hodge-podge of small trails and footpaths. The roads ran through narrow defiles, were cut into hillsides, and twisted up and down heights with many hairpin turns. They often led through towns with narrow streets lined by masonry houses. Opportunities for delay by demolitions were unlimited.[96]

Given the terrible nature of the terrain, it is not surprising that many Tigers broke down during their retrograde operation. What is surprising is that the Germans (primarily moving along Highway 439) were unable to recover or

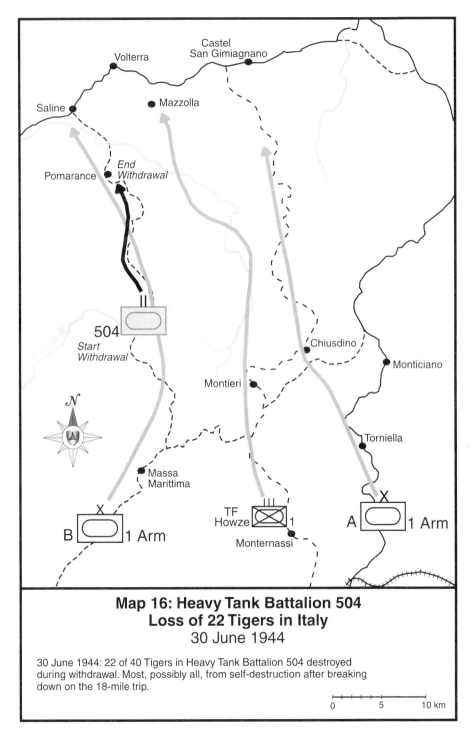

Map 16: Heavy Tank Battalion 504
Loss of 22 Tigers in Italy
30 June 1944

30 June 1944: 22 of 40 Tigers in Heavy Tank Battalion 504 destroyed during withdrawal. Most, possibly all, from self-destruction after breaking down on the 18-mile trip.

repair those Tigers faster than the advancing U.S. forces (moving on roads which were little more than goat paths). An indication of the obstacles that the 1st Armored Division's two engineer companies had to overcome is provided in the following excerpt.

> The engineers were heavily worked, as indicated by the record of the 16th Armored Engineer Battalion's accomplishments before the attack was completed. The battalion had swept more than 500 miles of road for mines (finding two new types), bulldozed passage through the rubble in 11 towns, improved 8 fords, repaired 12 enemy bridges, constructed 37 steel treadway bridges, and built or graded about 150 miles of bypasses.[97]

Despite this, the 1st Armored Division was able to maintain an average rate of advance of five miles (six kilometers) per day.[98]

During their delaying operations against the 1st Armored Division, Heavy Tank Battalion 504 lost 28 of their 45 Tigers.[99] Of these 28, it is likely that only one was knocked out and totally destroyed in direct combat. Others broke down during roadmarches, broke through bridges, or slid off the sides of roads.[100] Only a few were reported as having been slightly disabled in direct combat and were unable to be recovered, forcing their crews to destroy them.

This great loss of Tigers was repeated on a similar scale during the same withdrawal of German forces north of Rome by Heavy Tank Battalion 508. This battalion, operating east of Heavy Tank Battalion 504, supported German forces withdrawing against U.S. pressure. The terrain in this area was also rugged, so this battalion lost heavily from breakdowns. During its withdrawal, the battalion lost 13 of its 23 Tigers, most from self-destruction.[101]

In 40 days of combat, two heavy tank battalions fighting in Italy lost 64 Tigers.[102] Possibly as few as five of these were destroyed in direct combat! Although there were clearly more than five that were damaged in combat and subsequently had to be destroyed to avoid capture, it is clear that the vast majority of the 64 were destroyed for reasons other than combat damage.

Regardless of reason, two heavy tank battalions that were each at a full strength of 45 Tigers on 23 May 1944, were reduced to a total strength of ten for Heavy Tank Battalion 508 and 17 for Heavy Tank Battalion 504 by 1 July 1944. This was done primarily through rapid maneuver which kept the Germans off balance and did not allow the heavy tank battalions time to recover. U.S. forces in Italy found that what was extremely difficult to overcome frontally was relatively easy to overcome through maneuver, especially in terrain that favored the more mechanically-reliable tanks of the U.S. Army.

During the British 8th Army's offensive in September 1944, Heavy Tank Battalion 508 lost a further 11 Tigers during its retreat to the Gothic Line, all were destroyed by their own crews to avoid capture.[103] Although not specifically mentioned, it appears that the Germans attempted to overcome the Tiger's mechanical weaknesses in the latter stages of the Italian campaign by employing it primarily on good roads. During the fighting along the Gothic Line, the battalion was employed mainly along Route 9, between Bologna and Cesena.[104]

During the majority of these two battalion's employment in Italy, they were not employed as a battalion, or even as companies and platoons. To provide tank-killing coverage along the entire front, they were widely dispersed, often using single tanks.[105] This violated the principle of concentration that the Germans called for in the employment of their armor. It also caused extraordinary problems for command and control and for logistics for the battalion.

Log entries in the unit histories indicate that this was a misuse of the battalion. It may have been a misuse of the battalion based on its original purpose, but given the situation in terms of mission and terrain, the employment in Italy was probably more effective than concentrating the unit at a single point. Small groups and even single Tigers proved they were capable of defending against heavy enemy attacks, especially in restrictive terrain. Given the mechanical difficulties of the Tiger, getting to a good defensive location seems to have been more than half the battle. If the Germans had concentrated these battalions along a single sector of the front, the Allies would have found it easier to break through in another sector and a repeat of the major losses during withdrawals may have occurred, which is exactly the strategy that the Allies wished to employ against these powerful formations.

The heavy tank battalions were not as successful in Italy at destroying enemy tanks as they were elsewhere. Heavy Tank Battalion 508 lost 70 Tigers in Italy and only managed to destroy a little more than one hundred enemy tanks.[106] This gives this battalion a kill ratio of only 1.43 to 1. Of the 70 Tigers lost, however, almost 50 were destroyed by their own crews to avoid being captured.[107] Thus, the kill ratio of direct combat losses was 3.3 enemy tanks for every Tiger destroyed in combat.

Heavy Tank Battalion 504 lost 87 Tigers during its employment in Italy and destroyed 100 enemy tanks during that time.[108] Of the 87 Tigers, probably only 13 were destroyed by enemy fire.[109] Of the 74 Tigers that were destroyed by their own crews, 29 of these were destroyed during the final month of the war when the strategic situation was hopeless for the Germans.[110] Until the final month of the war then, this battalion destroyed 7.7 enemy tanks to every Tiger lost in direct combat and almost two enemy tanks for every Tiger lost, regardless of the reason.

With the exception of the withdrawals where large numbers of Tigers broke down, these two battalions were able to maintain a fairly high operational rate for their vehicles. Heavy Tank Battalion 508 was able to maintain a 60 percent operational rate for their Tigers while Heavy Tank Battalion 504 maintained almost an 82 percent operational rate for theirs.[111] Notably, this was achieved despite being so widely dispersed across the front. Of course, once in place, these vehicles also were not required to conduct long roadmarches from one spot to another, which helped to reduce the number of breakdowns. Also, despite several spectacular advances by the Allies, the Italian theater was primarily static, with German forces defending prepared lines. Undoubtedly, this static nature was also a factor in raising the maintenance status of the battalions.

Conclusion

The increased Tiger production capability allowed Germany to more than double the number of heavy tank battalions from the summer of 1943 to the summer of 1944. Of the ten army heavy tank battalions, all but two were committed in the east fighting the Soviets.[112] Although the German military was on the defensive, heavy tank battalions were still employed offensively in leading counterattacks, spearheading relief attacks, or attacking to eliminate bridgeheads, beachheads, or to restore the previous main defensive line.

Tiger tanks continued to suffer from several deficiencies of equipment. Specifically, the inability to develop and field a mine roller or plow to assist the Tiger in overcoming the increasing Allied use of mines caused Tigers to suffer damage. This, in turn, resulted in a sharp decline in the number of operational Tigers after their commitment to battle. The lack of an armored recovery vehicle, and the inadequate number of recovery vehicles overall, presented heavy tank battalions with many challenges in recovering disabled Tigers. Often, these challenges could not be overcome, with the end result being a large number of Tigers destroyed by their own crews to avoid capture.

By the summer of 1944, almost two years had passed since the Tiger began being produced. Despite several improvements to the Tiger, the mechanical reliability remained poor, especially during rapid movements over extensive distances. This resulted in more Tigers being destroyed by their own crews during several withdrawals.

In many instances, heavy tank battalions were able to successfully defend against attacks in which they were vastly outnumbered, often with only a few operational Tigers. Despite being primarily on the defensive, however, the doctrinal guidance for the employment of heavy tank battalions was not revised to address this reality.

Chapter 5

The Last Year of the War

The employment of "Tigers" in individual groups (spread over the corps sector and frequently shifted from one division to another) succeeded for the most part in keeping the main battle line of the corps intact. Wherever "Tigers" were employed, the Russians called off their attacks or only repeated them with infantry in suitable terrain (woods and the area around lakes).[1]

Major Hans-Joachim Schwaner,
Commander, Heavy Tank Battalion 502

By the end of May 1944, the Germans had built up an impressive number of heavy tank battalions to counter the expected Soviet summer offensive in the east and the Allied invasion of France. Six independent heavy tank battalions and the *Grossdeutschland*'s heavy tank battalion were on the Eastern front preparing for the inevitable Soviet attack.[2] In the West, the Germans positioned SS-Heavy Tank Battalion 101 and 102 (redesignated 501 and 502 in November 1944) in Belgium and the Netherlands respectively, prepared to react to an invasion in the Pas de Calais.[3] In addition to the two heavy tank battalions operating in Italy, Heavy Tank Battalion 503 was reestablished after its near destruction in the East and fully reequipped with 45 new Tigers by 17 June 1944. *OKH* also formed its last new heavy tank battalion, Heavy Tank Battalion 510, which, coincidentally, was fully manned and equipped by 20 July 1944.[4]

This period marked a high point in the number of heavy tank battalions available and in the strength of the battalions overall. The Allied offensive known as Operation OVERLORD in the West and the Soviets' Operation BAGRATION in the east led to heavy losses in heavy tank battalions.[5] By the end of July 1944, three heavy tank battalions, namely 501, 505, and 506, had been decimated in action against the Red Army. These battalions either had no tanks left or had so few that they handed them over to other heavy tank battalions. In some instances, the few remaining tanks were so badly damaged that they were transported back to factories in Germany to be overhauled.[6] In the West, of the three heavy tank battalions committed to Normandy, only a handful of Tigers made it across the Seine River, and probably none of these made it all the way back to Germany, although one managed to get as far as Brussels.[7]

By the last year of the war, the heavy tank battalions encountered more weapons capable of penetrating the Tiger, and even the newly-issued King Tiger. Tiger crews were so confident in their vehicle that they did not adhere to the same tactics that more lightly-armored tanks did. This was beginning to cause losses from a general lack of care in adhering to such basic tactical principles as overwatch, use of terrain, and adequate reconnaissance.[8] To counter this, the Inspector of Panzer Troops wrote an article, stressing the importance of Tiger's adherence to accepted tactical principles.[9]

The Allied offensives forced the German military and the heavy tank battalions to operate primarily on the defensive, although heavy tank battalions did participate in some offensives during the last year of the war. However, an examination of the last year's major operations reveals that Tigers and heavy tank battalions gradually became less effective.

Operation BAGRATION

As a result of Soviet deception efforts, the Germans concentrated their armored forces south of Belorussia with Army Groups North Ukraine and South Ukraine and left few armored units with Army Group Center, where the main Soviet offensive known as Operation BAGRATION was focused.[10] When the Soviet attack began on 22 June 1944, only one heavy tank battalion, Heavy Tank Battalion 501, was assigned to Army Group Center.[11] OKH assigned four heavy tank battalions, Heavy Tank Battalions 505, 506, 507, and 509, to Army Group North Ukraine.[12] More fateful for the Germans, in the early part of June, Heavy Tank Battalion 501 gave up nine of its Tigers to Heavy Tank Battalion 509, attached to Army Group North Ukraine to bring it up to full strength. This left Heavy Tank Battalion 501 with only 20 Tigers in the battalion.[13]

Army Group Center committed Heavy Tank Battalion 501 immediately upon commencement of the Soviet attack, and it fought in the vicinity of the Orscha junction, along with the 14th and 256th Infantry Divisions and the 78th Sturm Division, beginning on 23 June 1944.[14] Because these units were overwhelmed and destroyed within the first few days of fighting, reports concerning this battalion are incomplete. Probably only six Tigers from this battalion ever made it back across the Berezina River, ferrying over on 1 or 2 July 1944.[15] On 4 July 1944, the battalion received five new Tigers and fought near Minsk with several recently-repaired tanks. The battalion's last two Tigers were destroyed when they ran out of fuel on 5 July 1944 fighting near Molodechno.[16] In less than two weeks of fighting, this battalion was completely destroyed. (see map 17)

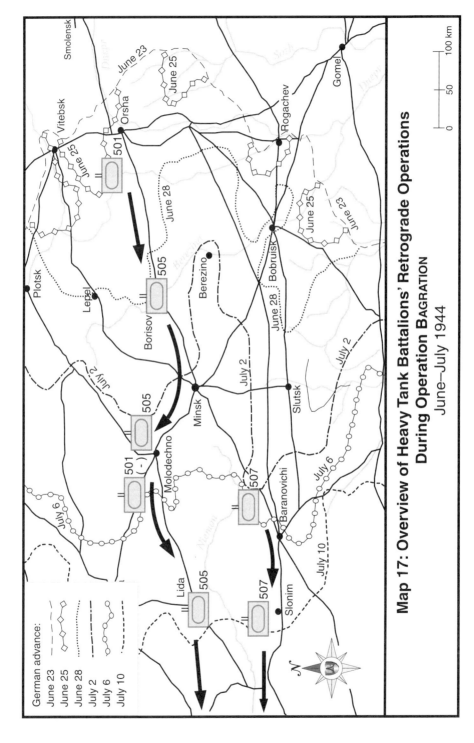

Map 17: Overview of Heavy Tank Battalions' Retrograde Operations During Operation BAGRATION
June–July 1944

Information is so incomplete for this unit that no reasonable assessment can be made about its employment. It is clear, however, that the 25 Tigers fielded by this battalion were wholly inadequate to stop the Soviet attack against Army Group Center.

Once the Germans realized that the main Soviet attack was focused on Army Group Center, Heavy Tank Battalion 505 and 507 were loaded onto trains for transport from Army Group North Ukraine on 24 and 22 June 1944, respectively. Army Group Center attached Heavy Tank Battalion 505, the first heavy tank battalion to arrive, to the 5th Panzer Division and employed it as a blocking force northeast of Borisov.[17] Initially, its task was to keep open the primary route from Minsk to Orscha. It was also tasked with stopping the Soviet armored attacks along the Minsk-Orscha highway and with defending the bridges across the Berezina River near Borisov.[18]

From 27 to 30 June, the battalion fought against the 11th Guards Army of the 3d Byelorussian Front near Krupki and Borisov. During this time, its crews destroyed more than 70 enemy tanks while losing nine Tigers, all due to enemy action.[19] More importantly, as part of the 5th Panzer Division, they held open the major Minsk-Orscha highway crossings of the Berezina River for four days, allowing other German units to withdraw to the west.

After the Soviets crossed the Berezina north and south of Borisov, the 5th Panzer Division and Heavy Tank Battalion 505 withdrew northwest of Minsk. From 1 to 6 July 1944, the battalion fought around Molodechno.[20] On 7 July 1944, Soviet forces cut the battalion's line of communication, forcing them to destroy 12 Tigers that were damaged and to retreat to the west.[21] The battalion, greatly dispersed, finally arrived in Grodno, around 200 kilometers west of Minsk, on 9 July 1944.[22] Sources vary, but at least 11 and probably 24 Tigers from the battalion survived the retreat.[23] OKH ordered the survivors of the battalion back to Germany to be reequipped with the new King Tiger.[24]

During Operation BAGRATION, Heavy Tank Battalion 505 destroyed 128 enemy tanks while losing approximately 21 Tigers. During desperate defensive and retrograde actions where it was always outnumbered, this battalion managed to achieve a 6.1-to-1 kill ratio.

The other heavy tank battalion to arrive from Army Group North Ukraine was Heavy Tank Battalion 507. This battalion detrained at Baranovichi on 2 July 1944 after Soviet forces cut the main road to Minsk.[25] The battalion fought around Baranovichi and Slonim until 10 July 1944.[26] After Soviet forces captured Lida and Vilna (Vilnius, Lithuania), the battalion withdrew, finally arriving across the Narev River at Trzeszczotki on 20 July 1944.[27]

In all, the battalion lost 10 Tigers, with one Tiger being destroyed by its own crew.[28] Available records do not provide information on the damage inflicted upon the enemy forces, so a kill ratio cannot be computed reliably. The battalion was successful in delaying the Soviet advance for more than seven days along the Soviet southern axis of attack, although by this point the Soviets were probably very close to achieving their operational goals anyway.[29]

It is difficult to judge these battalions' effectiveness because records are incomplete. Two of these battalions fought against the most powerful Soviet attacks, Heavy Tank Battalion 501 around Orscha and Heavy Tank Battalion 505 northwest of Minsk. It can be inferred that all three battalions were locally and temporarily successful at stopping the Soviet advance. Both Heavy Tank Battalion 505 and 507 only withdrew to avoid encirclement after their line of retreat was cut or threatened. Also worthy of mention is the relatively low number of Tigers destroyed because they could not be recovered. This is especially impressive considering the fluid nature of the battle and the great distances these battalions traveled during their withdrawals.

In the Aftermath of Operation BAGRATION: Heavy Tank Battalion 502 Defending Dünaburg

As a result of the success of Operation BAGRATION, a huge gap was torn in the German defenses between Army Group Center and Army Group North. The situation was summed up by a report from Army Group North to *OKH* on 29 June 1944:

> The development of the situation in the Army Group Center area of operations has decisively changed the situation of Army Group North. The right flank of the army group hangs in the breeze. South of here, the enemy has achieved operational freedom on a wide front and can quickly advance strong forces to the west. The chance of reestablishing the former contact with Army Group Center does not exist.[30]

On 2 July 1944, Heavy Tank Battalion 502 was transported by rail from Ostrow to Dünaburg. That same day, after overcoming the German strongpoint at Polozk, the Soviet 6th Guards Army was exploiting the breakthrough toward Dünaburg (Daugavpils, Latvia).[31] In this area between the army groups, there were only small, disorganized, German units that were desperately attempting to combine to form a coherent defensive line. The II Corps was ordered to build a new front with units pulled from throughout Army Group North.[32]

A study of the employment of Heavy Tank Battalion 502 in and around Dünaburg between 4 and 27 July 1944 highlights the weaknesses and deficiencies of the heavy tank battalions and indeed, the Tiger itself, in the conduct of warfare. At the same time, such an examination highlights the incredible tank-killing capability of small groups of Tigers.

Two companies, the 2d and 3d, of this battalion arrived in Dünaburg on 4 July 1944 and occupied assembly areas to the southeast of Dünaburg in the towns of Peski and Laucesy.[33] (see map 18)

The first limitation that challenged the battalion's ability to conduct mobile operations was the Düna (western Dvina) River. More specifically, it was the absence of bridges strong enough for Tigers to cross over the river. As the battalion commander stated:

> At the time, the railroad bridge in Dünaburg represented the only crossing possibility for Tigers over the Düna. Not only was a crossing not available for a distance of 100 kilometers east of Dünaburg, but there was also none for at least the same distance northwest of that town. Fording possibilities across the Düna were out of the question. Because of these reasons, the construction of a 60-ton ferry over the Düna northwest of Dünaburg was planned.[34]

This was important because the Düna River ran generally along the route of march of the Soviet attack. To defeat Soviet attacks, the battalion had to be able to move quickly across the river to the north or the south. The existence of a single crossing site severely restricted the battalion's ability to deal effectively with the Soviet attack. Consequently, the battalion's scout and engineer platoon began construction of a 60-ton ferry northwest of Dünaburg.

Beginning on 9 July 1944, the battalion began counterattacking, reinforcing German defensive positions, and relieving encircled German strongpoints. These missions involved road marches across long distances and subsequently strained the mechanical reliability of the Tigers themselves. At 1000 hours on 9 July 1944, the battalion was ordered to conduct a road march to Deguziai, a distance of 50 kilometers.[35] The battalion requested postponement of the movement until later in the day when it was cooler, but because the situation was critical and the battalion was urgently needed by the 205th Infantry Division, this request was denied. The battalion after-action report stated:

> Towards 1900 hours, the combat elements of the 2d and 3d Companies arrived in the sector ordered with a large number of road march breakdowns (motor damage, running gear damage). These were bound to occur as a result of the high temperature and the long march distance. Of the 22 Tigers that originally participated in the road march, only five Tigers from the 2d Company and three Tigers from the 3d Company were combat ready.[36]

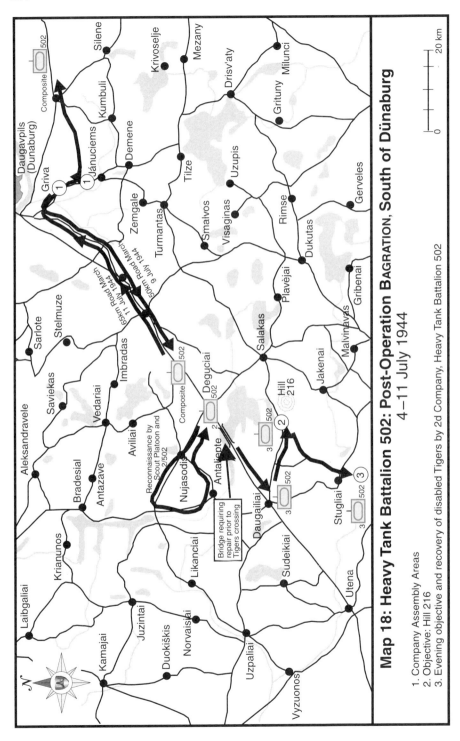

Map 18: Heavy Tank Battalion 502: Post-Operation BAGRATION, South of Dünaburg
4–11 July 1944

1. Company Assembly Areas
2. Objective: Hill 216
3. Evening objective and recovery of disabled Tigers by 2d Company, Heavy Tank Battalion 502

This meant that 64 percent of the Tigers broke down during a 50-kilometer roadmarch along a primary road.

Upon reaching the town of Deguziai, the 205th Infantry Division ordered the battalion to move further southwest to Daugailiai and defeat enemy forces near there.[37] To reach their objective, the battalion encountered another bridge three kilometers southwest of Deguziai. Engineers reinforced it so that it was strong enough to support Tigers. This required time, however, and the Tigers did not cross the bridge until 0600 hours the next morning.

On 10 July 1944, the 3d Company, with a total of nine operational Tigers, drove 19 kilometers from Deguziai to Garniai. In consonance with an infantry battalion, it attacked enemy forces southwest of Garniai in an attempt to break through to an encircled German combat group. Despite destroying a large number of antitank guns and mortars, the German forces were unable to break through the Soviet force. In addition to failing to accomplish their mission, two Tigers were destroyed by flank shots from antitank guns.

Early in the afternoon, the battalion commander ordered this company to establish contact with another German combat group to the south. After receiving additional ammunition, the 3d Company and an infantry battalion from the 205th Infantry Division's Grenadier Regiment 335, began their movement around 1800 hours. This combat group also met stiff Russian resistance and was unable to break through to their objective.

Until the onset of darkness, a large number of antitank guns were destroyed and several artillery pieces were put out of action. Enemy infantry, making a counterattack out of the woods, were successfully engaged. The enemy lost nearly 200 men. When it became dark, the attack had to be stopped at the line reached, because only two Tigers out of the original seven operationally-ready ones were still capable of fighting. Five vehicles broke down due to the heavy demands placed on the powerplants, the summertime heat, and the long road march on the previous day.[38]

The 3d Company started the day with nine operational Tigers and moved at least 32 kilometers throughout the day. The five mechanically-inoperable Tigers presented a further problem for the battalion because they were close to enemy forces and far away from recovery assets.

The maintenance woes for the battalion continued when the 2d Company was ordered from Deguziai, where they guarded the bridge, to assist in recovering the five broken down Tigers of 3d Company. The 2d Company started with only five operational Tigers and reached the 3d Company positions after midnight on 11 July 1944 with only two Tigers.[39] The others had broken down on the road march.

Throughout 11 July 1944, recovery an d maintenance elements worked at towing and fixing the disabled Tigers, which was eventually completed with great difficulty. By the early morning of 11 July 1944, the battalion had seven operational Tigers. The battalion ordered these to move from Deguziai back to Dünaburg. From there they moved via Peski, their old assembly area, to Tarzeka, to support a counterattack by the 215th Infantry Division to regain the village of Karasino and restore the old front line. This march, although on primary roads, was 65 kilometers long.[40]

Of the seven operational Tigers that began the march, only two made it without breaking down. Although two other Tigers from the battalion maintenance repair shop were brought forward in time to participate in the attack, these four Tigers represented the majority, if not all, of the battalion's combat strength after only three days of mobile defensive combat. This attack was successful, with the few Tigers destroying 10 Soviet tanks and six antitank guns for the loss of two Tigers.[41]

The battalion's 1st Company arrived on 12 July 1944 in Dünaburg from X Corps in Idriza. It added ten operational Tigers to the battalion's combat power. From 12 through 21 July 1944, Heavy Tank Battalion 502 continued to conduct operations south of Dünaburg. These operations consisted of several small groups of Tigers spread throughout the area of operations, usually consisting of between two and five Tigers. During this first period of employment south of the Düna River, the battalion destroyed 12 Soviet tanks, 53 antitank guns, and 15 mortars. This was accomplished at the price of losing seven Tiger tanks. (see map 19)

A Soviet breakthrough on the north bank of the Düna on 21 July 1944 forced the battalion to focus their efforts to the north. They were given the following mission by II Corps:

> Cross over to the northern bank of the Düna with all operationally-ready Tigers and, using the Dünaburg-Isvalta road, reach the 290th Infantry Division command post at Ohmelnickaja as soon as possible. Hold up further enemy armor penetrations in the direction of Dünaburg.[42]

The battalion was further cautioned that enemy contact along the route to Ochmelnickaja was to be expected.

The battalion moved along the designated route in at least three march columns. During the movement, they received information that approximately 20 Soviet tanks had penetrated west of the new defensive line. The 2d Company, under Leutnant Carius, moved back to Dünaburg to protect the main road north of that city. In the small town of Malinava, Carius and two other Tigers encountered 20 T-34s and JS-IIs. Without losing any Tigers, these

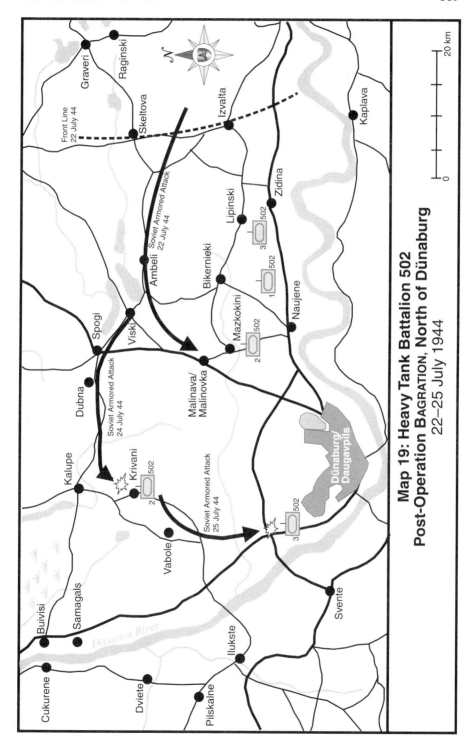

Map 19: Heavy Tank Battalion 502
Post-Operation BAGRATION, North of Dünaburg
22–25 July 1944

three tanks destroyed 17 of the Soviet tanks.[43] This action effectively defeated the Russian attack on Dünaburg, for the day at least.

Another substantial Soviet breakthrough occurred on the north side of the Düna River on 23 July 1944. The next day was spent moving groups of Tigers to intercept the Soviet armored formations to block their movement to Dünaburg, primarily along the main roads. The area around Krivani was the scene of another major defeat of Soviet armor. This time, Leutnant Nienstedt, with six Tigers, defended the town.

> Nienstedt was able to initiate a firefight between his Tigers and the enemy tanks which had broken through. He was able to knock out 17 of the 20 attacking tanks, among them 2 assault guns. He himself knocked out 10 enemy tanks with his Tiger. Using his 6 Tigers, he conducted a counterattack in conjunction with Engineer Battalion 44. By evening, the old positions had been regained.[44]

On the next day, 25 July, it was the turn of 3d Company's Leutnant Eichhorn to distinguish himself. He led an attack on a Soviet tank unit that was preparing to attack along the Dünaburg-Kreutzberg (Krustpils) road. This unit, probably consisting of five Tigers, destroyed 16 JS-II heavy tanks within ten minutes at close range, without losing any Tigers.

On 26 July 1944, Lieutenant Eichhorn supported an infantry regiment in an attack on strong Soviet positions in the same area. Although his force of four Tigers managed to destroy 12 T-34s, one SU-122, and ten antitank guns, the attackers were forced to withdraw, with the infantry moving back across to the west side of the Düna River.[45] Also, two of the four Tigers were totally destroyed and the other two were badly damaged.

During the battalion's employment on the north side of the Düna River, they destroyed 73 Soviet tanks and 24 antitank guns while losing only four Tigers. The 18.25-to-1 kill ratio from 22 to 26 July 1944 was probably aided by the restrictive terrain that made movement difficult, if not impossible, off of the primary roads. The battalion also operated in a much smaller area than they did south of the Düna, reducing the number of movements and the distances required to travel during those movements.

The initial period of employment required rapid and extensive movement in a fluid and uncertain battlefield. This type of combat stressed the Tigers mechanically and consequently inflicted problems on the battalion's maintenance and recovery assets. Throughout the battalion's combat operations around Dünaburg, it was only able to maintain a 44.53 percent operational readiness rate for its Tigers.[46] The outstanding penetrative capability of the Tiger's main gun allowed very small elements of the battalion to destroy large numbers of Soviet tanks, thereby delaying the eventual Soviet capture of Dünaburg.

Normandy

Three heavy tank battalions were involved in combat in Normandy. Two of these were SS battalions assigned to I and II SS-Panzer Corps. The last was Heavy Tank Battalion 503, which was attached to the 21st Panzer Division throughout the campaign.[47] This makes the employment of these battalions unique in that they were not shuffled around the front from unit to unit, but were assigned permanently, in the case of SS Heavy Tank Battalion 101 and 102, or kept in support of the same division, as was the case of Heavy Tank Battalion 503. Another unique aspect is that these were the battles in which the King Tiger tank was introduced, fielded by the 1st Company and the headquarters element of Heavy Tank Battalion 503.[48] The final unusual aspect about the heavy tank battalions in Normandy is that they were all employed almost exclusively against the British around Caen.[49]

Tiger tank losses in direct combat action during the Normandy campaign increased in absolute numbers and thus reduced the combat kill ratio of heavy tank battalions, relative to previous engagements against British and American forces. This was due in large part to the static nature of the German defensive posture that allowed heavy tank battalions to recover damaged or disabled Tigers and repair them in maintenance facilities behind the line. The result was that fewer Tigers required destruction to avoid capture during hasty withdrawals, and thus a higher percentage of Tigers were destroyed by direct fire than in previous battles. Another factor in this dynamic was that the Allied forces, particularly the British, fielded more weapons with better tank-killing abilities.

Since the battles in North Africa, the British Army had sought to develop and employ tanks and antitank guns with high penetrative capabilities. After encountering more Tigers and their first Panthers in Italy, this necessity was only reinforced. By 1944, the British issued a 76mm (the so-called "17-pounder," after the weight of the cartridge and projectile) towed antitank gun to their antitank regiments at a ratio of two to every 57mm ("6-pounder") antitank gun that was already in use.[50]

This already excellent weapon was improved by developing new ammunition. Adding to the basic armor piercing (AP) round, the British introduced an armor piercing capped (APC) and also an armor piercing capped ballistic capped (APCBC) round.[51] The last round had a second cap which gave it better penetration beyond 500 meters. Later in the war, the British developed an even better round, the armor piercing discarding sabot (APDS). To increase muzzle velocity, a sub-caliber shot was placed inside an aluminum shoe (or "sabot") that detached itself after leaving the muzzle of the gun. Thus, the sub-caliber round was propelled forward with all the force available to a larger projectile's surface area, but with the reduced friction of only the sub-caliber round itself. This increase in muzzle velocity greatly increased the kinetic penetration capabilities of the round, giving it the ability to penetrate 170mm of armor at 1,000 meters. The impressive nature of this is evident when compared to the 100mm of armor that a Tiger's 88mm main gun, firing a *PzGr. 39* round, was capable of penetrating at the same range.[52]

Both the American and British leadership realized that this 76mm antitank gun had twice the penetrative capability of the low-velocity 75mm gun mounted in the Sherman tank to that point, as well as some versions of the British Cromwell and Churchill. After several unsuccessful attempts, the 76mm was eventually mounted in a Sherman. These up-gunned Shermans were called the "VC" or "Firefly," and a rush conversion program was undertaken. The Royal Ordnance Factories were able to provide every British armor regiment with 12 Fireflies by D-Day for OVERLORD or shortly afterwards.[53] This was enough for each British tank platoon (a "troop" in British parlance) of four tanks to have one Firefly, greatly enhancing the overall lethality of the unit. This was extremely important in the fighting to come because it provided each platoon with a weapon that was capable of destroying a Tiger.

The final area of emphasis on tank-killing ability for the Allies was in man-portable antitank infantry weapons. The British fielded the "Projector, Infantry, Antitank," or PIAT. This was a 34-pound weapon that launched a two-and-one-half-pound projectile with a shaped charge warhead to a maximum effective range against tanks of 100 meters.[54] The Americans fielded the improved M9 Bazooka. This famous weapon fired a high-explosive rocket capable of penetrating 75mm of armor and had a maximum effective range of 100 meters.[55] Later improvements on the rocket increased the penetrating ability to close to 100 millimeters.

Although both of these weapons were in service prior to the commencement of OVERLORD, they were available in much greater numbers than previously. More importantly, the nature of the Normandy battlefield enhanced their effectiveness because engagement ranges were generally greatly reduced in the compartmentalized terrain. These weapons were still unable to destroy a Tiger, except in extraordinary circumstances, usually involving a lucky shot. They did, however, provide the infantryman with a weapon that could disable a Tiger. To do so required a skilled and courageous operator, firing from very close range. Even then, the best chance of disabling a Tiger involved hitting the track or roadwheels to disable it or hitting it in the rear armor to damage the engine. Chances of damaging a Tiger could be improved by employing them *en masse,* with two or three fired at the same time at the same aiming point.

SS-Heavy Tank Battalion 101 was the first heavy tank battalion to reach the invasion area. This unit roadmarched from its training area at Beauvais, near the Belgian-French border, through Paris, and finally to Normandy. Alerted on 6 June 1944, the battalion started to move the next day.[56] In recognition of Allied air superiority, the unit moved primarily at night, but was still attacked numerous times by fighters and bombers.[57] The lead elements only arrived behind the front on the evening of 12 June 1944, with many vehicles mechanically broken down enroute.[58] By dawn on 13 June 1944, the 1st Company deployed eight Tigers 10 kilometers northwest of Villers-Bocage on the N175 Highway, while 2d Company deployed six Tigers just a few kilometers northwest of the same town.[59] The 3d Company was still enroute in the vicinity of Falaise and did not reach the front until 15 June 1944. It took six days to travel the 400 kilometers from their staging area to their combat assembly area. During this roadmarch, despite the air attacks, SS-Heavy Tank Battalion 101 lost no Tigers to fighter-bombers during the movement. (see map 20)

The battalion's baptism of fire, the battle of Villers-Bocage, took place on 13 June 1944, only hours after most of their Tigers and crews arrived in their assembly areas. This legendary engagement is often cited, but seldom well documented. Most versions address the battle in broad generalizations, and accordingly, the accounts vary greatly. When specific accounts are given, they almost universally focus on the initial engagement, led by the commander of the 2d Company, Obersturmführer Michael Wittmann, and fail to mention the details of the entire battle. (see map 21)

What is indisputable is that two understrength companies of SS-Heavy Tank Battalion 101, along with elements from the *Panzer-Lehr* Division and the 2d Panzer Division, managed to defeat the lead brigade of the British 7th Armoured Division. This was vitally important because this unit was attempting to exploit a break in the German line between the I SS-Panzer Corps' *Panzer-Lehr* Division and the 352d Infantry Division of the XLVII Corps.[60]

This gap began to develop when the 352d Infantry Division was forced to withdraw under American pressure. This caused a break in the line between the two German divisions as well as between American and British forces, which was noticed by both sides as early as 9 June 1944. The British 2d Army planned to use the 7th Armoured Division to envelop the German forces' left flank and use the main highway, the N175, to attack toward Caen. Key to this operation was seizure of the important town of Villers-Bocage and the high point 2.5 kilometers to the northeast of the town. From this high point, Hill 213, the road led straight down to Caen. Headquarters, British 2d Army, issued

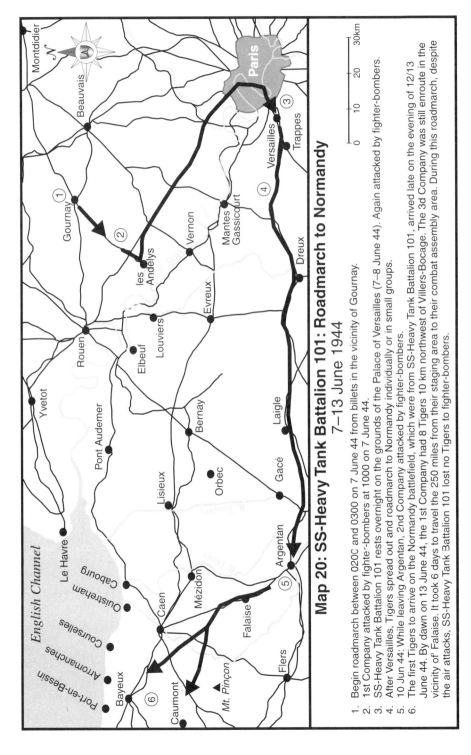

Map 20: SS-Heavy Tank Battalion 101: Roadmarch to Normandy
7–13 June 1944

1. Begin roadmarch between 020C and 0300 on 7 June 44 from billets in the vicinity of Gournay.
2. 1st Company attacked by fighte-bombers at 1000 on 7 June 44.
3. SS-Heavy Tank Battalion 101 rests overnight on the grounds of the Palace of Versailles (7–8 June 44). Again attacked by fighter-bombers.
4. After Versailles, Tigers spread out and roadmarch to Normandy individually or in small groups.
5. 10 Jun 44: While leaving Argentan, 2nd Company attacked by fighter-bombers.
6. The first Tigers to arrive on the Normandy battlefield, which were from SS-Heavy Tank Battalion 101, arrived late on the evening of 12/13 June 44. By dawn on 13 June 44, the 1st Company had 8 Tigers 10 km northwest of Villers-Bocage. The 3d Company was still enroute in the vicinity of Falaise. It took 6 days to travel the 250 miles from their staging area to their combat assembly area. During this roadmarch, despite the air attacks, SS-Heavy Tank Battalion 101 lost no Tigers to fighter-bombers.

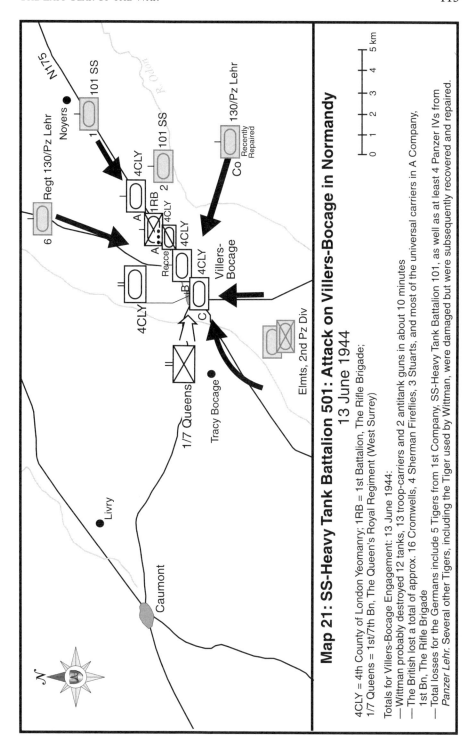

Map 21: SS-Heavy Tank Battalion 501: Attack on Villers-Bocage in Normandy 13 June 1944

4CLY = 4th County of London Yeomanry; 1RB = 1st Battalion, The Rifle Brigade; 1/7 Queens = 1st/7th Bn, The Queen's Royal Regiment (West Surrey)

Totals for Villers-Bocage Engagement: 13 June 1944:
— Wittman probably destroyed 12 tanks, 13 troop-carriers and 2 antitank guns in about 10 minutes
— The British lost a total of approx. 16 Cromwells, 4 Sherman Fireflies, 3 Stuarts, and most of the universal carriers in A Company, 1st Bn, The Rifle Brigade
— Total losses for the Germans include 5 Tigers from 1st Company, SS-Heavy Tank Battalion 101, as well as at least 4 Panzer IVs from *Panzer Lehr*. Several other Tigers, including the Tiger used by Wittman, were damaged but were subsequently recovered and repaired.

the order to execute this operation at noon on 12 June 1944 and by that evening, the 7th Armoured Division was attacking deeply into the open flank of the *Panzer-Lehr* Division, stopping overnight in the vicinity of Livry.

The Germans were aware of the gap in their lines, but were unable to do anything about it because all available units were engaged. Because of this, as elements of SS-Heavy Tank Battalion 101 arrived, they were positioned generally along the N175 behind the *Panzer-Lehr* Division. The closest element to Villers-Bocage, the 2d Company under Wittmann, was "instructed to stand by in the Villers area, ready to attack and destroy an eventual enemy attack from the northeast and northwest."[61] Both the 1st and 2d Companies probably arrived after dark and established assembly areas in the hope of conducting maintenance and resting from the long road march. This hope was not to be realized for Wittmann's company. This company received heavy artillery fire throughout the night and, because they were under the mistaken assumption that they were being observed by the British, moved twice in an attempt to avoid it. In reality, this was pre-planned, unobserved interdictory fire against obvious geographical targets, fired in support of the British attack.[62]

The British continued their attack at 0500 hours the next day, 13 June 1944.[63] By 0900, the lead unit, the 4th County of London Yeomanry (The Sharpshooters), had passed through the town of Villers-Bocage and were sitting on top of their most important initial objective, Hill 213.[64] At this point, they were arrayed along the N175 from Hill 213 back through town and along the road leading back to Livry. A company-sized unit of The Sharpshooters, A Squadron, occupied the geographical crest of Hill 213. Behind them, on the main road stretching back to the east edge of Villers-Bocage, was their attached infantry company, A Company, 1st Battalion, The Rifle Brigade, in infantry carriers and half-tracks. They were followed by The Sharpshooters' regimental Headquarters Section and elements of the regimental Reconnaissance Troop, which took up most of the main road in the town. The next tank companies, B and C Squadrons of The Sharpshooters, started on the western edge of Villers-Bocage and stretched back toward Livry. Behind The Sharpshooters on the road back to Livry was the 1st/7th Battalion, The Queens Royal Regiment (West Surrey), followed by the 5th Regiment (a battalion-sized unit) of the Royal Horse Artillery.[65]

Michael Wittmann and his 2d Company watched in awe as the British armored units passed by them, a few hundred meters north of their assembly area. Had Wittmann known that the British column was stopped temporarily for a leaders' reconnaissance and orders group on Hill 213, he may have taken the time to coordinate a hasty attack by his understrength company. Probably because he believed that the British were going to continue toward Caen without pausing, he attacked the column alone in a single Tiger. In an after-action report written by Wittmann later that day, he said:

> I had no time to assemble my company; instead I had to act quickly, as I had to assume that the enemy had already spotted me and would destroy me where I stood. I set off with one tank and passed the order to the others not to retreat a single step but to hold their ground. Drove up to the column, surprised the English as much as they had me. I first knocked out two tanks from the right of the column, then one from the left and attacked the armored troop carrier battalion in the middle of the armored regiment. I drove toward the rear half of the column on the same road, knocking out every tank that came towards me as I went. The enemy was thrown into total confusion. I then drove straight into the town of Villers, got to approximately the center of town where I was hit by an antitank gun. My tank was disabled. Without further ado, I fired at and destroyed everything around me that I could reach; I had lost radio contact and was unable to summon my company. My tanks were out of sight. I then decided to abandon my tank. We took all the weapons we could carry, but didn't destroy the tank as I believed that we could regain possession of it.[66]

This attack was a very decisive portion of the battle because his actions forced the British to abandon all hope of continuing the planned attack and forced them onto the defensive. During this attack, Wittmann destroyed portions of the lead British tank company, the infantry company, the regimental headquarters element, and portions of the reconnaissance troop. In all, he destroyed no fewer than 12 enemy tanks, 13 armored troop carriers, and two antitank guns.[67] More importantly, he caused tremendous confusion throughout the British forces remaining out of contact and panic in those units that he did engage.

While Wittmann was engaging the units west of Hill 213 and in the town of Villers-Bocage, other Tigers from his company attacked from the south and southwest toward A Squadron of The Sharpshooters on Hill 213. By about 1100 hours, an ad hoc tank company from the *Panzer-Lehr* Division attacked from the northeast against the same objective. Some sources indicate that another company-sized tank unit was scratched together by the *Panzer-Lehr* Division, using tanks that were in its repair facility. This unit allegedly advanced south of the N175 and attacked Hill 213 from the south and southeast.

Finally, around 1300 hours, Hauptsturmführer Rolf Möbius' 1st Company of SS-Heavy Tank Battalion 101 attacked down the N175 from the east and northeast, and the hill was retaken.

This is the point where accounts normally stop. The Germans had been wildly successful up to this point, with SS-Heavy Tank Battalion 101 destroying 23 or 24 British tanks, as well as numerous troop carriers and antitank guns.[68] The real achievement, however, was the fact that it halted the 7th Armoured Division's attack.[69] A major problem remained for the Germans, however, in that while their forces were busy eliminating the British on Hill 213, infantry from 1st/7th Battalion, the Queens Royal Regiment and B and C Squadrons of The Sharpshooters occupied Villers-Bocage itself. Throughout the town, Sherman Fireflys and antitank guns were positioned at key intersections and alleys, many positioned for flank shots. Also, the infantry were armed with the PIAT, giving them a tank-killing capability as well.

During the afternoon, the 1st Company of SS-Heavy Tank Battalion 101 and the ad hoc tank company from the *Panzer-Lehr* attacked to seize the town. Because there were none available, this attack was virtually unsupported by any panzergrenadiers or other dismounted troops. As could be expected, the Germans lost heavily in the town and were unsuccessful in pushing out the British. Engagements were at such close ranges that on several occasions, vehicle loaders had to sight down their guns' tubes because the gunners could not use their telescopic sights.[70] Late in the day, British forces did withdraw to defensive positions in the vicinity of Livry, but this was probably because of a perceived threat from lead units of the 2d Panzer Division arriving from the south near Villers-Bocage, as well as a continuing German force build up throughout the area.[71]

By halting the British operation to outflank German forces, the tactical engagement initiated by Michael Wittmann was sensational and definitely had much larger implications. In stopping the British offensive, however, SS-Heavy Tank Battalion 101 paid the price of at least five Tigers destroyed, and may have lost as many as seven.[72] This fact is often overlooked when some recount the stirring story of Wittmann's attack. Wittmann's Tiger was reportedly the only Tiger damaged in his company, and it was indeed subsequently recovered and repaired.[73]

In Möbius' 1st Company, which attacked into Villers-Bocage, losses were much heavier. This company attacked Hill 213 with eight to ten Tigers and succeeded in destroying British forces there without any losses.[74] Möbius left two Tigers in the vicinity of Hill 213 to secure the feature and attacked into the town with the remainder of the company. This means that six to eight Tigers entered the town. It is difficult to differentiate the Tigers that were destroyed from the ones that were totally disabled, but five Tigers were probably totally destroyed and another two were disabled but repairable.[75] British forces in the town, possibly aware of the resiliency of the Tigers, made every effort to ensure that the damaged Tigers were rendered irreparable. Sergeant

Bobby Bramwell describes how the leader of his troop dismounted and ensured that the disabled Tigers that he encountered were totally destroyed:

> It now began to rain heavily. One of the panzers had caught fire, the crew was either dead or had got out, but the Germans would be able to come back and tow the tank away. Bill Cotton, therefore, took a German gas can and a few wool blankets and we went out to destroy the panzer. Bill opened up an umbrella on account of the rain; we must have been crazy! We went from panzer to panzer, Bill with his open umbrella and the blankets and I with the gas can. We soaked a blanket with gasoline and tossed it inside the turret, followed by a match.[76]

Of the nine Tigers that entered the town of Villers-Bocage throughout the day's battle, including Wittmann's Tiger, all but one was either damaged or destroyed.[77]

Whatever the exact number of tanks that were totally destroyed, it is indisputable that the 1st Company of SS-Heavy Tank Battalion 101 was combat ineffective by the end of the day. Far from being the resounding and overwhelming German success that many accounts portray, when looked at in total, although they undeniably did stop the British advance, the Germans' victory was essentially Pyrrhic. Further, the Tigers lost during this battle were never replaced throughout the remainder of the Normandy campaign. The losses of the British, however, were quickly replaced. For example, three days later, on 16 June 1944, the 4th County of London Yeomanry was issued replacement vehicles and manned them with reserve crews.[78]

The other two heavy tank battalions in Normandy, Heavy Tank Battalion 503 and SS-Heavy Tank Battalion 102, also experienced difficulties in reaching the front because of Allied air superiority. Trains had to be unloaded around Paris for SS-Heavy Tank Battalion 102, but the ones transporting Heavy Tank Battalion 503 managed to get to Dreaux, 80 kilometers west of Paris. Measures taken to evade Allied aircraft and mechanical breakdowns caused these battalions to "trickle" to the front. For example, although most of the trains carrying SS-Heavy Tank Battalion 102 were unloaded by 27 June 1944, as late as 20 July the battalion still reported that ten Tigers were enroute to the front.[79] Although few, if any, Tigers were destroyed completely en route to the Normandy front, Allied air power played an important role in interdicting their movements and thus delayed and disrupted their commitment to battle as coherent and cohesive organizations.

General Guderian, the Inspector of Armored Troops at the time, appropriately described the difficulties that the heavy tank battalions had to overcome in getting to, and fighting in, Normandy. On 19 June 1944, he wrote to Hitler, "by itself, the highest bravery of the armored forces cannot make up for the loss of two branches of the *Wehrmacht*."[80] In this passage he was lamenting the absence of *Luftwaffe* and German naval participation in stopping the Allied Normandy invasion and was probably implying that German armored forces were being asked to do too much considering the many obstacles they had to overcome.

During the remainder of the fighting in Normandy, all three heavy tank battalions were employed primarily as mobile reserves, countering enemy penetrations. They accomplished this by counterattacking to defeat the enemy so that the previous front line could be reestablished. It was not uncommon for a battalion to array its three companies in a dispersed pattern behind the front of the division or corps it was supporting so that each could react quickly to enemy penetrations. This was probably also done to reduce the size of the potential target. An entire heavy tank battalion in a single assembly area would surely have brought a massive response from the Allied air forces and artillery.

Even General Guderian seems to have supported this dispersion. In a departure from his principle of concentration, he recommended a change of tactics for all tank forces, presumably based upon the restrictive terrain of Normandy:

> Whenever armored forces go into action on the Invasion Front, the *Panzer-Kampf-Trupp-Taktik* is to be used instead of the previous tactic of employing concentrated forces. The latter tactics are still to be used in most other circumstances. The *Panzer-Kampf-Trupp-Taktik* consists of close cooperation of small armored units combined with panzer-grenadiers [mechanized or motorized infantry assigned to *Panzer* or *Panzer-Grenadier* divisions or *Panzer* brigades] or Infantry units.[81]

Fortunately for the Germans, the heavy tank battalions and the individual heavy tank companies were spread out behind the main defensive line when the British began Operation GOODWOOD on 18 July 1944. This attack was preceded by massive aerial and naval bombardment involving 2,077 bombers dropping 7,800 tons of bombs and 720 medium and heavy artillery pieces firing 250,000 shells.[82] The British ground attack was then spearheaded by three armored divisions, the 7th, 11th, and the Guards Armoured Divisions. Including the tanks assigned to support the flank attacks, the British attack threw 1,100 tanks at the German defenders.[83] (see map 22)

Closest to the front, Heavy Tank Battalion 503, supporting the 21st Panzer Division, played an important part during GOODWOOD. The 3d Company of Heavy Tank Battalion 503 was hit hardest from the massive bombing in their assembly area outside of Manneville, near Caen.[84] The 1st Company, just outside of the town of Emiéville, also received damage. The British plan called for different types of ordnance to be dropped in different areas depending upon

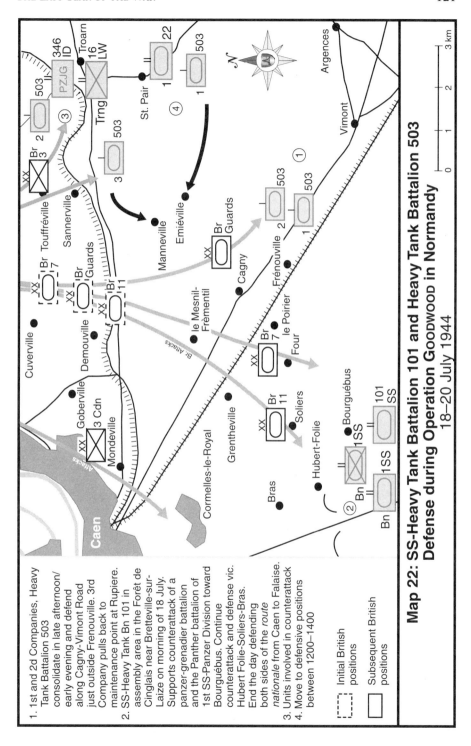

1. 1st and 2d Companies, Heavy Tank Battalion 503 consolidate in late afternoon/early evening and defend along Cagny-Vimont Road just outside Frenouville. 3rd Company pulls back to maintenance point at Rupiere.
2. SS-Heavy Tank Bn 101 in assembly area in the Forêt de Cinglais near Bretteville-sur-Laize on morning of 18 July. Supports counterattack of a panzer-grenadier battalion and the Panther battalion of 1st SS-Panzer Division toward Bourguébus. Continue counterattack and defense vic. Hubert Folie-Soliers-Bras. End the day defending both sides of the *route nationale* from Caen to Falaise.
3. Units involved in counterattack
4. Move to defensive positions between 1200–1400

Initial British positions

Subsequent British positions

Map 22: SS-Heavy Tank Battalion 101 and Heavy Tank Battalion 503 Defense during Operation Goodwood in Normandy 18–20 July 1944

the type of target and the scheme of maneuver of the attacking British forces. The town of Manneville was inside, and Emiéville was just outside, of Bombing Area H, an area encompassing nearly 1,000 acres. The British plan called for this area to be captured by a follow-on unit, the 3d Division, and was not to be used as a route of march by the leading armored divisions. This was important because—as the area was not required to be traversable by armored vehicles in the initial stages of the attack—cratering was allowable and the RAF bombers dropped large 1,000- and 500-pound high-explosive bombs in Area H.[85]

The British bombed Area H from approximately 0545 until 0630 hours. For heavy tank battalions, this was the worst day for losses from air attack during the Normandy campaign. This battalion probably lost seven Tigers from air attacks during this bombing, four in the 3d Company and three in the 1st.[86] In yet another, albeit unusual, testament to the survivability of the Tiger, one Tiger was flipped over by the bombing, ending up resting on its turret. Incredibly, the three crew members inside survived.[87] More importantly for the success of the British attack, the bombing damaged virtually all of the Tigers in the 1st and 3d Companies. It took several hours just to dig out the buried tanks.

The British ground attack began at 0745 and encountered virtually no resistance up to the railway line from Caen to Troarn, which they reached at about 0939. Oberleutnant von Rosen, the Commander of the 3d Company, moved eight of its damaged Tigers toward the town of Cagny in an attempt to attack the British advance in the flank. Six of those eight Tigers made it to a defensive position northeast of Cagny by 1000, as the other two suffered engine fires during the march.[88]

When they began engaging British tanks, they found that their Tigers had suffered more than just external damage. As Oberleutnant von Rosen stated:

> It was only then that it became clearly evident what hitherto unseen damage the tanks had received during the carpet bombing. The worst result was that all of the tanks' guns were completely out of alignment with the sights. We needed three rounds now where only one would have been adequate before.[89]

Nevertheless, British accounts testify to the effectiveness of these six Tigers in disrupting their attack. Much credit, however, must be given to a *Luftwaffe* battery of 88mm antiaircraft guns positioned in Cagny.[90] These four guns and the six Tigers were stationed in a key position that allowed them to engage the attacking British armor before they were able to deploy properly. In effect, the British armored divisions "stacked up" behind one another, from the leading elements around Cagny to behind the railway embankment.

The lethality of the four *Luftwaffe* 88s is reinforced by the fact that they also accounted for the only two Tigers in the 3d Company's defensive position that were lost throughout the day.[91] These Tigers were penetrated in their frontal armor while they were repositioning around a small wooded area. The *Luftwaffe* gunners, understandably weak in armored fighting vehicle identification, mistook them for British tanks. Even at the range of 1,200 meters, the *Luftwaffe* 88mm antiaircraft guns were able to penetrate the Tigers' frontal armor.[92]

The German counterattacks conducted into the enemy's left flank also added to the confusion of the British command. Supported by the 1st and 2d Companies of Heavy Tank Battalion 503, starting in the early afternoon, these counterattacks played a large part in protecting the wide open gap in the German right flank and containing the British advance.[93]

The 1st Company paid a heavy price, however, losing four King Tigers during the counterattack.[94] Two of these were destroyed by direct fire, although the exact source is unknown. These two were the first King Tigers ever lost to direct fire, on any front. Another King Tiger drove or slipped into a bomb crater and could not be towed out. The last King Tiger was lost in a very unusual manner. It was rammed by a Sherman tank of the 2d Battalion, The Irish Guards, although German and British accounts over who rammed or backed into whom.[95]

By late in the afternoon, the 3d Company, Heavy Tank Battalion 503, only had one Tiger still operational. Some Tigers could move but could not shoot, while others could shoot but could not move.[96] The battalion commander, therefore, ordered them to pull back to the battalion maintenance point. The 21st Panzer Division ordered the remaining two companies to consolidate in the Frenouville area to protect the Cagny-Vimont road.[97] There, these two companies prevented a further advance by the British to the southeast.

Meanwhile, during the same day, SS-Heavy Tank Battalion 101 began the day in assembly areas around Bretteville-sur-Laize. This battalion, along with several other armored battalions, comprised the 1st SS-Panzer Corps' reserve. Starting the day with around 19 Tigers operational out of 28 on hand, the battalion escaped the destruction of the morning carpet bombing.[98] Around midday, they supported a counterattack toward Bourguebus being conducted by a combat group consisting of a Panther battalion and a panzergrenadier battalion of the 1st SS-Panzer Division *Leibstandarte Adolf Hitler* (*LSSAH*). Throughout the day they continued to defend in the Hubert Folie–Soliers–Bras area against attacks by the British 11th Armoured Division.[99] By the end of the day, after losing only one Tiger to a British Firefly, the battalion occupied defensive positions on both sides of the *Route National* from Caen to Falaise to block any British attacks toward the southeast.[100]

Although General Montgomery did not formally call off Operation GOOD-WOOD until 20 July 1944, it was essentially stopped by the evening of 18 July 1944. Both heavy tank battalions involved played a pivotal role in successfully defending against the massive British attack. Heavy Tank Battalion 503 contributed heavily to delaying and disrupting the British attack and in protecting the German right flank. SS-Heavy Tank Battalion 101 then reinforced and greatly assisted German units in halting the British advance.[101] The exact number of British tanks destroyed by each heavy tank battalion is unknown, but altogether, the British forces suffered 1,500 casualties of all ranks and lost around 200 tanks.[102] Many of these tanks were destroyed in the vicinity of Cagny.[103]

The third heavy tank battalion employed in Normandy, SS-Heavy Tank Battalion 102, did not even begin to arrive near the front until 6 July 1944. At that time, the battalion occupied assembly areas near the Orne River, southwest of Caen. From 10 July 1944 until the end of the month, this battalion fought on and around the key terrain feature known as Hill 112. This point was key because it was "high ground which separates the valleys of the Odon and the Orne [Rivers]."[104] The battalion conducted offensive and defensive operations in the vicinity of Maltot. This town, along with Eterville, was one of the objectives of the British attack to expand their Odon bridgehead. The capture of these two towns was also important for the establishment of a bridgehead across the next river, the Orne.[105]

The British seized Hill 112 on 10 July 1944, but lost it to a German counterattack, supported by SS-Heavy Tank Battalion 102, on 11 July 1944.[106] It continued to change hands many times throughout the month. SS-Heavy Tank Battalion 102 played a prominent role in all of these battles, destroying 48 British tanks, 27 antitank guns, and at least 15 armored troop carriers.[107] Although many of its tanks became disabled, sometimes being reduced to having only five Tigers ready for combat, the battalion only had seven Tigers that were completely destroyed during the month's fighting around Hill 112.[108] The fact that the battalion only maintained a 33-percent operational rate throughout the month is indicative of the ferocity of the fighting.

By the first week of August, the overall situation for German forces in Normandy had deteriorated significantly. The Americans were successfully exploiting their breakthrough after Operation COBRA and were continuing to advance, despite the German counterattack around Mortain. In an effort to coordinate American, British, Canadian, and Polish forces in an attempt to envelop German forces in Normandy, General Montgomery ordered the 1st Canadian Army to renew their attack toward Faliase from the direction of Caen.[109] This mission, known as Operation TOTALIZE, was awarded to General Guy D. Simonds' II Canadian Corps. (see map 23) The direction, objective,

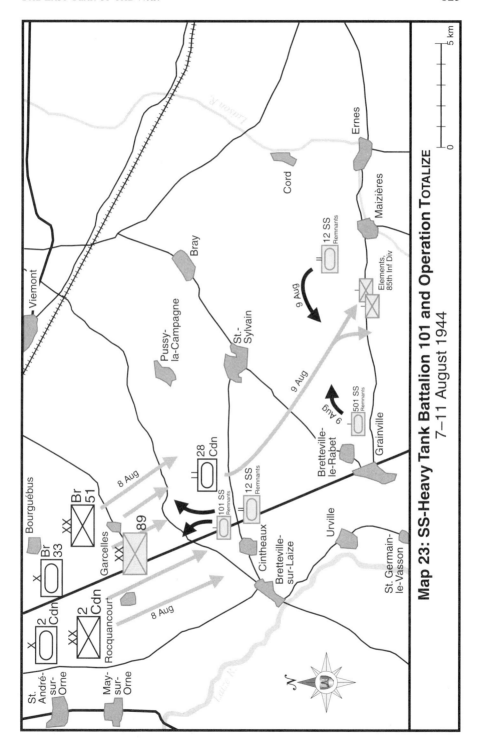

Map 23: SS-Heavy Tank Battalion 101 and Operation TOTALIZE
7–11 August 1944

and imminence of this attack were readily apparent to everyone, therefore, General Simonds attempted to overcome these disadvantages by an unusual plan that incorporated innovative tactics.

This attack started at dusk and was supported by heavy bombers and massed artillery in support of the advancing armored columns. This was the first-ever use of heavy bombers at night in close support of advancing troops. Also, in an attempt to enhance the ability of infantry to operate in close coordination with tanks, obsolete self-propelled artillery chassis were used as battlefield transport.[110]

Operation TOTALIZE was divided into two distinct phases, each of which relied heavily upon massive and carefully-planned artillery and bomber support. The ground attack plan of the first phase called for the British 51st Highland Division and the 33d Armoured Brigade to attack on the east side of the main Caen-Falaise road to seize the important German strongpoints at St. Aignan de Cramenil.[111] On the west side of the road, the 2d Canadian Infantry Division and the 2d Canadian Armoured Brigade were ordered to seize the towns of Gaumesnil and Caillouet. After these objectives were seized, the 1st Polish Armoured and the 4th Canadian Armoured Divisions, again supported by massive preplanned bomber and artillery support, would attack toward Falaise.[112]

The initial bombing attacks began at 2300 hours on the night of 7 August 1944, and was followed half an hour later by the Allied ground attack. By first light, the attacking forces captured the main objectives of St. Aignan and Cremesnil, although the western attack did not achieve its objectives until later in the morning.[113] Even so, these successes came considerably more quickly than anticipated. The second phase, also supported by pre-planned bomber strikes, was not to begin until 1400 hours on 8 August, so there was an unexpected pause in the attack. This allowed German forces time to consolidate their forces, reorganize, and conduct a counterattack.

The German unit defending the front line area, the 89th Infantry Division, was effectively destroyed in the first phase of the attack. Behind them, in reserve, were the remnants of both the 12th SS-Panzer Division "Hitler Youth" and SS-Heavy Tank Battalion 101. SS Brigadeführer Kurt Meyer, the Commanding General of the "Hitler Youth" Division, organized the counterattacks.[114] On the morning of 8 August 1944 he issued the order for Combat Group Waldmüller, including the 1st Battalion, SS-Panzer Regiment 1 and the remnants of the Corps' 101st SS-Heavy Tank Battalion, to seize the high ground south of St. Aignan."[115]

The 2d Company of SS-Heavy Tank Battalion 101 was involved in attacks against British forces in the vicinity of Grimbosq and was therefore not readily available on the morning of 8 August.[116] The battalion commander, newly promoted Hauptsturmführer Michael Wittmann, had only 10 Tigers available in the vicinity of the town of Potigny.[117] Wittmann was thrust into the battalion commander's position on 10 July 1944 because he was the senior ranking officer left in the battalion.[118] This is indicative of the heavy losses incurred by the battalion in the Normandy campaign. Further, the sole company commander in the area was a newly-assigned Obersturmführer with no previous experience leading armored units.[119]

Sometime after 0600 hours on 8 August, Wittmann ordered the battalion's operational Tigers to assemble in the vicinity of Cintheaux. After conferring with and receiving orders from Kurt Meyer, Wittmann arrived in his Tigers' assembly area at 1100 hours. Although the battalion, minus the 2d Company, started the day with ten operational Tigers, only eight are recorded as arriving at the Cintheaux assembly area. They consisted of five Tigers from the 3d Company; the battalion commander's and signal officer's tanks from the battalions headquarters element; and one other Tiger from another unit.[120]

Even though Wittmann and Meyer observed masses of British, Canadian, and Polish tanks, or perhaps because they observed them and instinctively wanted to attack before being attacked, they ordered the attack to proceed. Meyer states that they were

> aware that we can not allow the enemy tank squadrons to attack again. An enemy armored division stands ready to attack down both sides of the road [Caen to Falaise], this attack must not start, we must take the initiative.[121]

Had they been aware of the odds and taken into account the fact that the British elements they were preparing to attack on the east side of the Caen-Falaise road had been in place for at least six hours preparing defensive positions, they may have reconsidered. Including the tanks of the 12th SS-Panzer Division, the Germans had no more than 50 tanks which, essentially, attacked more than 900 British, Canadian, and Polish tanks of all kinds and more than 30,000 men.[122] Wittmann showed supreme leadership when he commandeered a tank and led the attack, saying "I must go along, for Heurich [the new and inexperienced company commander] can scarcely cope."[123] (see map 24)

Whether it was because of the haste in preparing the operation or due to a flawed plan, the German counterattack was conducted in an uncoordinated fashion. The attack began at about 1230 hours with Wittmann's Tigers attacking astride the Caen-Falaise road toward Gaumesnil. A battlegroup built around the 2d Battalion, SS-Panzer Regiment 12 attacked toward Cremesnil while Combat Group Waldmüller (built around Waldmüller's 1st Battalion, Panzer-Grenadier Regiment 25) attacked toward St. Aignan.[124] British sources state—and the results of the attack reinforce the assertion—that these attacks did not support one another, thus dispersing their effectiveness.[125] Of all the attacks, Wittmann's may have had the best chance of success because the

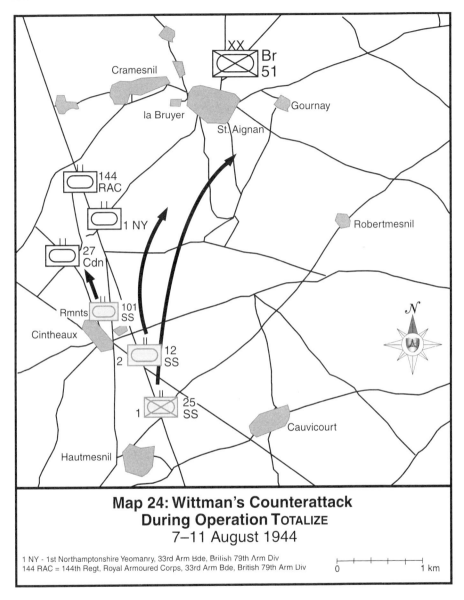

**Map 24: Wittman's Counterattack
During Operation TOTALIZE
7–11 August 1944**

1 NY - 1st Northamptonshire Yeomanry, 33rd Arm Bde, British 79th Arm Div
144 RAC = 144th Regt, Royal Armoured Corps, 33rd Arm Bde, British 79th Arm Div

0   1 km

Caen-Falaise road appears to have been the boundary between Canadian and British divisions and brigades.

Wittmann's Tigers attacked down the Caen-Falaise road toward Gaumesnil with five Tigers on the east side and two more on the west side of the road.[126] Waiting in good defensive positions were three Allied tank battalions: the 27th Canadian Armoured Regiment (The Sherbrooke Fusilier Regiment) on the west side of the road; the British 144th Royal Armoured Corps Regiment, situated essentially astride the road; and the 1st Northamptonshire Yeomanry on the east side of the road.[127] Counting all type of tanks, the eight Tigers of SS-Heavy Tank Battalion 501 attacked 216 British and Canadian tanks, all of which were likely to be within direct-fire range.[128] Of this impressive number however, it should be noted that "only" 36 were VC Fireflies, the only tanks that stood any chance of penetrating the Tiger.[129]

It would be an understatement to say that accounts vary on what happened to the Tigers during their attack. Based upon a wide variety of sources, it is likely that the Tigers received fire from Canadian tanks on the west side of the road and became focused on them.[130] Regardless of what the Germans' focus was, they failed to detect elements of the Northamptonshire Yeomanry in an orchard to their east. The Tigers continued to move parallel to the road and ultimately provided A Squadron of the Yeomanry with excellent flank shots.

At 1240 hours, the company commander of A Squadron, Captain Boardman, took personal control of his 3d Platoon and ordered the three Shermans, plus his own, to "pepper" the turrets of the Tigers.[131] This, he hoped, would cause the commanders to retreat inside their turrets and close their hatches, severely restricting their vision. Because these Shermans were armed with the standard low-velocity 75mm main gun, their rounds would have had little effect upon the Tiger's armor. Judging from the results, however, it did have the desired effect of causing the tank commanders to "button up" and cause confusion.

At the same time, the sole Firefly in the platoon began engaging Tigers from the rearmost one forward.[132] This single Firefly destroyed three, and possibly four, Tigers on the east side of the road.[133] Whether the destruction of the fourth Tiger is credited to this Firefly or not, the fact remains that there was a fourth Tiger destroyed on the east side of the road and another Tiger destroyed on the west side of the road. Only three of the original eight attacking Tigers survived, with the Yeomanry claiming the destruction of all five Tigers.[134] Even if the single Firefly destroyed only three of the five Tigers that were destroyed, it would likely make the gunner of this Firefly, Trooper Joe Ekins, the top British "Tiger Killer" in World War II.[135]

This small engagement illustrates the difficulty in attacking even hastily-prepared defensive positions. The eight Tigers led by Wittmann could easily be classified as one of the most, if not the most, combat-experienced and lethal small units in the German military at the time. Despite this, they were quickly and easily defeated. The few hours between dawn and the 12:30 P.M. German attack was enough time for the Canadian and British tanks to establish a good, hasty, defensive position. Although they attacked against overwhelming odds, in the end, little more than one severely under-gunned platoon was needed to defeat the attack. As one historian aptly described:

The usual roles in Normandy, of GOODWOOD, EPSOM, COBRA, and so on [Allied offensive breakthrough attempts], had been reversed. Instead of the Allies being the vulnerable attackers, they had placed themselves in a position of the advantaged defenders, with German armor constrained to attack. Although the Germans knew the ground, both the Northamptonshire Yeomanry and the Sherbrookes had found their way into good defensive positions in woods and orchards. The destruction of Wittmann's Tiger Troop is the best example of this.[136]

When the second phase of the Allied attack began, the several Tigers that survived the Wittmann attack, plus a few more that may have been brought forward from maintenance repair facilities, as well as Tigers that had been recalled from the 2d Company in the Grimbosq area, assisted in stopping the attack of the 1st Polish Armoured Division. Three Tigers destroyed seven Polish tanks attacking south of St. Aignan.[137] During this phase of the Allied attack, two more Tigers were destroyed, for a total of seven Tigers lost during the first day of Operation TOTALIZE.[138] By the end of the day, SS Heavy Tank Battalion 101 had 18 Tigers on hand, of which only eight were operational.[139] An indication of the poor condition of the battalion in terms of personnel losses is the fact that after the death of Captain Michael Wittmann, the battalion surgeon, as the senior ranking officer in the battalion, was given command of the battalion by the chief of staff of the 1st SS Panzer Corps.[140]

The next day, 9 August 1944, five Tigers assisted in the total defeat of an element of the 4th (Canadian) Armored Division. During this engagement the Tigers occupied good defensive positions on the flank of the attacking Canadian forces and took advantage of their extended range advantage over the Sherman tank. While the Tigers maintained their stationary firing positions, effectively containing the attacking Canadian forces, Panthers from SS-Panzer Regiment 12 as well as infantry from the 85th Infantry Division maneuvered on, and eventually destroyed the Canadian force. During this engagement, 47 Canadian tanks were destroyed while German forces lost no tanks.[141]

The remnants of SS Heavy Tank Battalion 101 continued to defend the Caen-Falaise road for the next week. By 16 August 1944, German forces were in danger of being enveloped and they began to withdraw toward the Seine River. As in other theaters of the war at other times, rapid withdrawals over vast distances resulted in the loss of many Tigers.

After more than two months of combat, the first Tiger was destroyed by its own crew on 16 August 1944.[142] During the withdrawal to the Seine River, Heavy Tank Battalion 503 lost 28 of its Tigers from either abandonment or destruction by their own crews.[143] After 20 August 1944 during their retreat, the SS heavy tank battalions destroyed or abandoned 22 of their Tigers.[144] An additional two Tigers sank attempting to cross the Seine River by ferry.[145] Only four Tigers were lost to direct combat after 20 August 1944.[146]

These statistics lead to the conclusion that the heavy tank battalions had improved in their vehicle-recovery efforts, especially when employed along a fairly static front, but were still extremely vulnerable when forced to retreat. A possible reason for the relatively high number and ratio of Tigers destroyed in direct combat, compared to previous encounters, was the fact that the Western Allies were fielding more weapons capable of destroying a Tiger, especially in close-range combat, as was the norm in Normandy. The following chart provides a breakdown of the cause of loss of Tigers in each heavy tank battalion in Normandy (see table 4).

These three heavy tank battalions managed to destroy around 510 Allied tanks as well as numerous other vehicles and pieces of equipment.[147] Other than the few Tigers that were shipped back to Germany for factory maintenance, every one of the three battalions' tanks were lost. The overall kill ratio for the loss of every Tiger was 3.9 to 1 while the kill ratio for direct combat was 10.6 to 1.

Until the strategic situation became hopeless then, the employment of the heavy tank battalions has to be judged as successful. For the most part, they were employed in accordance with the portion of their doctrine that called for heavy tanks to form mobile reserves to counter enemy breakthroughs. They adapted this doctrine to the terrain and to the operational situation by splitting the battalions apart into company assembly areas. Prior experience showed, and their employment in Normandy validated, that a handful of Tigers were able to defeat or delay a large enemy armored attack. Also, by assigning companies behind the front but across the width of it, they

	SS Heavy Tank Battalion 101	SS Heavy Tank Battalion 102	Heavy Tank Battalion 503	Total
Destroyed by direct or indirect fire	29	24	7	60
Destroyed or abandoned by crew	12	18	28	58
Destroyed by air attack	4	2	7	13
Transported back to Germany for maintenance	0	0	3	3
Total	45	44	45	134

Table 4. Tiger Tank Losses in Normandy
Source: Schneider, *Tigers in Combat I and Tigers in Combat II.*
Note: This covers the period of initial employment on 13 June 1944 until 30 August 1944. The last Tiger in SS Heavy Tank Battalion 102 was abandoned on 1 September 1944.

minimized the distance necessary to travel in order to react to enemy penetrations. Although this reduced the concentration of the entire battalion, in violation of their doctrine, this must have helped the maintenance status of the battalions because of reduced vehicular movement.

Poland

Although the King Tiger first saw action against in the west against the British forces during Operation Goodwood on 18 July 1944, it was not until 13 August 1944 that King Tigers were first employed in the east against Soviet forces. This battalion, Heavy Tank Battalion 501, was the first heavy tank battalion to receive the full authorization of 45 King Tigers. Its initial combat action illustrates the problems and weaknesses of the King Tiger, especially in its initial fielding, before all the technical problems could begin to be rectified.

As part of the subsequent offensive operations after Operation Bagration, Soviet forces established several small bridgeheads across the Vistula River in Poland in early August. One of the few initial bridgeheads was located in the Baronow area.

After experiencing shattering losses during Operation Bagration, the German Army was short of forces to counter the Soviet bridgehead. Additionally, units were in the process of being encircled in the Falaise pocket in Normandy. Finally, German forces were still attempting to stabilize the front in Italy north of the Arno River, retreating to the Gothic Line after the breakthrough at Cassino and Anzio a few months prior.

Heavy tank battalions, as well as the German Army, were spread out and stretched thin. Of the 13 heavy tank battalions in existence at this point of the war, nine were engaged and unable to move to this threatened sector. Against the Western Allies, three heavy tank battalions were in the process of being totally destroyed in Normandy and two heavy tank battalions were in Italy.[148] In the east, three heavy tank battalions were defending against Soviet attacks in Lithuania and East Prussia, and two were in Poland.[149] Of the two in Poland, one was retreating against Soviet pressure in the north part of Poland while the other was employed against the Soviet offensives across the Vistula in the Sandomierz and Baronow areas. The final three heavy tank battalions were back in Germany, at the Ohrdruf Training Area, receiving the new King Tiger.[150]

Given the desperate situation on almost all fronts, it is interesting to note that the *OKH* employed the first of these King-Tiger-equipped heavy tank battalions against Soviet forces around the Baronow bridgehead in Poland. This may have been because the Soviet forces in this bridgehead at that time were the closest Allied forces to Berlin.[151] By the first week of August, Heavy Tank Battalion 501 had received all 45 of its King Tigers.[152] Of the two other heavy tank battalions drawing King Tigers at Ohrdruf, only Heavy Tank Battalion 505 had received any King Tigers, drawing six to train upon on 26 July 1944.[153] The last heavy tank battalion, Heavy Tank Battalion 506, was still enroute from the Budapest area after having turned over their few remaining Tigers to Heavy Tank Battalion 507.[154] They did not start receiving any King Tigers until 20 August 1944.

During these battalions' training on the King Tiger at Ohrdruf, they experienced many mechanical problems. Of the six King Tigers issued to Heavy Tank Battalion 505, three caught fire during training and were complete losses.[155] When Heavy Tank Battalion 501 was ordered to deploy to Poland during the first days of August 1944, they had to combine the entire battalion's King Tiger fleet to field two companies of operational vehicles.[156] Additionally, Heavy Tank Battalion 505 was forced to transfer two of its remaining King Tigers to Heavy Tank Battalion 501 to help it achieve this objective.[157]

Heavy Tank Battalion 501's 2d and 3d Companies departed Germany on 5 August 1944 and arrived in Kielce, Poland on 9 August 1944. The 1st Company remained at Ohrdruf with the broken King Tigers and joined the battalion later in the month. Upon its arrival in Poland, Heavy Tank Battalion 501 was attached to the 16th Panzer Division and was tasked to attack Soviet forces to eliminate the Baronow bridgehead. During the 50-kilometer roadmarch from Kielce to their forward assembly area, almost every one of the battalion's King Tigers broke down.[158] These breakdowns caused the counterattack to be delayed for several days while the battalion's maintenance sections conducted repairs. (see map 25)

Despite the maintenance section's efforts, only 11 King Tigers were operational when they attacked with the 16th Panzer Division on the morning of 11 August 1944. Terrain in this area was extremely sandy, forcing the King Tigers to stay primarily on the existing roads. The German forces attacked from the town of Ogledow toward Staszow. Soviet forces defending in this area consisted of the 53d Guards Tank Brigade reinforced by the 71st Independent Guards Heavy Tank Regiment. Although this sounds like a large force, they consisted of only nine T-34/76s in the 53d Guards Tank Brigade; and eleven JS-2 Heavy Tanks and one JS-85 Heavy Tank in the 71st Independent Guards Heavy Tank Regiment.[159]

Soviet forces in this area primarily used defensive tactics, positioning tanks and assault guns in hidden ambush positions focused on the known German avenues of approach, the roads. This tactic was extremely effective and resulted in the destruction of three King Tigers during the initial attack that started at 0700 hours, and one more during a subsequent attack a few hours later.

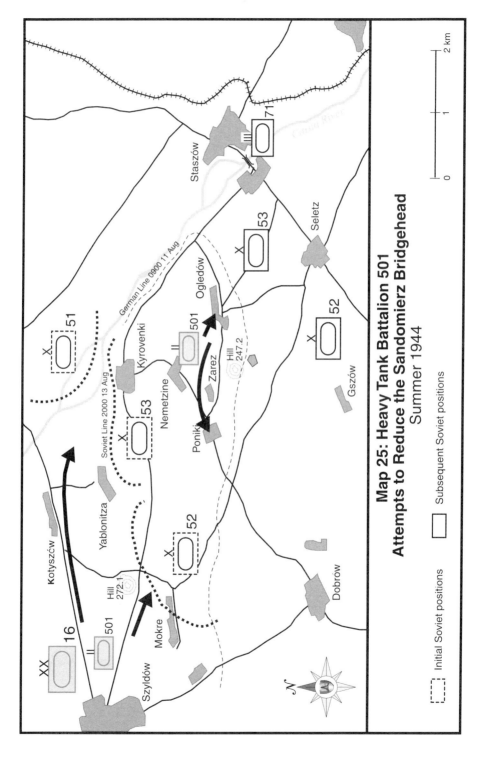

**Map 25: Heavy Tank Battalion 501
Attempts to Reduce the Sandomierz Bridgehead**
Summer 1944

Most of these were destroyed by fire from JS-2s, but at least one was knocked out by a T-34/76 at a range of less than 400 meters.[160]

Later in the day, Soviet forces counterattacked and seized the town of Ogledow where they found three abandoned King Tigers.[161] Two of these were broken or damaged, and were repairable. They had obviously been abandoned before they could be totally destroyed. Worse still, the third abandoned King Tiger still had fuel and ammunition on board and Soviet soldiers were able to start the engine without any trouble.[162] During the Soviet attack and subsequent German counterattack, a JS-II destroyed another King Tiger from a distance of 1,000 meters.[163]

The next two day's fighting moved toward the town of Szydlow. During several counterattacks, Heavy Tank Battalion 501 lost seven more King Tigers.[164] Virtually all of these were destroyed by Soviet tanks occupying a defensive position against those German attacks. Throughout three days of fighting, Soviet forces destroyed or captured 14 King Tigers out of a total strength of around 30 or 31 King Tigers in two companies of Heavy Tank Battalion 501.

In combat that pitted Soviet heavy tanks against German heavy tanks, the Soviet JS-II definitely came out on top during their initial contact. Of the 11 JS-IIs in the 71st Independent Guards Heavy Tank Regiment on 11 August 1944, three were totally destroyed and seven were damaged.[165] Four of the seven damaged tanks were so badly damaged that they were transported back to a factory to be repaired.[166]

Soviet sources credit the maneuverability of their tanks as a primary attribute that led to their success, allowing them to move to key defensible terrain instead of staying tied to the roads like the King Tigers. The Soviets appear also to have combined the technical strengths of their vehicles with sound tactical employment in dealing with the German counterattacks. Even though the Soviets were on the offensive at the operational level, they occupied strong defensive positions and defeated German counterattacks before resuming attacks at the tactical level. Once they had captured more terrain, they reverted to the defense and repeated the process.

This inauspicious loss of the 14 King Tigers in their first battalion-sized engagement cost the battalion commander his job, although he may also have been implicated in the plot to kill Hitler.[167] More costly to the German war effort was the capture of three operational King Tigers that allowed the Soviets to conduct tests to evaluate its strengths and weaknesses. They were transported back to the main testing area at Kubinka and overall, the tests on the King Tiger did not impress the Soviets.

Just getting the King Tigers to a railhead for transport was challenging and illustrated their mechanical unreliability. On the lone operational King Tiger, the left idler wheel's bearing failed, the mounting bolts on the left drive sprocket sheared, and the engine overheated causing damage to the engine as well as the gearbox.[168] It was repaired, but the right side running gear failed and was fixed with parts from one of the damaged King Tigers.[169] Finally, the drive shaft roller bearing failed, causing the replaced running gear to fail again. During this ordeal, the track had to repaired numerous times because it kept breaking due to the vehicle's weight. Reportedly, the King Tiger's track tension mechanism did not maintain tension and had to be adjusted every 10 to 15 kilometers.[170] Track problems apparently increased when pivoting or turning the vehicle.

The results of the Soviet testing indicated a low mechanical reliability in terms of the King Tiger's chassis, engine, and transmission. Additionally, the performance specifications that were published for the King Tiger by the Germans were found to be extremely inflated or optimistic, for example:

> It was determined that 860 liters of fuel was sufficient for 90 kilometers of movement over a dirt road, even though the vehicle's manual indicated that this amount of fuel should have been sufficient for 120 kilometers. Fuel consumption per 100 kilometers was 970 liters instead of the 700 liters according to this same [captured] manual. Average rate of movement along the highway was 25–30 kilometers per hour, 13.4–15 kilometers per hour along a dirt road. The average speed when moving over rough terrain was even worse: 6–7 kilometers per hour. The maximum speed, given as 41.5 kilometers per hour in the tank's technical documentation, was never achieved in the maneuverability tests.[171]

The sole favorable point for the King Tiger in the Soviet tests was the impressive accuracy and armor-penetration capability of the 88mm *Kwk* 43 L/71 main gun, comparing it to the Soviet 122mm D25 gun mounted on the JS-II Heavy Tank.

Although many mechanical deficiencies were eventually rectified, the King Tiger continued to be a relatively unreliable tank. These mechanical weaknesses dictated their tactical employment throughout the war. Also, the high fuel consumption and consequent limited radius of action reduced their effectiveness in conducting mobile operations across large distances. The King Tiger may, therefore, have been better suited for defensive operations than for offensive ones. Heavy Tank Battalion 501 learned this lesson in August 1944 in Poland when they were not only unable to eliminate Soviet forces in their bridgehead, but actually lost ground to Soviet forces while losing 14 expensive King Tigers. This battalion continued to operate against the Soviet bridgeheads across the Vistula until they were destroyed in the Soviet offensive breaking out toward the Oder River in January 1945.

The legendary Tiger tank. Introduced in late 1942, its powerful main gun and thick, resilient armor made it a threat to any Allied tank throughout the war. However, its voracious fuel consumption, limited maneuverability, mechanical unreliability, and limited operational or strategic mobility detracted from Tiger battalions' combat potential. (*Patton Museum of Cavalry and Armor*)

A Tiger advances during Operation ZITADELLE in July 1943. After this massive offensive, Tiger battalions were used almost exclusively in defensive missions, a role for which they were not designed. (*Patton Museum of Cavalry and Armor*)

A Tiger from Heavy Tank Battalion 504 in Tunisia, January 1943.
(Patton Museum of Cavalry and Armor)

This Tiger is from
SS-Heavy Tank
Battalion 101. It is
towing a second
Tiger through the
debris of a French
town in Normandy.
*(Patton Museum of
Cavalry and Armor)*

In July 1943 near Merefa/Ukraine, 18-ton halftracked recovery vehicles of Heavy Tank Battalion 503 tow Tiger 114. Tiger 114 was commanded by Fahnenjunker-Feldwebel Alfred Rubbel, and had been damaged during the fighting in Operation ZITADELLE. *(Dale Ritter Collection)*

Tigers were prone to an unusually high breakdown rate when traveling even relatively short distances on roads, so rail movement was essential for long-distance transfers. Of course, rail movement included its own special challenges, including the need to use special narrow tracks on every tank, and a paucity of the unique rail cars which could carry Tigers. Here, a Tiger is entrained on the reinforced Ssyms rail car, awaiting transport to the front, March 1944. This particular tank is from the 3d Company, Heavy Tank Battalion 505. March 1944—Leutnant Hilbig is facing the camera. *(Dale Ritter Collection)*

The King Tiger tank, also called the "Tiger II" or the "Royal Tiger." Appearing in 1944, it was the successor to the Tiger in every way: its main gun was even more lethal; its armor thicker and better designed; its motor and drive train more fragile; and its fuel consumption greater. *(Patton Museum of Cavalry and Armor)*

A newly-issued King Tiger of Heavy Tank Battalion 505. The new vehicles are being strenuously tested at the Ohrdruf Training area in August, 1944. *(Dale Ritter Collection)*

King Tigers were employed in a few offensive operations in the last six months of the war. Here, a King Tiger from Heavy Tank Battalion 501 carries forward paratroopers from Parachute Regiment 9 during the Ardennes Offensive. This picture was reportedly taken just south of Ligneuville, Belgium on 18 December 1944.
(Patton Museum of Cavalry and Armor)

The 88mm L/71 main gun was the most effective weapon mounted on any tank during WWII. (The 128mm L/55 was only mounted on the Hunting Tiger tank destroyer.) Here, King Tigers conduct gunnery exercises. These are from the 3d Company, Heavy Tank Battalion 503, which received new King Tigers in July 1944. The tank in the foreground has the Porsche turret, as did 12 of the 14 initially issued to the company; the other two had the more common Henschel turret. *(Patton Museum of Cavalry and Armor)*

A King Tiger and crew in Budapest, Hungary, October 1944. The tank crew from 2d Company, Heavy Tank Battalion 503 prepares its King Tiger for movement. The soldier straddling the gun tube is covering the muzzle to protect it from the elements. This battalion was employed in Hungary's capital for four days in mid-October 1944 in the bloodless coup to reinstall a pro-Nazi government. The heavy tank battalion was probably chosen for this task because of the psychological impact on the local population of the King Tiger. *(Patton Museum of Cavalry and Armor)*

Both the Tiger and King Tiger required a great deal of main-tenance. In this instance, men of Heavy Tank Battalion 505 are replacing a motor of a newly-issued King Tiger at Ohrdruf Training Area, late summer, 1944. *(Dale Ritter Collection)*

Early "Organization D" Tiger battalions were partially equipped with Panzer IIIs, Version (*Ausführung*) N. This model of the Panzer III was armed with a low-velocity 75 mm L/24 gun. (*Patton Museum of Cavalry and Armor*)

A *Sonderkraftfahrzeug* (*Sdkfz*) 2 *Kettenrad*. Six *Kettenräder* were authorized in the scout and engineer platoon of Organization E battalions. Intended for reconnaissance missions, each one carried two men. (*Patton Museum of Cavalry and Armor*)

The *Sdkfz* 251/7 was armed with two 7.92mm MG34s or 42s and one 7.92mm PzB39 anti-tank rifle. It had racks to carry small assault bridges, mines, and other heavy equipment of the engineer platoon. There were three *Sdkfz* 251/7s in the heavy tank battalion scout and engineer platoon. Each vehicle carried one non-commissioned officer and eight other soldiers. *(Patton Museum of Cavalry and Armor)*

Seven of these *Sdkfz* 250s were assigned to Organization E battalions, replacing the Panzer IIIs in the headquarters company. These were the primary vehicle of the battalion armored reconnaissance platoon. Each *Sdkfz* 250 carried one non-commissioned officer and five soldiers. *(Patton Museum of Cavalry and Armor)*

Ninety "Porsche Tiger" hulls were converted to heavy tank destroyers armed with the 88mm L/71 main gun. These were issued to Heavy Tank Destroyer Battalions 653 and 654, which first saw action in the battle of Kursk in July 1943. *(Patton Museum of Cavalry and Armor)*

The *Panzerjäger VI "Jagdtiger"* ("Hunting Tiger") was the tank-destroyer variant of the King Tiger. With a combat weight of over 79 tons, it was slow and lacked agility, but its nearly 10 inches of frontal armor and mammoth 128mm L/55 main gun made it a formidable opponent. *(Patton Museum of Cavalry and Armor)*

The Panther medium tank (Model A shown here) was probably the most successful armored vehicle the Germans developed. It had a relatively high speed and excellent maneuverability. These characteristics were combined with sloped and relatively heavy armor and a high-velocity 75mm L/70 main gun which had better penetrative capability than the 88 mm *KwK 36 L/56* mounted on the Tiger I. *(Patton Museum of Cavalry and Armor)*

The tanks in the M4 Sherman series were those primarily used by U.S. armored forces throughout WWII. Designed as a weapon of exploitation to be used in long-range thrusts deep into the enemy's rear, it could attack his supply installations and communications. This required great endurance, low consumption of gasoline, and ability to move long distances without a breakdown. It was never intended to be used in direct combat against heavy tanks such as the Tiger. As such, it was originally armed with a low-velocity 75mm main gun (above left). To deal with the superior German tanks like the Panther, Tiger, and Tiger II, many Shermans (such as this M4A3E8, above right) were ultimately armed with a higher-velocity 76mm gun or with the much more effective British 17-pounder. *(US Army Signal Corps)*

A Sherman VC arrives in Normandy. Nicknamed the "Firefly," this was a British modification of the American M4A4 tanks that were delivered under the Lend-Lease agreement. Its outstanding feature was its high velocity 76mm L/58 main gun which could penetrate a Tiger's armor at ranges far greater than any other tank available to the Western Allies until the appearance of the Pershing in the closing days of the war. (*The Tank Museum, Bovington*)

This lend-lease Sherman in the hands of the Soviets was knocked out by the 5th SS Panzer Division "Viking" on the eastern front. Like the crews of T-34/76s, until later versions of the Sherman were fitted with US 76mm or British 17-pounder main guns, Sherman crews were all but completely helpless against Tigers.
(*Dale Ritter Collection*)

The T-34/76 first saw action against opposing German forces during Operation BARBAROSSA, the invasion of the Soviet Union. the German invasion of the Soviet Union. The combination of relatively thick, angled armor, a main gun with good armor penetrating capability, and superb mobility placed it in a class above any German tank available in 1941. This led the Germans to develop the Panther and to reinvigorate its previously dormant heavy tank program. *(Patton Museum of Cavalry and Armor)*

By the end of 1942, when the Soviets encountered the first German Tigers, they realized that the 76mm main gun on the T-34 was inadequate. To improve armor penetration, an 85mm gun in an improved and more heavily armored three-man turret was mounted on the T-34 chassis. Production began on the first models in December 1943. *(Patton Museum of Cavalry and Armor)*

The JS-2 was armed with a 122mm gun derived from the A-19 field gun. These vehicles were issued to special Guards heavy tank regiments whose role was to assist in breaking through German defenses. The JS-2's thicker frontal armor protected it against Tiger I fire at ranges over 1,500 meters while the Tiger I was still vulnerable to the JS-2's fire. Against the Tiger II, there was no clear advantage to either tank.
(Patton Museum of Cavalry and Armor)

A German officer inspects an SU-152 while several of his soldiers look on. The appearance of the German Tiger spurred the Soviets to develop an armored vehicle capable of dealing with it on the battlefield. The SU-152 first saw action in the battle of Kursk where it quickly earned the nickname "Animal Hunter," for its reputed abilities to kill Tigers, Panthers, and Elephants.
(Patton Museum of Cavalry and Armor)

The Soviets built the SU-122 by wedding the standard 122mm howitzer to a T-34 chassis. Although excellent in the infantry support role, it had limited antitank capability. *(Patton Museum of Cavalry and Armor)*

The Cromwell first went into action in Normandy and became a mainstay of British armored units for the rest of the war in the European Theater. This Cromwell is typical, as it is armed with a 75mm main gun. The Cromwell, although technically a "cruiser" design, was a solid and steady medium tank.
(The Tank Museum, Bovington)

The Americans, British, and Soviets all developed specialized vehicles for clearing lanes through minefields. Most were highly effective. The Germans never did develop such a vehicle, and using Tigers to bull their way through minefields was an often costly alternative.

American Sherman (below) with a "mine roller" *(US Army Signal Corps Photo)*

British Valentine "Scorpion" mine flail (above) *(Patton Museum of Cavalry and Armor)*

Soviet T-34/76 with mine exploder (left) *(Patton Museum of Cavalry and Armor)*

Chapter 6

The Final Battles

> The fighting at Karniewo lasted a total of 3 days. During the course of
> the fighting, the Russians lost 134 tanks to our battalion alone. As far as
> I know, we had hardly any losses. Of course, there were quite a few
> mechanical problems. . . . . Although we had prevented the break-
> through of the enemy up to that point, the front had to be pulled back.
> The Russians had broken through on both sides of our sector.
>
> *Kurt Kramer, 3d Platoon, Heavy Tank Battalion 507*[1]

During the last six months of the war, heavy tank battalions were intensely
engaged in fighting on all fronts. The missions given to them were predomi-
nantly as mobile reserves, held behind the front lines. As the war neared its
end, heavy tank battalions were split apart, being employed across wide areas,
and continually shifted from one area to another.

There are notable exceptions when battalions took part in offensive operations, albeit usually very limited ones. Two heavy tank battalions took part in
the Ardennes Offensive in December 1944, which the Germans codenamed
Operation WACHT AM RHEIN (WATCH ON THE RHINE). Two heavy tank battalions also participated in Operation SÜDWIND (SOUTHWIND), the offensive
against the Soviet Gran bridgehead in Hungary. Ultimately, three heavy tank
battalions took part in at least one of the several German attempts to relieve
Budapest throughout 1945. Coincidentally, SS-Heavy Tank Battalion 501 (formerly 101) participated in every one of these offensives.

Hungary: The Early Battles

Heavy Tank Battalion 503 moved back to Germany after losing all of its tanks
during combat in Normandy and the subsequent withdrawal. While waiting
for new vehicles, veterans were allowed to go on leave and new personnel
arrived from the Heavy Tank Training unit at Paderborn. The battalion
received 45 new King Tigers between 19 and 22 September 1944.[2] After a short
period of training, including the production of a propaganda film, the battalion loaded trains in Germany on 12 October.[2]

152

The battalion arrived in Budapest, Hungary, on 13 and 14 October.[4] Whether intentional or not, the battalion's first employment was probably due to the high psychological value of the King Tiger. From 14 to 16 October 1944, the battalion assisted in suppressing the *coup d'etat* of the Imperial Regent, Admiral Horthy, who started peace negotiations with the Soviet Union and other Allied powers. Positioning their King Tigers at key locations throughout the city, such as bridges and the hilltop palace on the Burgberg, they helped to reinstall a pro-Nazi government in Hungary.[5] Based upon the results, which consisted of little armed resistance, the King Tigers rolling through the streets of Budapest had the desired effect on the local population.

The temporary peace overtures by Admiral Horthy resulted in many Hungarian Army units leaving the front lines. This left numerous German units in untenable positions and the already-fluid battlefields on the Hungarian steppes southeast of Budapest became even more uncertain. After completing operations in Budapest, Heavy Tank Battalion 503 was ordered to move southeast to support the 4th SS-Police Panzer-Grenadier Division and the 24th Panzer Division.

Due to a shortage of the special railway cars required for transporting Tigers, only one company at a time was able to be sent to the battalion's forward assembly area, with the lead company arriving on 18 October 1944.[6] As a result, the elements of the battalion were divided between the two divisions that it supported.

The German attack on 19 and 20 October 1944 was led by two companies of Heavy Tank Battalion 503. On 19 October 1944, the 1st Company led, followed and supported by the 3d Company.[7] The attack, beginning at 0500 hours east of the town of Szolnok, succeeded in penetrating the initial defensive positions held by Romanian troops and seized their objective for the day, the town of Mezotur. (see map 26) The Commander of the 3d Company describes the success of the day:

> Shortly after the lead tank had crossed the main line of resistance, the first Rumanians [*sic*]—they were the ones who held the positions in that sector—approached the tanks with their hands raised. . . . The next village was rapidly reached, from which the Rumanians tried in vain to flee. They were waved to the rear since the tanks had no time to concern themselves with prisoners. An antitank belt facing the direction of the attack was overrun. As it turned out, the entire depth of the defensive position had been penetrated. Mines were discovered twice on the avenue of advance, but it was possible to drive around them. As a result, the Tigers thrust ever deeper into the hinterland. Enemy trains were surprised; entire columns swept from the road. Nothing could halt the forward advance.[8]

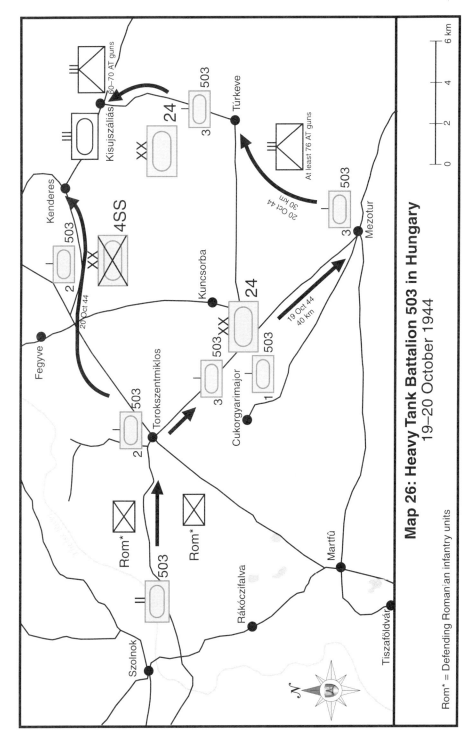

Map 26: Heavy Tank Battalion 503 in Hungary
19–20 October 1944

Rom* = Defending Romanian infantry units

Later in the day as the attack continued, the lead elements of the battalion encountered a train loaded with a Soviet Guards cavalry division and wrought havoc on the train and the troops.[9] The battalion also encountered and destroyed several rear-area columns and logistics units during the day. The attack on this day succeeded in penetrating 40 kilometers deep into the Soviet defenses.

On 20 October 1944, the 3d Company assumed the lead in the attack toward the town of Turkeve. Soviet forces recovered from the day's previous attack and established strong antitank defenses between Mezotur and Turkeve. Additionally, the muddy terrain conditions restricted the King Tigers from movement off of the road. Only a few tanks in the lead, therefore, were able to effectively engage Soviet forces during the attack. Despite the increased resistance and the restrictions on off-road movement, the company successfully defeated at least three separate Soviet antitank belts. The company commander praised the King Tiger during this day's action:

> If the Panzer IVs of the 24th Panzer Division had been forced to take the lead, not a single one of them would have made it through. The strong frontal armor of the King Tiger withstood the antitank rounds. Nothing could stop them and the tanks at the point chewed their way right through the strong antitank defense until they could gain open and negotiable terrain.[10]

After breaking through the Soviet defensive positions, the attack succeeded in capturing the town of Turkeve and even continued on 15 kilometers further to the outskirts of the town of Kisujszallas. Extremely strong Soviet forces in and around the town of Kisujszallas prevented its capture, however. Also, the supporting attack by the 4th SS-Cavalry Division, led by the 2d Company of Heavy Tank Battalion 503, failed to reach Kisujszallas from the west. Throughout the day, the German attack penetrated a total of 30 additional kilometers.

The next day, 21 October 1944, the Soviet capture of Mezotur in the German rear forced the leading German elements to withdraw. Over the course of two days, led throughout by elements of Heavy Tank Battalion 503, the German attack successfully penetrated the Soviet defenses to a depth of 70 kilometers. This relatively obscure attack is noteworthy because it was probably the deepest penetration of the war that was spearheaded by a heavy tank battalion.[11]

There were several reasons for this exceptional success. Foremost, the battlefield situation was uncertain and fluid after many Hungarian Army units left their defensive positions. In many places, there were not even defined front lines.[12] Also, the morale of the Romanian defenders on 19 October 1944 appears to have been low, with many surrendering easily.[13] More importantly, the Germans had done little to equip their former allies with first-quality anti-tank weapons, so the Romanians' few, small-caliber guns were incapable of dealing effectively with the attacking King Tigers. During the two days of offensive operations, the only mention of the battalion encountering any Soviet tanks was at the end of the second day in and around Kisujszallas.

This attack was conducted under very favorable conditions for Heavy Tank Battalion 503. Having just completed refitting with the King Tiger, it had its full authorization of equipment and personnel. To the battalion's credit, they penetrated several defensive lines each day and destroyed at least 36 antitank guns on the second day's attack. Although no King Tigers were totally destroyed during the operation, many received damage from the numerous antitank guns. By the time that the 3d Company made it to the town of Turkeve on the second day of the attack, there were only three King Tigers operational.[14]

After this attack, Heavy Tank Battalion 503 withdrew gradually to the west with other German forces. Initially, they defended along the Theiss River around Szolnok, finally withdrawing from those positions on 31 October 1944.[15] The battalion spent the month of November 1944 withdrawing from their positions along the Theiss River, eventually occupying a new defensive line northeast of Budapest.

As could be expected, the battalion's combat power dramatically decreased after continual employment without providing or allocating any appreciable time to conduct major maintenance efforts. Continuing its tradition through-out the war, this battalion's crews and ordnance personnel did an excellent job of recovering damaged and broken vehicles. The battalion destroyed its first King Tiger to avoid capture on 2 November 1944, after it became stuck in the muddy terrain.[16] That day marked the first time also that a King Tiger from the battalion was destroyed by direct fire, namely, from a Soviet antitank gun.[17] On 30 November 1944, Army Group South ordered Heavy Tank Battalion 503 to move to the vicinity of Lake Balaton to defend against Soviet forces that had broken out of their Danube bridgeheads south of Budapest.[18]

The battalion loaded trains on 30 November 1944 and arrived in Balatonkenese, on the east side of Lake Balaton, on 3 December 1944.[19] Their redeployment presented the battalion with a major problem, however.

> Fifteen damaged tanks were in the maintenance facility at Kurt. It would take at least 14 days to repair them since replacement parts had to be brought from Germany in the unit's own trucks. The corps ordered that the Maintenance Company had to remain in Kurt until the tanks were repaired. For the time being, the enemy situation in that section of the front did not cause any concern. There was, indeed, no other alternative, since that number of tanks could not be towed the approximately 50

kilometers to a railroad station where they could be rail loaded. There were no prime movers available for that. As a result, the maintenance facility remained in Kurt.[20]

The "enemy situation in that section" changed dramatically on 5 December 1944 when the Soviets began their largest offensive operation in Hungary up to that time.[21] Although the King Tigers at the repair center were towed into defensive positions and managed to destroyed several Soviet tanks, on 7 December 1944, eight King Tigers had to be destroyed to avoid capture.[22] Fortunately for the battalion, they were somehow able to transport the remainder of the damaged vehicles to the relative safety of the battalion's new area of operations.[23]

The battalion contributed greatly in stopping the Soviet offensive and stabilizing the front in the Lake Balaton area. Soviet antitank guns and self-destruction of vehicles after they had become stuck in the mud were the two primary causes of King Tiger losses throughout their time around Lake Balaton.[24] Heavy Tank Battalion 503 continued to operate in and around the Lake Balaton region until 11 February 1945 when they were moved north to participate in Operation SÜDWIND, the reduction of the Gran Bridgehead.

Operation WACHT AM RHEIN

Both of the heavy tank battalions that took part in the Ardennes offensive, namely SS-Heavy Tank Battalion 501 and Heavy Tank Battalion 506, were equipped with new King Tiger tanks. As an organic unit of the I SS-Panzer Corps, SS-Heavy Tank Battalion 501 was attached to the 1st SS-Panzer Division which in turn attached it as the second battalion of SS Panzer Regiment 1.[25] This unit, known as Combat Group Peiper for its commander, Obersturmbannführer Joachim Peiper, was assigned as a spearhead of the attack for the 6th Panzer Army.[26]

The King Tiger, however, was not suited for the type of operation envisioned in the German plan. They were very slow and continued to be mechanically unreliable. The hilly terrain in the Ardennes further exacerbated the mechanical difficulties. The soft-surfaced, narrow roads were also insufficient for such large, heavy vehicles needing to move quickly. Peiper realized these deficiencies and considered the King Tiger too slow and too heavy for the rapid advance that was required of his unit, therefore, he placed the entire battalion at the rear of his column.[27]

Combat Group Peiper's mission was to move through the penetration in the American front lines to be made by the 12th Volks-Grenadier Division and advance through Trois-Pont and Werbomont. Peiper's ultimate goal was to reach the Meuse River between Liege and Huy.[28] There, his combat group was to establish a bridgehead for follow on forces to continue the advance to Antwerp. Peiper planned to have his Panzer IVs, Panthers, and panzer-grenadiers do most of the initial fighting. After penetrating the most difficult terrain of the Ardennes, SS-Heavy Tank Battalion 501 would move forward and spearhead the final portion of the breakthrough to the Meuse River.[29] Throughout the initial stage of the operation, the primary difficulty that SS-Heavy Tank Battalion 501 faced was road movement behind the lead elements of Combat Group Peiper, and doing so with as much speed as possible.

The German offensive began early on the morning of 16 December 1944, but the lead elements of Combat Group Peiper did not begin moving until 1630 hours. As the trail elements, the King Tigers of SS-Heavy Tank Battalion 501 did not begin their movement until well after dark. The battalion's order of march was 2d Company, the battalion headquarters element, 3d Company, and then 1st Company.[30] (see map 27)

From the very beginning of the march, King Tigers started to break down with mechanical problems, mainly failures of the final drive.[31] In an attempt to keep pace with the lead elements, the battalion continued forward throughout most of the night and on into 17 December 1944. The battalion destroyed two American antitank guns in the town of Honsfeld that must have occupied the town after the lead elements of Combat Group Peiper had already passed through the town or had been bypassed by the lead German elements. The first King Tiger damaged by enemy action occurred outside of the town of Bullingen when U.S. Army Air Force P-47s attacked the column. This vehicle was damaged, but not destroyed completely, although it was never repaired and was eventually abandoned by the battalion.[32]

By 18 December 1944, Combat Group Peiper had broken through the defenses of the 526th Armored Infantry Battalion and 202nd and 291st Engineer Combat Battalions around Stavelot to push on to Trois Ponts. When the only bridge over the Ambleve there was destroyed by elements of the American 51st Engineer Combat Battalion, Peiper turned his tanks down the narrow, winding road toward the only remaining exit from the Ambleve Valley near La Gleize. Here, engineers of the 291st Engineer Combat Battalion demolished the only bridge capable of holding Tigers; although there were many days of fighting left, this was the furthest extent of Combat Group Peiper's advance, over 60 kilometers from the Meuse.

The King Tigers of SS-Heavy Tank Battalion 501 had great difficulty in following Combat Group Peiper's advance even to this point. As a result of the many mechanical breakdowns, the battalion fragmented and large gaps in the march column developed. Subunits and individual vehicles continued

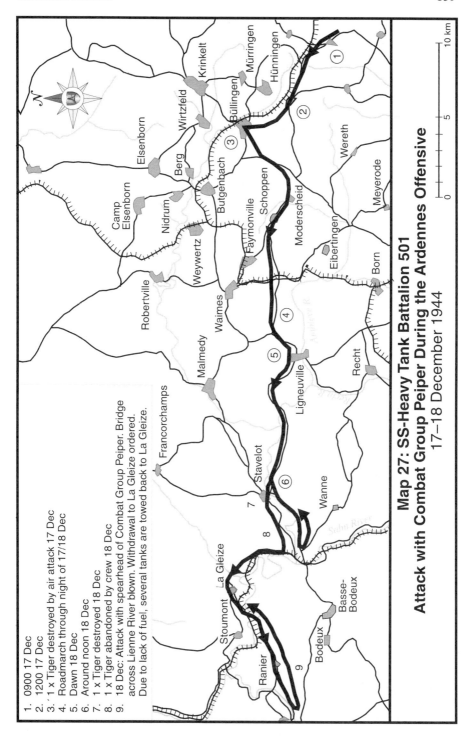

1. 0900 17 Dec
2. 1200 17 Dec
3. 1 x Tiger destroyed by air attack 17 Dec
4. Roadmarch through night of 17/18 Dec
5. Dawn 18 Dec
6. Around noon 18 Dec
7. 1 x Tiger destroyed 18 Dec
8. 1 x Tiger abandoned by crew 18 Dec
9. 18 Dec: Attack with spearhead of Combat Group Peiper. Bridge
   across Lienne River blown. Withdrawal to La Gleize ordered.
   Due to lack of fuel, several tanks are towed back to La Gleize.

**Map 27: SS-Heavy Tank Battalion 501
Attack with Combat Group Peiper During the Ardennes Offensive
17–18 December 1944**

forward as best they could, along whatever route they could find by themselves.[33] Shortly after the lead portion of Combat Group Peiper drove through Stavelot enroute to Trois Ponts and La Gleize, the 1st Battalion, 117th Infantry Regiment of the American 30th Infantry Division, drove out the small detachment Peiper had left there and established defensive positions in the town, blocking the sole bridge over the Ambleve River.[34]

Only six King Tigers were close enough to the lead elements of Combat Group Peiper to make it through Stavelot before that route was closed by the counterattacking American forces. The attack by these six King Tigers was enhanced by the presence of unusually high-ranking vehicle commanders. The platoon leaders and company commanders had continued to switch to King Tigers that were still operational when theirs broke down. Consequently, the six tank commanders who made it through to Combat Group Peiper in the La Gleize area consisted of the battalion commander, the battalion adjutant, the three tank company commanders, and a platoon leader from the 2d Company.[35] (see map 28)

The trailing King Tigers continued to move forward as best they could, repairing broken down and damaged tanks as they progressed. Several King Tigers barely missed making it through the town of Stavelot and supported attacks on that town aimed at seizing the bridge across the river. This bridge was eventually blown up by the engineers attached to the 1st Battalion, 117th Infantry Regiment, effectively cutting off supplies to the rest of Combat Group Peiper. Two other King Tigers moved south of Stavelot with the 1st SS-Panzer Division's Reconnaissance Battalion toward Trois Ponts, but found that route blocked by strong American defensive positions. These King Tigers ended up guarding a light bridge across the Ambleve between Trois Ponts and Stavelot for the next few days.

A few King Tigers with Combat Group Peiper in La Gleize followed an attack southwest through Cheneux toward Werbomont on 18 January 1945. The column turned back when they found the bridge over the Lienne Stream had been destroyed by the 291st Engineers; although there were other bridges over the Ambleve in the area, neither were Tiger-capable.[36] These King Tigers did not have enough fuel to return to La Gleize, so fuel was drained from several and they were towed back by the others during the night.[37]

On 19 December 1944, American forces closed in around Combat Group Peiper, effectively trapping the German units in the vicinity of La Gleize-Stoumont-Werbomont-Cheneux area, with the Tigers around La Gleize. From 19 through 23 December 1945, these six King Tigers defended against increasingly-intense counterattacks mounted by elements of the 30th Infantry Division and 3d Armored Division. These Tigers' crews, as well as the rest of Combat Group Peiper, suffered from a lack of resupply (especially fuel),

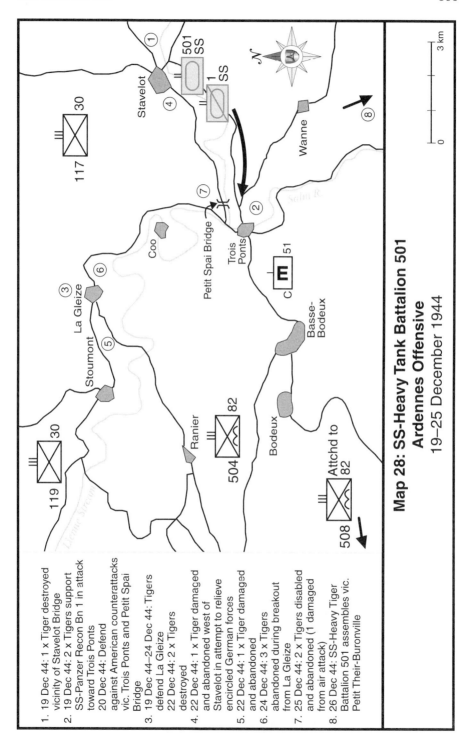

**Map 28: SS-Heavy Tank Battalion 501
Ardennes Offensive
19–25 December 1944**

1. 19 Dec 44: 1 x Tiger destroyed vicinity of Stavelot Bridge
2. 19 Dec 44: 2 x Tigers support SS-Panzer Recon Bn 1 in attack toward Trois Ponts
   20 Dec 44: Defend against American counterattacks vic. Trois Ponts and Petit Spai Bridge
3. 19 Dec 44–24 Dec 44: Tigers defend La Gleize
   22 Dec 44: 2 x Tigers destroyed
4. 22 Dec 44: 1 x Tiger damaged and abandoned west of Stavelot in attempt to relieve encircled German forces
5. 22 Dec 44: 1 x Tiger damaged and abandoned
6. 24 Dec 44: 3 x Tigers abandoned during breakout from La Gleize
7. 25 Dec 44: 2 x Tigers disabled and abandoned (1 damaged from air attack)
8. 26 Dec 44: SS-Heavy Tiger Battalion 501 assembles vic. Petit Their-Buronville

ammunition, and repair parts. Although American operations were supported by some armor, the battle around La Gleize was primarily an infantry battle. The King Tigers supported the defense as best they could, but a severe lack
of fuel restricted their movement. Early on the morning of 24 December 1944,
the trapped elements of Combat Group Peiper broke out of the pocket on
foot, leaving all of their vehicles and heavy equipment.

The part played by SS-Heavy Tank Battalion 501 in the early portion of the
Ardennes offensive has to be judged as a failure. Numerous mechanical breakdowns caused vehicles to trickle forward. The great fuel requirements of the
King Tigers imposed a huge logistical burden on the German forces. Even
though this battalion was assigned with the lead unit (Combat Group Peiper),
it essentially did not contribute to any consequential combat action until the
fourth day of the offensive. By this time, the offensive had turned into a defensive struggle for Combat Group Peiper. Of the 45 King Tigers that began the
offensive from their initial assembly area, only six were able to keep up and not
break down, joining Combat Group Peiper around La Gleize.

The second heavy tank battalion involved in Operation WACHT AM RHEIN,
Heavy Tank Battalion 506, started the offensive with only 41 King Tigers.[38]
This battalion had been in action against American and British forces since
September 1944 and was transferred from the vicinity of Aachen to participate
in the offensive. Because of this, it is likely that the number of operational
vehicles was much lower than the number of King Tigers on hand.Heavy Tank
Battalion 506 saw action in the Eifel Region, attacking southwest through the
American 14th Cavalry Group on 17 and 18 December 1944, to encircle elements of the 106th Infantry Division defending the Eifel Mountains.[39] As part
of the 5th Panzer Army, Heavy Tank Battalion 506 supported the encirclement
of these forces in the Schnee Eifel region through 20 December 1944, blocking the withdrawal of American forces to St. Vith. (see map 29)

The greatest contribution this battalion made was in its support of the 18th
Volks-Grenadier Division's Grenadier Regiment 294 during its attack to break
through American defenses toward St. Vith on 21 December 1944.[40] Due to
the restrictive terrain, it is doubtful whether more than a few King Tigers took
part in this attack.

The main breakthrough occurred along the Schönberg Road. The American official history states that only three Shermans of Combat Command B,
7th Armored Division defended this key road during this attack and that they
were easily destroyed by the attacking King Tigers.[41] This attack successfully
penetrated the American defenses, forcing the withdrawal of American forces
from St. Vith. After this, the battalion moved south toward Bastogne where it
supported attacks on the defenses around this key town, as well as defending
against American relief attempts.

Both battalions were largely ineffective during the Battle of the Bulge. Because of breakdowns, problems in supply, and the restrictive terrain, only small numbers of King Tigers ever fought together as a unit. From 17 December 1944 to 13 January 1945, both battalions lost a total of 22 Tigers.[42] Heavy Tank Battalion 506 lost six to direct fire and one more from an Allied air attack.[43] The SS battalion also lost six to direct fire, but abandoned or destroyed another nine King Tigers.[44] Until 17 January 1945 when American forces attacked around Bastogne, Heavy Tank Battalion 506 did not destroy or abandon any of its tanks. In the face of the American attacks and the battalion's subsequent hasty withdrawal, they destroyed three of their own Tigers.[45]

Probably only a handful of American tanks—possibly as few as 20—were destroyed by these two heavy tank battalions during the Ardennes Offensive.[46] This was due to a number of factors: first, only a portion of each heavy tank battalion managed to make their way forward to engage the enemy, especially

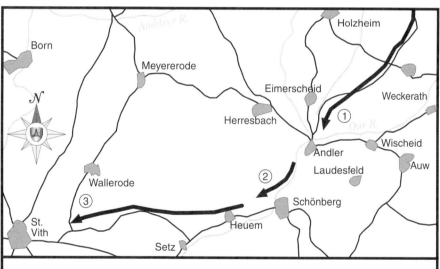

Map 29: Heavy Tank Battalion 506
Ardennes Offensive
17–22 December 1944

1. 17 Dec 44: Roadmarch from northern Eifel. Skirmish with elements of Troop B, 32nd Cavalry Squadron, 14th Cavalry Groupvic. Andler
2. 18–20 Dec 44: Support consolidation of encirclement of American forces in Schnee Eifel. Block withdrawal to St. Vith.
3. 21–22 Dec 44: Attack with Grenadier Regiment 294, 18th Volksgrenadier Division. Breaks through American defenses and seizes St. Vith

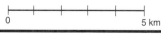

0   5 km

during the initial stages of the offensive; also, during those initial stages, the Americans committed little of their own armor. These aspects of the situation make the contribution of the heavy tank battalions difficult to judge. Whatever their contributions, it is doubtful that those accomplishments sufficiently offset the loss of 25 King Tigers.

Hungary 1945

While the Germans units that participated in WACHT AM RHEIN were being driven back or destroyed in the snows of the Ardennes, the Germans launched a series of attacks in Hungary with the goal of relieving forces encircled in Budapest. Two heavy tank battalions took part in these attacks, namely Heavy Tank Battalions 503 and 509. Heavy Tank Battalion 503 was assigned as an organic unit of the Panzer Corps *Feldherrnhalle* (*FHH*) on 19 December 1944.[47] It was officially renamed Heavy Tank Battalion "*Feldherrnhalle*" (or *FHH*) but continued to be referred to as Heavy Tank Battalion 503.[48] This meant that it was only the second army heavy tank battalion to be assigned as a permanent component of a corps, although it did not operate exclusively with this corps until Operation *SÜDWIND* in mid-February 1945.[49] This battalion had operated in Hungary since mid-October 1944 after its reconstitution in the wake of its total destruction in Normandy.[50]

Throughout January 1945, the main effort for the German attacks toward Budapest fell to IV SS-Panzer Corps.[51] The overall German relief effort was divided into three offensives, dubbed Operations KONRAD I, II, and III, respectively.[52] The first attack started on 1 January and lasted until 8 January 1945, with IV SS-Panzer Corps attacking to the southeast from starting positions west of Budapest.[53] (see map 30)

A supporting attack was made by III Panzer Corps, attacking on the IV SS-Panzer Corps' right flank. A very-weakened Heavy Tank Battalion 503, attached to the 4th Cavalry Brigade, attacked as part of III Panzer Corps in a supporting attack.[54] These attacks originated out of the vicinity of Lake Balaton and had a general orientation of east and northeast. Of the 26 King Tigers on hand in Heavy Tank Battalion 503, the battalion started the offensive on 1 January 1945 with only 10 operational tanks. The largest quantity operational on any single day was 13, on 4 January 1945.[55] This battalion supported the 4th Cavalry Brigade during the other days with only small numbers of King Tigers. For example, on 2 January 1945 only three King Tigers saw action; on the next day, only two were involved in a night attack.[56]

Operation Konrad II started on 9 January and lasted until 14 January 1945.[57] This time, IV SS-Panzer Corps shifted further north of their original

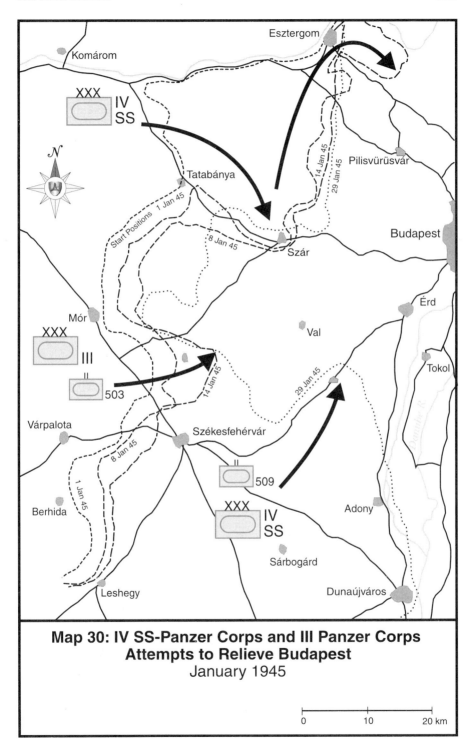

**Map 30: IV SS-Panzer Corps and III Panzer Corps
Attempts to Relieve Budapest
January 1945**

axis of attack and focused on a narrow front 25 to 30 kilometers northwest of Budapest.[58] Although the main attack by IV SS-Panzer Corps began on 10 January 1945, the supporting attack by III Panzer Corps occurred on 9 January 1945, again from the southwest of Budapest from the vicinity of Lake Balaton.[59]

Heavy Tank Battalion 503, as part of the III Panzer Corps, attacked in concert with the 4th Cavalry Brigade and the 23d Panzer Division on 9 January 1945, and as part of Combat Group Weymann on 11 January 1945.[60] On 9 January 1945, one company supported the 4th Cavalry Brigade while the remainder of the battalion supported the 23d Panzer Division.[61] Although limited in scope, it appears that both attacks achieved their objectives, with the company supporting the 4th Cavalry Brigade destroying seven Soviet tanks during their attack. The King Tigers supporting the 23d Panzer Division, although apparently achieving their objective for the day, encountered a Soviet unit equipped with SU-152 assault guns situated in a reverse-slope defense.[62] These well-sited Soviet assault guns managed to destroy three King Tigers and damaged a fourth that was ultimately recovered by the Germans.[63]

Throughout these attacks toward Budapest in January, German units were able to achieve numerical superiority in terms of tanks, but had difficulty achieving numerical superiority in infantry.[64] This affected the success of the armor attacks such as the ones conducted by Heavy Tank Battalion 503. Lack of effective infantry support put extra strain on the armor crewmen when they encountered trenches or minefields, and when recovering disabled or damaged vehicles close to enemy units. When Heavy Tank Battalion 503 encountered a strong enemy trench line on 9 January 1945, the battalion commander personally attempted to motivate the supporting infantry and lead them in the attack:

> Our own infantry remained behind our tanks and made no move to leave that cover. Then I saw how Hauptmann von Diest-Körber climbed out of his tank and, right arm gesticulating forward, tried to urge the infantry forward with him. A scene like something out of an old battle painting! I couldn't breathe. We tried to hold the Russians down with our fire and give him cover. The infantry, however, did not follow him. He was all alone in front of the trench. He hastened back again behind our tanks.[65]

As the battalion commander relates, he continued to attempt to rally the infantry and finally motivated several infantrymen to follow him:

> Finally, I succeeded, with the help of three decent corporals and a machine gun, in getting to the ditch and eventually taking about 300 prisoners. About 100 dead or wounded lay around in it.[66]

On 11 January 1945, 13 King Tigers of Heavy Tank Battalion 503 led Combat Group Weymann in its attack toward Zamoly. During this attack, the battalion's crews successfully destroyed 21 Soviet tanks, 20 antitank guns, three airplanes, and one multiple rocket launcher.[67] More importantly, they accomplished their mission, seizing the town of Zamoly. This was done at a heavy cost to the battalion, having three King Tigers totally destroyed and another seven severely damaged. By the end of the day, out of a total of 23 King Tigers on hand in the battalion, only three were operational.[68] With the exception of a few operational King Tigers employed along the front, Heavy Tank Battalion 503 spent the remainder of the time during the second German offensive repairing vehicles to increase their combat power.

Operation Konrad III started on 18 January and lasted until 29 January 1945. This time, IV SS-Panzer Corps' main effort originated from the same general area in which Heavy Tank Battalion 503 had been operating during the first two relief efforts. The IV SS-Panzer Corps, supported by Heavy Tank Battalion 509, attacked toward Budapest to the northeast. This effort reached an area south of the Soviet-held town of Stuhlweissenburg (Szekesfehervar, Hungary). Still attached to the 4th Cavalry Brigade, and the 23d Panzer Division, Heavy Tank Battalion 503 participated in the supporting attack north of Stuhlweissenburg.

After heavy fighting along the Vistula River in Poland during the summer of 1944, Heavy Tank Battalion 509 turned over their few remaining Tigers to Heavy Tank Battalion 501 in early September 1944 and moved back to Germany.[69] They spent several months in Germany, waiting for new King Tigers to arrive and on training with the few that they received. This battalion did not receive their full authorization of King Tigers until 1 January 1945 and only arrived in Hungary on 15 January 1945, just in time to take part in the third offensive toward Budapest.[70]

Allocated to IV SS-Panzer Corps, Heavy Tank Battalion 509 must have been a welcome addition by this time. With its 45 brand new King Tigers, the battalion contributed a major portion of the entire combat power of the corps during this attack. The IV SS-Panzer Corps consisted of two SS panzer divisions, namely the 3d (*Totenkopf,* or "Death's Head") and the 5th (*Wiking,* or "Viking"). For this attack, the corps controlled the 1st, 3d, and 6th Panzer Divisions.[71] These five panzer divisions sound like an impressive array of combat power, but in reality all the units were severely depleted and suffered from a low number of operationally-ready tanks and assault guns. These divisions combined to field only 116 tanks and assault guns at the beginning of this attack.[72] (see map 31)

In Operation KONRAD III, IV SS-Panzer Corps attacked with both *Waffen-SS* divisions in the center as the main effort, with the 1st Panzer Division

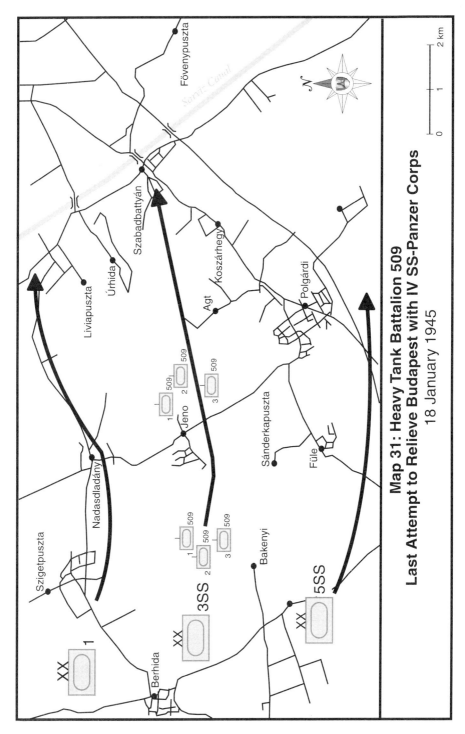

Map 31: Heavy Tank Battalion 509
Last Attempt to Relieve Budapest with IV SS-Panzer Corps
18 January 1945

protecting the left, or northern, flank and the 3d Panzer Division protecting the right flank.[73] Heavy Tank Battalion 509 attacked as the spearhead in the vanguard of the 3d SS-Panzer Division. The battalion's mission on the first day was to seize the bridges over the Sarviz Canal south of Stuhlweissenburg.[74] Their ultimate objective was to achieve a penetration to the Stuhlweissenburg–Budapest highway, presumably to allow the following panzer divisions to continue to exploit that penetration toward Budapest.

This battalion's attack on 18 January 1945 is a rare example of an entire, fully-equipped heavy tank battalion, operating under its own commander, attacking to accomplish the mission for which it was doctrinally intended (creating a breakthrough). In other operations, elements of other battalions were used to effect breakthroughs, but were only deployed piecemeal, with separate companies being attached to different divisions.[75] Still other battalions were employed in a breakthrough role, but were not at, or usually anywhere near, their authorized combat strength of 45 tanks.[76]

Heavy Tank Battalion 509 initiated its attack at 0800 hours on 18 January 1945 in a battalion "V" formation, with 1st and 3d Companies leading, or in the first "wave."[77] The 2d Company trailed in the center as the second "wave." This must have been an impressive sight as 45 King Tigers started the mission.[78] The battalion's initial objective was a ridgeline between two hills south of the town of Jeno.

After fighting through several Soviet defensive belts that included minefields, antitank guns, and tanks, the battalion reached its initial objective sometime around noon. The regimental engineers from the SS-Panzer Regiment 3 assisted in clearing the mines, reportedly taking heavy casualties in the process.[79]

Heavy Tank Battalion 509 also suffered heavy losses during this phase of the attack. In terms of key personnel, the battalion commander was wounded and the adjutant was killed. All of the officers in the 3d Company were wounded, as was the commander of the 1st Company.[80] The trailing company in the battalion attack, the 2d, fared the best. Its commander assumed command of the battalion and one of the platoon leaders in the 2d Company stepped up to lead the company. A senior non-commissioned officer assumed tactical leadership of the 3d Company.

When the battalion continued its attack at 1400 hours, only 18 King Tigers were operational.[81] In this attack the battalion adopted a wedge formation.[82] Due to its greater remaining combat power, the 2d Company assumed the lead and the remnants of the other two companies followed. They succeeded in seizing the town of Szabadbattyan, but Soviet forces managed to blow up the bridge over the Sarviz Canal when the leading King Tigers were only 50 meters away.[83]

Heavy Tank Battalion 509 had successfully penetrated the first echelons of the Soviet defenses during this day's operation. There was no intact bridge capable of holding King Tigers, however, so the German attack continued on without Heavy Tank Battalion 509 for the next few days. During the attack on 18 January 1945, the battalion lost seven King Tigers and destroyed at least 20 Soviet tanks and numerous other antitank guns.[84] Sources indicate only four other King Tigers were damaged by enemy fire, leading one to assume that mechanical failures caused the reduction of the battalion's operational strength to only 18 tanks. This would mean that 16 King Tigers broke down during their first day's combat operation.

Although this battalion achieved its objectives for the day, it cannot be viewed as a total success for the heavy tank battalion as a unit. Admittedly, the unit was given the most difficult mission of any unit in the entire corps, or in Army Group South for that matter. Despite the difficult nature of the mission, the battalion did penetrate Soviet defenses to a depth of 25 kilometers against prepared defensive positions. Doing so, however, cost the battalion 15 percent of its combat power in total losses. Also, after penetrating to a depth of around 12 kilometers during its initial attack, it was reduced in operational combat power to 40 percent of its original strength. Finally, the King Tiger's great weight prohibited it from crossing existing bridges and this limitation restricted it from crossing the Sarviz Canal and continuing to perform its mission of leading the IV SS-Panzer Corps' attack.[85]

The battalion supported several other attacks during this third German offensive and although they didn't lose any more tanks, the number available for combat continually declined. On 27 January 1945, when the Soviets launched major counterattacks in the 3d SS-Panzer Division's sector, there were only three King Tigers available to counter the Soviet armor.[86] The battalion commander joined these three later in the battle and their accomplishments on this day illustrates the effectiveness of the King Tiger in the defense when positioned along a major enemy axis of attack. Defending against the attacks of a Soviet tank brigade, these four King Tigers destroyed 41 Soviet tanks in and around the town of Pettend.[87]

By 29 January 1945, Soviet counterattacks forced the Germans to realize that further offensive actions were not possible, effectively ending the Germans' third attempt to break through to Budapest. By this time, Heavy Tank Battalion 509 only had five operational King Tigers out of a total of 38 on hand.[88] The battalion continued to operate between Lake Balaton and Lake Valence almost to the end of the war, participating in the final attempt toward Budapest, Operation FRÜHLINGSERWACHEN in March 1945.

After the Ardennes Offensive, Hitler ordered the 6th Panzer Army, now designated the 6th SS-Panzer Army, to displace to Hungary. This powerful formation was to launch an offensive, Operation FRÜHLINGSERWACHEN (Spring Awakening), the objective of which was to clear all Soviet forces from the area west of the Danube and north of the Drava Rivers, and to secure the Nagykanizsa oil fields.[89] Prior to that, however, German forces had to eliminate Soviet forces established in a strong bridgehead across the Gran River north of Esztergom. This almost 20-by-20 kilometer bridgehead was a potential assembly area for a major Soviet thrust toward Vienna, and to secure the German lines of communication, it had to be eliminated prior to the main offensive around Budapest.[90] The operation to eliminate this bridgehead was given the code name SÜDWIND (Southwind).

Two heavy tank battalions took part in SÜDWIND. SS-Heavy Tank Battalion 501 was still attached to Combat Group Peiper, a component of the 1st SS-Panzer Division. This division was also still part of the I SS-Panzer Corps, to which the SS-Heavy Tank Battalion 501 was permanently assigned. The second heavy tank battalion was Heavy Tank Battalion 503 (FHH) which had operated in Hungary since October 1944. For this operation, the battalion was placed under the operational control of the 44th Infantry Division, the Reichs-Grenadier Division "Hoch und Deutschmeister."[91]

Neither heavy tank battalion was at full strength for this operation. SS-Heavy Tank Battalion 501 had 36 King Tigers on its rolls, but only 19 were operational for the start of the attack.[92] Heavy Tank Battalion 503 (FHH) had 22 on hand, all of which were operational for the beginning of the attack.[93]

The attack began at 0500 hours on 17 February 1945 with Panzer Corps FHH leading and I SS-Panzer Corps following. Heavy Tank Battalion 503 (FHH) attacked in the vanguard and was successful in penetrating the Soviet defenses.[94]

During this attack, the battalion lost one Tiger to antitank gunfire.[95] This was the only Tiger lost to enemy action by either battalion during the entire operation. During the afternoon, both battalions led the attack to the Parizsky Canal.[96] This attack was probably the only instance during the war where two German heavy tank battalions attacked together toward a common objective. (see map 32)

On 18 February 1945, SS-Heavy Tank Battalion 501 attacked out of the small bridgehead over the Parizsky Canal to key high ground north of Muzsla. Around midnight, Heavy Tank Battalion 503 (FHH) linked up with elements of the 1st SS-Panzer Division in the same vicinity. During their attack south, they ran into an extensive minefield. Without the support of infantry or engineers, tank commanders and other crewmen dismounted and manually breached the minefield by clearing paths for the tanks.[97]

The next day, 19 February 1945, SS-Heavy Tank Battalion 501 continued its attack with the Leibstandarte to the confluence of the Gran and the Danube

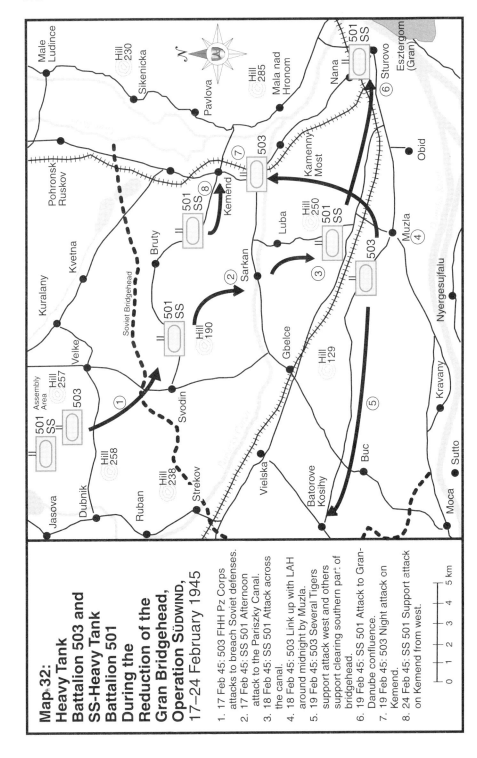

**Map 32:
Heavy Tank
Battalion 503 and
SS-Heavy Tank
Battalion 501
During the
Reduction of the
Gran Bridgehead,
Operation SÜDWIND,
17–24 February 1945**

1. 17 Feb 45: 503 FHH Pz Corps attacks to breach Soviet defenses.

2. 17 Feb 45: SS 501 Afternoon attack to the Pariszky Canal.

3. 18 Feb 45: SS 501 Attack across the canal.

4. 18 Feb 45: 503 Link up with LAH around midnight by Muzla.

5. 19 Feb 45: 503 Several Tigers support attack west and others support clearing southern par'. of bridgehead.

6. 19 Feb 45: SS 501 Attack to Gran-Danube confluence.

7. 19 Feb 45: 503 Night attack on Kemend.

8. 24 Feb 45: SS 501 Support attack on Kemend from west.

Rivers. During the day, Heavy Tank Battalion 503 (*FHH*) supported a number of lesser attacks to secure the entire southern portion of the bridgehead.[98]

That night, Heavy Tank Battalion 503 (*FHH*) conducted an unsupported attack against the Soviet strongpoint in the village of Kemend. It was halted by an extensive minefield.[99] The battalion then supported the further reduction of the bridgehead by assuming defensive positions to contain Soviet forces.

SS-Heavy Tank Battalion 501 took part in the final attack in the bridgehead that eliminated the Soviet strongpoint in Kemend. On 24 February 1945, the battalion attacked from the west with the rest of Combat Group Peiper and was successful in eliminating this Soviet strongpoint.[100]

Although records do not indicate how many enemy tanks were destroyed by each unit, this operation must be deemed as a complete success. The two heavy tank battalions led the two corps' attacks during the important stages of the operation and only suffered the loss of one Tiger to enemy action. This was achieved against a prepared Soviet defense that included 60,000 men; between 100 and 230 tanks and assault guns; and over 100 antitank guns.[101]

Although these battalions sustained only one Tiger destroyed, their maintenance elements had difficulty repairing damaged Tigers as well as conducting routine tank maintenance. At the end of Operation SÜDWIND, SS-Heavy Tank Battalion 501 only had four King Tigers operational out of 36 on hand.[102] What Russian tanks, guns, and troops could not accomplish, the ubiquitous mechanical and maintenance problems did.

Immediately following this operation, I SS Panzer Corps moved south to prepare for its next operation, FRÜHLINGSERWACHEN. This battalion only had nine days to recover from SÜDWIND before being thrown once again into major offensive activity requiring extensive cross-country and road movement. As a result, SS-Heavy Tank Battalion 501 was unable to increase the number of operational King Tigers, beginning FRÜHLINGSERWACHEN with four King Tigers.[103]

Heavy Tank Battalion 509 was also committed to FRÜHLINGSERWACHEN. As part of III Panzer Corps, this battalion operated in a supporting role in the northern zone of the German attack. Since participating in the third German relief attempt toward Budapest in January (Operation KONRAD III), it had been allowed time to conduct maintenance and was committed in primarily a defensive role, allowing it to begin this operation with 32 operational King Tigers.[104] (see map 33)

Both heavy tank battalions experienced great difficulties during the offensive because of the muddy and swampy terrain. The Soviets did not use very many armored vehicles to counter this offensive, so FRÜHLINGSERWACHEN turned out to be primarily an infantry battle on both sides.

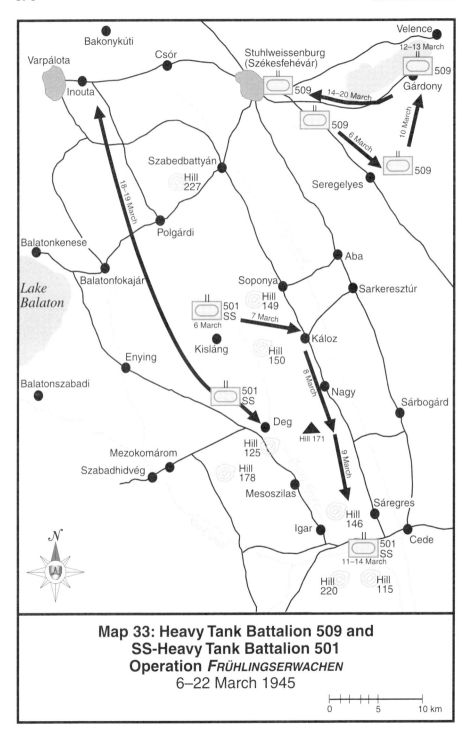

Map 33: Heavy Tank Battalion 509 and SS-Heavy Tank Battalion 501 Operation *FRÜHLINGSERWACHEN* **6–22 March 1945**

0   5   10 km

As part of the main attack, SS-Heavy Tank Battalion 501 did not contribute greatly during the offensive. Along with the rest of Combat Group Peiper, they generally trailed the two leading panzer-grenadier regiments of the 1st SS-Panzer Division during the attack. Even though the *Leibstandarte* was able to establish a bridgehead across the Sio River, the King Tigers of SS-Heavy Tank Battalion 501 did not cross, probably because a bridge capable of supporting the King Tigers did not exist.

German intelligence indicated the possibility of a Soviet counteroffensive, so the 1st SS-Panzer Division consolidated Heavy Tank Battalion 501 near the town of Deg on 14 March 1945. After the Soviets began their offensive the next day, I SS-Panzer Corps committed Combat Group Peiper and the eight operational King Tigers of SS-Heavy Tank Battalion 501 to stopping the enemy penetrations to the northwest around Stuhlweissenburg and Varpalota. These eight tanks were employed in a piecemeal fashion, with one or two King Tigers operating with other types of tanks from Combat Group Peiper.

On several occasions, a handful of Tigers knocked out large numbers of Soviet tanks and armored vehicles. On 20 March 1945, one King Tiger destroyed 15 Soviet tanks near Varpalota; on the next day, a single King Tiger supported by two Panthers destroyed another 17 enemy tanks.[105] On 21 March 1945, however, the battalion began a long series of delaying actions that eventually led to its surrender to the U.S. Army near Steyr, Austria.[106]

Heavy Tank Battalion 509 was either in the lead echelon or closely supported the lead units of III Panzer Corps and was directly responsible for the success of an attack on at least two occasions. On 6 March 1945, forward units of III Panzer Corps were not able to neutralize some JS-II Heavy Tanks near Seregelyes. Two King Tigers from the battalion rumbled forward and destroyed six JS-IIs, which allowed the attack to continue.[107]

On 13 March 1945, lead elements of III Panzer Corps encountered 24 SU-152s in prepared defensive positions protected by a minefield. During the battalion's attack on this complex, every one of the 16 operational King Tigers was severely damaged and three were totally destroyed. After lanes were cleared in the minefield, two King Tigers managed to destroy all of the SU-152s.[108]

During the offensive, Heavy Tank Battalion 509 lost three Tigers to enemy action, with many others damaged but repairable, and destroyed at least 30 enemy tanks or armored vehicles. This battalion was directly responsible for breaking through several layers of the Soviets' defense and managed to achieve a 10-to-1 kill ratio.

At this very late stage of the war, even when pitted against the newest and most formidable Soviet tanks, King Tigers could still be particularly deadly.

The Vistula-Oder Operation

In January 1945, two heavy tank battalions faced the Soviet bridgeheads of the 1st Ukrainian Front and the 2d Belorussian Front across the Vistula and Narew Rivers. In Army Group A's sector, Heavy Tank Battalion 501 was assigned to XXIV Panzer Corps, which was the operational reserve for the 4th Panzer Army. Its mission was to destroy enemy penetrations of the German defenses around the Sandomierz Bridgehead. Further north, as part of Army Group Center, Heavy Tank Battalion 507 was assigned to the 2d Army and faced a similar mission against Russian bridgeheads across the Narew River.[109]

Heavy Tank Battalion 501 was a powerful unit at this time. This battalion had between 41 and 45 King Tigers and had recently taken over Heavy Tank Battalion 509's former Tigers, so that it had a total strength of 52 Tiger and King Tiger tanks.[110] Along with the remainder of XXIV Panzer Corps, this battalion was concentrated well forward in the defensive sector so that they were near the front lines. Furthermore, their assembly area was in swampy terrain, which restricted the use of tanks primarily to the roads. The battalion occupied the same assembly area as the 17th Panzer Division, although it is unclear whether they were formally attached to this division.[111] (see map 34)

Records indicate that everyone in the chain of command from the battalion commander to the Commanding General of Army Group A disagreed with the deployment of these units so far forward.[112] Even though some members of Heavy Tank Battalion 501 claimed that they were being sabotaged, according to the Commanding General of the 17th Panzer Division, the orders came from Hitler. Others have speculated that they were ordered forward to bolster the confidence of the infantry manning the front line defenses in anticipation of the forthcoming Soviet offensive.

Whatever the case, when the main Soviet attack came on 12 January 1945, the German operational reserve units were quickly overrun or bypassed. After waiting most of the day, the commander of Heavy Tank Battalion 501 received word that the 17th Panzer Division headquarters was being overrun by Soviet tanks.[113] After an unsuccessful attempt that day, the attack to relieve the divisional command post was continued on 13 January 1945. During this attack, the battalion destroyed 27 tanks without losing a single Tiger to enemy action.[114] Nevertheless, the attack was halted and the battalion consolidated to begin its withdrawal, or more specifically—because it had been bypassed and was now surrounded—its attack to the rear. The battalion's objective was to reach the city of Kielce via the town of Lisow. During the movement to Lisow, several tanks got stuck in the mud and were ultimately abandoned.

Presumably the Soviets were aware of the battalion's existence because, based on available reports, they prepared an ambush for this battalion in the town of Lisow. By the end of the day, most of Heavy Tank Battalion 501 was

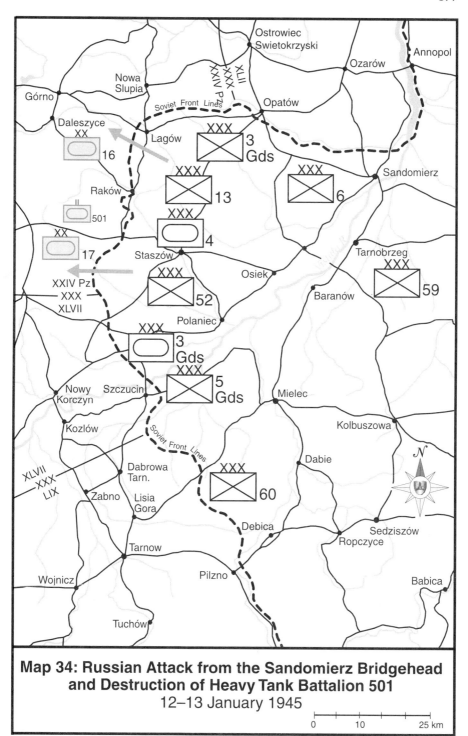

**Map 34: Russian Attack from the Sandomierz Bridgehead
and Destruction of Heavy Tank Battalion 501**
12–13 January 1945

0   10   25 km

destroyed. The few remaining tanks and crews continued to fight on and joined part of "Nehring's Wandering Pocket," named for the commander of XXIV Panzer Corps, General Walther K. Nehring.[115] The few vehicles that survived the Soviet ambush were reportedly destroyed later because they ran out of fuel, although one Tiger may have made it all the way back to Berlin.[116]

Further north, Heavy Tank Battalion 507, like Heavy Tank Battalion 501, was overstrength and fielded a total of 51 tanks, all Tigers. This battalion fared much better, in large part because they were not in the direct path of the main Soviet offensive. They were spread out behind the front in separate company assembly areas, similar to heavy tank battalion employment in Normandy. From 16 to 19 January 1945, this battalion destroyed 96 enemy tanks while losing only four Tigers.[117] Its efforts could not stop the Soviet offensive and it began to withdraw west on 19 January 1945. From 19 to 30 January 1945, 41 Tigers were lost with the majority being destroyed by their own crews. Of those 41 Tigers, 22 reached the east bank of the Vistula. Ferries were not available, however, so the battalion destroyed them to avoid capture.[118] By 13 February 1945, one month after the beginning of the Soviet Vistula offensive, Heavy Tank Battalion 507 was reduced to two Tigers.[119]

Obviously, Heavy Tank Battalion 501 was ineffective in its employment as a part of the mobile reserve defending the Sandomierz Bridgehead. It was positioned so far forward that it was unable to react to enemy penetrations of the front line before those penetrations bypassed them. Their assembly area also was in an area that degraded their mobility by limiting them primarily to existing roads. Also, although adhering to the concept of concentration by consolidating the entire battalion, the Germans were unable to counter, or even slightly influence, the many Soviet penetrations from the bridgehead. From the results, it is apparent that the Soviets exploited these poor German decisions, and thus eliminated Heavy Tank Battalion 501.

In contrast, Heavy Tank Battalion 507 appears to have been very effective in destroying enemy penetrations, although the deteriorating strategic situation to their south ultimately resulted in devastating losses during their retreat. Positioning elements of the battalion across a wider frontage and locating those elements further in depth helped them inflict significant, but by this stage of the war, wholly inadequate, losses upon the attacking Soviet armored forces. Prior to its retreat, this battalion destroyed 24 Soviet tanks for the combat loss of each Tiger.

Fragmented End

During the last six months of the war, 11 heavy tank battalions were destroyed in action against the Red Army. These heavy tank battalions usually fought with significantly fewer tanks than the 45 that they were authorized. Even with only a handful of Tigers, however, these units were sometimes able to destroy large numbers of enemy tanks. (see map 35)

Four heavy tank battalions—Heavy Tank Battalions 501, 503 (*FHH*), and 509; and SS-Heavy Tank Battalion 501—fought in Hungary and their remnants retreated to Austria or Czechoslovakia before the war ended. The 3d Battalion of Panzer Regiment *Grossdeutschland,* and Heavy Tank Battalions 502, 505, and 507 all fought in the northern part of Germany, Poland, and East Prussia. Their last battles, with only a few Tigers, were in places like Pillau, the Frische Nehrung, and Königsberg. Heavy Tank Battalion 510 fought as part of Army Group North (later called Army Group Kurland) in the Kurland Peninsula, ultimately surrendering to Soviet forces at the end of the war.[120] Prior to that surrender, one company was transported back to Germany and participated in the fighting in the Ruhr Pocket.

After Heavy Tank Battalion 501 was destroyed along the Vistula in January 1945, only two heavy tank battalions defended the front east of Berlin. These were the two remaining SS battalions, SS-Heavy Tank Battalions 502 and 503. Both of these battalions operated with far fewer tanks than the 45 authorized and what tanks they did have were usually employed in small elements. Although both battalions fought in a wide variety of places, from January until the end of the war, SS-Heavy Tank Battalion 503 was employed with its tanks very widely dispersed. This battalion, or elements of it, fought in the vicinity of Küstrin, in Gotenhafen, and Danzig. Some parts of the battalion even participated in the attack out of Pomerania, Operation SONNEWENDE (Winter Solstice), in February 1945.[121] At late as 2 May 1945, this battalion still had seven King Tigers fighting in Berlin.[122]

Also during the last six months of the war, three heavy tank battalions were destroyed fighting the Western allies. Two battalions, Heavy Tank Battalions 504 and 508, were gradually demolished in combat in northern Italy. The remaining battalion, Heavy Tank Battalion 506, fought in western Germany following its participation in Operation WACHT AM RHEIN, and surrendered to American forces in the Ruhr pocket.

Summary

The last two years of the war saw a dramatic increase in the number of heavy tank battalions. By the end of the war, some battalions had been destroyed and reconstituted two or three times. *OKH* and *OKW* committed the heavy tank battalions of the Army and *Waffen-SS* to almost every region of the European theater during the last two years of the war.

Officially, the doctrine for the employment of the heavy tank battalions did not change during this period. This doctrine continued to be focused solely on the offensive, even though the battalions participated primarily in defensive

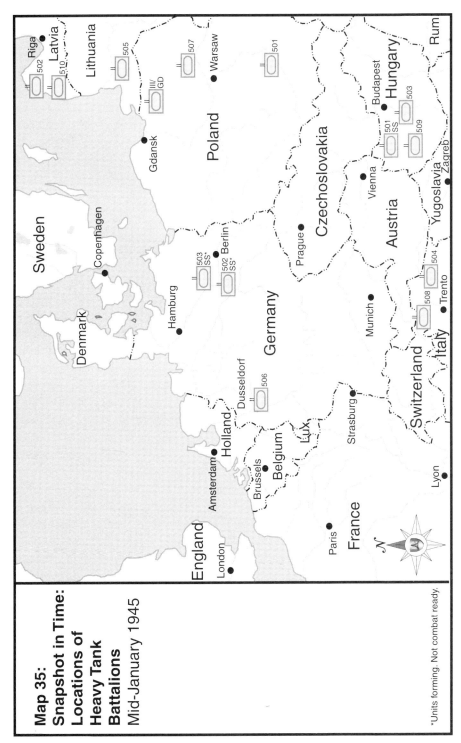

**Map 35:
Snapshot in Time:
Locations of
Heavy Tank
Battalions**
Mid-January 1945

* Units forming. Not combat ready.

battles. The principle of concentration, extremely important and valid in the offense, was also stressed in these defensive battles. Conceptually, this may have been a valid principle. In reality, however, the limitations of the Tiger and King Tiger, along with the vast defensive frontages along which they were employed, invalidated this principle in many situations.

When heavy tank battalions were concentrated in the defense, they were generally easier to bypass and/or were targeted for destruction by Allied armored units or from the air. The Allies naturally preferred to avoid the concentrated heavy tank battalions. When concentrated, deployment of heavy tank units to the threatened area reduced the operational number of Tigers because of their persistent mechanical problems.

In the defense, heavy tank battalions were most effective when employed as a reserve force to counterattack against enemy penetrations. They were also most effective when they were dispersed along the breadth of the defensive front, to diminish the distance they would have to travel to accomplish their missions. This was especially true when the terrain restricted vehicular movement to a few avenues of approach.

When employed in the offense, heavy tank battalions achieved mixed results. Their failure can be attributed primarily to the Tigers' and King Tigers' mobility limitations, but credit also has to be given to their enemies' ever-improving ability to destroy German heavy tanks through the introduction of antitank weapons of larger calibers firing improved projectiles at higher velocities. Also, the widespread employment of mines severely degraded the heavy tank battalions' effectiveness in breaking through the enemy's defenses.

Operation SÜDWIND and Heavy Tank Battalion 509's involvement in Operation FRÜHLINGSERWACHEN are two notable exceptions and examples of successful employment of heavy tank battalions in the offense. During Operation SÜDWIND specifically, heavy tank battalions were extremely effective and important in breaking through several echelons of prepared defenses.

This success must be attributed to the fact that this was one of the only instances where they were employed in accordance with their own doctrine. Specifically, two heavy tank battalions were used together toward common objectives, thus achieving the principle of concentration. The common objectives were also beyond the front lines and were focused on destroying both artillery and antitank weapons in depth. Both heavy tank battalions were also part of a mechanized or armored unit and were supported by infantry, artillery, and engineers, which met the guidance that heavy tank battalions be attached to mechanized or armor units and that breakthroughs be accomplished through the close coordination and cooperation with other arms.

Chapter 7

Assessment and Conclusion

"The Tigers!" The panic-stricken cry was flying from mouth to mouth.
"The Tigers are coming!"[1]

American Soldiers at Kasserine Pass

One hour of Tiger operation requires ten hours of maintenance.[2]
Alfred Rubbel

The German military developed and fielded the heavy tank battalion to break through an enemy's tactical defensive belt. These heavy tank battalions were rarely employed as a breakthrough force as originally envisioned, but rather, due to the changing strategic situation, the Germans used them primarily in the defense. Whether in the offense or the defense, its primary purpose was the destruction of enemy tanks in furtherance of operational goals.

Mission Accomplishment

There are only a few examples of heavy tank battalions employed as a breakthrough force. Therefore, it is difficult to accurately assess their effectiveness in the offensive role for which they were developed, organized, and fielded. In the few instances where the German leadership employed heavy tank battalions as consolidated units in the offense, they achieved credible results and were successful in penetrating at least one echelon of the enemy's defenses.[3] These attacks were successful tactical breakthroughs, but they did not lead to operational breakthroughs, that is, penetrations that would enable decisive results for entire campaigns as German theorists originally envisioned. The organization and equipment of heavy tank battalions themselves, however, were not solely to blame for this failure to achieve their designers' expectations. Additionally, the crews and leaders of these units cannot be held primarily liable for the shortcomings of the heavy tank battalions.

These units were tasked with the most difficult missions and many times, were expected to accomplish those tasks without adequate support from other branches and arms of the military. When a heavy tank battalion was employed as a consolidated unit in the offense, it achieved much greater results in breaking through the initial defensive echelon than when it was dispersed. Whether other German forces or units composed of other tank types could have accomplished these missions is arguable and largely dependent upon the situation, primarily the terrain and composition of enemy forces. It is fair to note that, throughout the war, the Germans assigned tanks in general—and the heavy tank battalions specifically—with the primary mission of breaking through enemy defenses.

German doctrine incorporated armor, artillery, infantry, and air power in breakthrough operations. In theory, all of these branches were to combine their effects to achieve a breakthrough. In practice, employment of armor units, especially the heavy tank battalions, gained ascendancy over the other branches during the war. The especially heavy reliance on armor in German breakthrough operations placed high expectations and tremendous burdens on heavy tank battalions.

These expectations may have been met if the German military had developed several relatively simple items to complement the heavy tanks and the heavy tank battalions. A mine plow or roller for the Tiger and King Tiger would have allowed these vehicles to effectively breach minefields along their axes of attack. Instead, many heavy tanks were disabled by implementing the "bull-through" breaching technique, severely reducing the number of operational vehicles available to continue offensive operations. When heavy tanks did become disabled, for whatever reason, the heavy tank battalion organization included insufficient numbers of armored recovery vehicles to efficiently recover and repair disabled vehicles. In fact, until mid-1944, recovery operations had to be conducted with only the unarmored, half-tracked 18-tons organic to heavy tank battalions; such vehicles were completely inadequate for recovery under fire. Committing the resources necessary to field adequate numbers of armored recovery vehicles, in sufficient quantities, would certainly have saved the loss of many disabled heavy tanks.

Every tank design is a compromise between the three essential elements of mobility, firepower, and protection. The Tiger series, with their 88mm main guns, had a great deal of firepower throughout the war. Although the Tigers were highly resistant to enemy fire, especially when each design was initially fielded, they paid for this high degree of protection with reduced mobility, in terms of both speed and range.

Heavy tank battalions possessed three major deficiencies for breakthrough operations for which they were intended. First, because they were unique and scarce resources, when the Tigers attacked, the enemy was able to accurately deduce the area of the German main effort. This allowed the Allies to move forces to counter the German effort.

Second, thanks to their Tigers' very poor mechanical reliability and large size, which both contributed to limiting the Tiger's tactical mobility, heavy tank battalions were unable to achieve quick breakthroughs; it usually required extended amounts of time to overcome enemy antitank guns, tanks, and minefields. If the Tigers had been able to quickly break through the enemy defenses, the first deficiency may not have mattered because other German armored forces would have been able to exploit the breakthrough before the enemy could react.

Even these two deficiencies might have been overcome if the Tiger had the ability to exploit their own breakthroughs. Although these units were not developed for this, their limited radius of action due to voracious fuel consumption, low speed (especially in the King Tiger) and intensive maintenance requirements precluded them from exploiting any breakthrough achieved.

When theorists conceived heavy tank battalions, they thought that defenses would only consist of one, or at most a few, defensive lines. As the war progressed, armies of all sides extended their defensive depth so that there were many defensive echelons to penetrate. This extension of the defense was an effective counter to the heavy tank battalions.

The increased number and effectiveness of antitank guns, as well as the proliferation of landmines, also limited the effectiveness of the heavy tank battalions in the offense.[4] These measures, employed in depth, made achieving a deep breakthrough extremely difficult. The Tiger helped in penetrating such defenses, but never really solved the problem of restoring offensive mobility and movement to the German Army on a tactical or operational level.

In the defense, heavy tank battalions achieved mixed results depending upon many different factors. Heavy tank battalions performed defensive missions far more frequently than offensive missions. These defensive missions included counterattacks to reestablish the front line; occupying front line defensive positions with or without infantry support; and as a reserve force to counterattack enemy penetrations behind the front line. Generally, even a portion of a heavy tank battalion could defend against an enemy force that possessed many more tanks. If there was an alternative, enemy units bypassed heavy tank battalions rather than attacking them. After being bypassed, the heavy tank battalions became a liability because they could not be repositioned easily and required a great deal of logistical and other support to do so.

The logical deduction from this is that heavy tank battalions may have been more effective in the defense if they were dispersed along a wide front. This would also lead to a conclusion that heavy tank battalions, as combined units, were unnecessary in the defense and heavy tanks would have been more effective had they been incorporated into other armored units. Indeed, they could have been organized much as *Panzerjäger*, or tank destroyer, units were assigned as integral parts of panzer, panzergrenadier, or even infantry formations. Incorporating them into an infantry unit would have added much needed firepower, especially antitank firepower. Their incorporation into panzer or panzergrenadier divisions would have added useful offensive and defensive capabilities, but would have significantly complicated an already hard-pressed supply and maintenance system, so there would have been logistical challenges which may have more than offset the tactical advantages of such an arrangement.

An example of the incorporation of the Tiger into a division actually exists in the heavy tank companies of the 1st, 2d, and 3d SS Divisions and the *Grossdeutschland* Division.[5] All of these divisions eventually lost their heavy tank companies except for the 3d SS *Totenkopf* Division, which retained its heavy company throughout the war.[6] These divisions, and their heavy tank companies, achieved notable results during their existence.

Despite its shortcomings, a measure of the heavy tank battalion's effectiveness, in the offense or defense, can be gauged by the emphasis and level of attention accorded them by their opponents. The Soviets fielded many new weapons and implemented numerous organizational changes to counter the heavy tank battalions. The British conducted several studies of the Tiger, and of the heavy tank battalions, in an attempt to identify weaknesses of each. General Montgomery went so far as to ban British combat reports that detailed the firepower of the Tiger tanks because he felt they undermined morale.[7] The Allied intelligence estimate of German forces in the west prior to D-day shows that the heavy tank battalions were the only unit below divisional size that the Allies posted on their theater intelligence map.[8] These examples show that Germany's enemies took the threat of the heavy tank battalions very seriously and thus provide testimony to their effectiveness.

A Statistical Perspective

The Germans kept detailed records on the loss of each Tiger and on the number of enemy tanks they destroyed. The claims of American and British tanks destroyed have been confirmed, to various degrees of reliability, from available records. For Soviet losses, very few records are available to confirm the German claims. In these instances, the German claims are generally accepted without the benefit of verification.

Whatever mission heavy tank battalions were given, their primary task was to destroy enemy tanks. In so doing, they were undeniably successful. The kill ratio of heavy tank battalions when measured against Tigers lost in direct combat is an impressive 12.2 to 1. The ratio as measured against all Tigers lost, regardless of reason, is still a credible 5.4-to-1 kill ratio.[9] Although the last ratio is based upon the total annihilation of every heavy tank battalion, it is probably the most accurate considering that a certain percentage of kills claimed by Tigers must certainly have been repaired and returned to service in the same way that Tigers were returned to service after being damaged. (see table 5)

As would be expected, some heavy tank battalions were more successful than others in destroying enemy tanks. Some battalions were able to destroy close to 13 enemy tanks for the loss of each Tiger and others were able to achieve only a one-for-one exchange. Variables that could account for this include the terrain, enemy, leadership, and missions assigned. Of these, the mission assigned to heavy tank battalions was the one area that the Germans

	TIGER LOSSES			NUMBER COMPARISON		RATIO OF TIGERS TO ENEMY TANKS (1: X)	
Unit	Lost in Action	Dest. by Crew	Unk. or Other	Total Losses	Enemy Tanks Dest.	Kill Ratio (in Action)	Kill Ratio (Total Lost)
3d Bn/Pz.Reg GD	62	32	4	98	<500	8.06	5.10
SS-Hvy Tk Bn 101/501	72	33	2	107	<500	6.94	4.67
SS-Hvy Tk Bn 102/502	38	29	9	76	~600	15.79	7.89
SS-Hvy Tk Bn 103/503	10	9	20	39	<500	50.00	12.82
Hvy Tk Bn 501	24	12	84	120	<450	18.75	3.75
Hvy Tk Bn 502	88	14	5	107	<1400	15.90	13.00
Hvy Tk Bn 503	113	123	15	252	<1700	15.00	6.75
Hvy Tk Bn 504	29	80	0	109	<250	8.60	2.29
Hvy Tk Bn 505	47	62	18	126	<900	19.10	7.10
Hvy Tk Bn 506	61	116	2	179	<400	6.56	2.23
Hvy Tk Bn 507	43	57	4	104	<600	13.95	5.77
Hvy Tk Bn 508	15	46	17	78	<100	6.67	1.28
Hvy Tk Bn 509	76	40	5	120	<500	6.58	4.17
Hvy Tk Bn 510	35	1	29	65	<200	5.71	3.08
Grand Totals	713	654	214	1580	8600	12.16	5.44
Total Percentages	45%	41%	14%	100%			

Table 5. Tank Kill Ratio Comparison.
Sources: Schneider, *Tigers in Combat I*, 47, 78, 100, 144–45, 173, 226–27, 242, 263, 279, 311, 323, 344, 357, 372, 381, 408, 421, 439, 447, 456; idem, *Tigers in Combat II*, 56, 83, 268, 320, 336, 365, 375, 398.
Notes: Of all of the unit's claims, SS-Heavy Tank Battalion 503's is the most difficult to verify, but if accurate, the most impressive. This battalion was never fully equipped and only fought from January 1945 until the end of the war. Committed to the Eastern Theater, it was split apart to many different areas under many different commands. Its records are incomplete and cannot be verified. This battalion fought in places like Küstrin, the Seelow Heights, and in Berlin, in addition to many others. It is difficult to imagine how the battalion destroyed more than 500 Soviet tanks in a little over three months of combat.

could most influence. In general, heavy tank battalions were most successful when they were concentrated for offensive missions and dispersed behind the front for defensive missions. Even though results differ greatly from battalion to battalion, when taken as an overall average, heavy tank battalions were undeniably effective at destroying enemy tanks.[10]

Flaws

Deficiencies in organization and equipment detracted from the success of the heavy tank battalions throughout their existence. Almost all of these deal directly or indirectly with Tiger and King Tiger technical and mechanical problems.

These tanks were effective as tank-killing weapons, which is evident from the kill ratios. Another virtue of the tanks was that they were very durable. Frequently when a Tiger was damaged and was subsequently destroyed by its crew, the crew managed to escape capture and return to its unit. This had the benefit of creating experienced crews. These benefits came at a cost in other areas, however.

The high degree of maintenance required to keep the Tiger and King Tiger tanks operating was one of their biggest deficiencies. This usually resulted in a low operational rate for tanks within the heavy tank battalions, especially after extended periods of combat. The tendency of the Tigers to break down, coupled with the weight of the tanks, made recovery difficult. The failure to field a suitable recovery vehicle, with the exception of the Bergepanther after mid-1944, or to field them in sufficient quantities, resulted in the loss of Tigers in many instances.

Another deficiency of the Tiger was its extremely limited radius of action.[11] When this was included with the Tiger's maintenance requirements, heavy tank battalions were limited in their ability to conduct mobile operations across an extended area. The Allies exploited this fact during the numerous and frequent operational and strategic withdrawals of the heavy tank battalions. The result of these deficiencies is clearly seen by the number of tanks destroyed by their own crews. (see Table 6)

In many instances in the offense, the Germans failed to adhere to their published doctrine. During Operation ZITADELLE, for example, III Panzer Corps divided Heavy Tank Battalion 503's three companies among the corps' three armored divisions. This violated the principle of concentration that was published as being necessary for successful breakthroughs. Even though Heavy Tank Battalion 505 fought as a unit during Operation ZITADELLE, it was attached to an infantry division. This violated the guidance directing heavy tank battalions be attached only to other armored units. Thus, when this

	PERCENTAGE LOSSES			RAW NUMBERS			
Unit	Lost in Action	Dest. by Crew	Unk. or Other	Lost in Action	Dest. by Crew	Unk. or Other	Total Losses
3d Bn/Pz.Reg GD	63%	33%	4%	62	32	4	98
SS-Hvy Tk Bn 101	67%	31%	2%	72	33	2	107
SS-Hvy Tk Bn 102	50%	38%	12%	38	29	9	76
SS-Hvy Tk Bn 103	26%	23%	51%	10	9	20	39
Hvy Tk Bn 501	20%	10%	70%	24	12	84	120
Hvy Tk Bn 502	82%	13%	5%	88	14	5	107
Hvy Tk Bn 503	45%	49%	6%	113	123	15	252
Hvy Tk Bn 504	27%	73%	0%	29	80	0	109
Hvy Tk Bn 505	37%	49%	14%	47	62	18	126
Hvy Tk Bn 506	34%	65%	1%	61	116	2	179
Hvy Tk Bn 507	41%	55%	4%	43	57	4	104
Hvy Tk Bn 508	19%	59%	22%	15	46	17	78
Hvy Tk Bn 509	63%	33%	4%	76	40	5	120
Hvy Tk Bn 510	54%	>1%	45%	35	1	29	65
Grand Totals				713	654	214	1580
Total Percentages				45%	41%	14%	100%

Table 6. Tiger Losses
Sources: Schneider. *Tigers in Combat I*, 78, 144–45, 226–27, 263, 311, 344, 372, 408, 439, 456; idem, *Tigers in Combat II*, 83, 320, 365, 398.

battalion penetrated the Soviet first echelon defenses, there were no other armored units available to exploit that breach. The first instance where an entire, consolidated heavy tank battalion attacked to break through enemy defenses, as part of an armored force, was not until February 1945 during Operation SÜDWIND.

After considering the limitations of the Tiger and recognizing that the preponderance of missions given to heavy tank battalions were defensive in nature, it is puzzling that the Germans did not develop and publish more guidance and doctrine to more effectively deal with these realities.

German military doctrine stressed the concept of concentration, whether in the offense or the defense. In several instances, due to Tigers' mobility challenges, adherence to this principle during defensive operations significantly limited heavy tank battalions' flexibility; they just couldn't respond in time or with sufficient combat power to stop the enemy penetrations.

A prerequisite for employing heavy tank battalions, either as a mobile reserve or as a counterattack force employed to defeat enemy penetrations, was for them to have greater, or at least comparable, mobility and radius of action than the enemy formations they were attempting to defeat. If this criterion was met, then the principle of concentration in the defense might also be applicable. In many instances, because of the deficiencies and limitations of the Tiger, this criterion was not met. In these cases, enemy armored formations attacked where Tigers were not present. This led to many forced operational and strategic withdrawals, during which many Tigers broke down or ran out of fuel. Often, because they could not be recovered, this led to their destruction.

In light of these facts, heavy tank battalions may have been more effective if they had adopted a principle of dispersion in the defense in order to cover more avenues of approach or more defensive frontage. A prime example of the effectiveness of this tactic was Heavy Tank Battalion 502, which operated primarily with Army Group North around Leningrad and in the Baltic states. This area was heavily wooded and swampy, and armored mobility was reduced to the roads. Because of this, the battalion rarely operated as a concentrated unit. Instead, it was spread out and broken down to very small elements to effectively cover all the available armored avenues of approach. This battalion achieved the second highest kill total of all of the battalions and produced the highest overall kill ratio.

In this example, the terrain favored, and in actuality it forced, the dispersion of the battalion. Even across extended defensive frontages encompassing terrain that offered good armored mobility, dispersion may have been more effective than concentrating a heavy tank battalion. A handful of Tigers proved many times that they were capable of stopping a numerically-superior enemy. Across an extended frontage, a concentrated heavy tank battalion may have had difficulty getting to an area prior to the enemy forces that were breaking though the front-line defenses. In this case, it was probably preferable to counter an enemy penetration with a smaller-than-desired force than not being able to counter that same penetration at all.

Fulfilling a wide variety of missions in the defense proved to be challenging for the heavy tank battalions. On one hand, the Organization E battalion may have been the optimal organization for a battalion attacking forward of the main lines into prepared defenses because it included only heavy tanks. Many heavy tank battalions, however, were tasked with defensive missions on or near the front line. Sometimes these missions were unsupported by other types of units, either infantry or lighter armored forces. In these instances, the Organization D battalion would have provided the battalion with a much higher degree of flexibility to accomplish these defensive missions. Since the majority of missions assigned were defensive, it may have been worthwhile for the battalions to return to the Organization D. This would have allowed the creation of more battalions, each with a higher degree of flexibility in the performance of missions.

Synthesis and Conclusion

During WWII, German heavy tank battalions were effective at killing enemy tanks. They achieved a high kill ratio during both offensive and defensive missions. Their overall kill ratio was severely reduced, however, due to forced withdrawals over extended distances. These withdrawals caused the loss of many Tigers and highlighted the deficiencies in the Tiger and in the lack of recovery assets within the heavy tank battalions themselves.

The heavy tank battalions were hindered by the failure to adhere to German doctrine on their employment in the offense. German commanders often did not commit consolidated, concentrated heavy tank battalions in support of a major attack. During their few offensive missions, heavy tank battalions failed to achieve the expected operational breakthroughs, although they were often able to penetrate the first echelon defenses.

German heavy tank battalions were also hindered by the lack of a coherent, published defensive doctrine based upon the realities and weaknesses of the Tiger. German commanders continued to stress the importance of concentration in the defense. This was not always an invalid concept, but the lack of dispersal in the defense often denied heavy tanks the ability to counter enemy penetrations in time and with sufficient force. Conversely, in numerous cases where heavy tank battalions dispersed their forces behind the entire frontage, they were very successful at destroying enemy tanks and thus had a better chance to stop the enemy penetration.

One alternative that may have been more effective for the German military than the fielding of heavy tank battalions was a change in doctrine that provided for universal tank types to accomplish all missions. One can only hypothesize about whether this would have been more successful in achieving breakthroughs. It would have surely allowed the Germans to produce a much greater number of Mark IVs or Panthers. They then could have used these vehicles, in a greater quantity, to possibly achieve better results than they were able to achieve with the limited number of Tigers produced.

The strategic decision to develop and field the Tiger and the King Tiger was important because it was a massive investment in resources, time, money, and labor. The Germans ultimately lacked, or failed to commit, the production facilities and raw materials to mass produce the Tiger in large numbers.[12] German sources, and most histories of the war, continually emphasize the fact that the Germans were severely outnumbered in terms of tanks, as well as other vehicle types, on all fronts. Given the fact that they decided to build immensely-resource-intensive vehicles like the Tiger and the King Tiger, it is difficult to imagine that they would have expected for the situation to have been otherwise. Even if the Germans had resources equal to their opponents, the decision to build vehicles like the Tiger and the King Tiger ensured that they would be outnumbered.

The Tiger and the King Tiger tanks were engineering marvels and extraordinary fighting vehicles throughout the war. A single Tiger or a small number of Tigers at the right time, place, and in the right circumstances, accomplished extraordinary, even phenomenal feats numerous times throughout the war. This has led to a great number of anecdotal stories heralding the prowess of the Tiger and King Tiger. While this is only natural, because they are interesting tales and rightly recognize the crews' bravery and abilities, it fails to adequately portray the overall contribution of the organization to which these tanks belonged to the war effort.

In the end, one is left to wonder why the German military fielded heavy tank battalions. According to theorists like Guderian, and German doctrine, heavy tanks were only one tool to be used to achieve a breakthrough. If heavy tanks battalions were fielded during the war to achieve a breakthrough, the other arms and branches of the military were not developed, fielded, and incorporated as equal components in that effort.

By the time that heavy tank battalions were fielded in significant numbers, the strategic situation had changed so that even if a breakthrough was possible at the tactical level, the German military was no longer capable of exploiting that breakthrough on an operational scale. This should have signaled that there was no longer a need for heavy tank battalions, but the realities did not slow the production of heavy tanks or the fielding of heavy tank battalions.[13]

Given these facts, it is interesting that the German military did not reevaluate many aspects related to heavy tank battalions. Like the Soviet, American, and British military establishments, the German Army should have balanced the strategic realities they faced, with their limited resources, to develop a plan to achieve their strategic objectives. If that plan included heavy tanks, and allocated resources to field heavy tank battalions, the *Wehrmacht* should have at least developed and published new doctrinal guidance. This guidance should have further clarified the role of heavy tank battalions in what had become for Germany—at the strategic and operational levels—a primarily defensive war. As a result of this inaction, the German Army and *Waffen-SS* were left with expensive, important organizations built for offensive operations, operating on the defensive, and excelling not in the conduct of maneuver for which the *Wehrmacht* is so often praised, but at achieving attrition of enemy tanks.

Epilogue
Through the Eyes of Tiger Killers

A Soviet View

AUTHOR'S NOTE: *Heavy Tank Battalion 506 saw its first combat actions in the Zaporozhe Bridgehead in southern Ukraine in late September 1943. Formed from the 9th Panzer Division's 3rd Battalion, Panzer Regiment 33, it was fortunate to be attached to that same division for its first 10 days of combat. Arriving at the front with 45 brand new Tigers, the battalion was a welcome addition to the 9th Panzer Division's combat power, which fielded between 3 to 8 operational tanks during this time. Their primary mission during those first ten days was to defeat Soviet penetrations of the German lines, but on 26 September, they launched a surprise attack to break through Soviet lines to destroy Soviet artillery units—both missions being strictly in accordance with the doctrinal guidance on their employment. This attack was conducted with nine Tigers and was possibly supported by several other tanks from the 9th Panzer Division.*

During this unsuccessful attack, three Tigers were destroyed and the other six were damaged. One of these was so severely damaged that it had to be sent back to the factory in Germany to be rebuilt. After this attack, at the end of its seventh day in combat, Heavy Tank Battalion 506 had no operational Tigers remaining. Then-Captain Viktor Iskrov of the 116th Guards Artillery Regiment was commanding a battalion of 76mm field guns that opposed Heavy Tank Battalion 506's attack.

Viktor M. Iskrov was born on 23 October 1915 in Petrograd (later Leningrad, now St. Petersburg). He graduated from the Leningrad Artillery School and was commissioned as a lieutenant in June 1938. He joined the Communist Party in August 1939, and participated in the campaign in Poland in September of 1939, and the campaign in Finland in 1939–40. Serving in various combat field artillery assignments, Iskrov was seriously wounded in a firefight against German infantry on 18 November 1941. He recovered from his wounds in time to participate in the Kharkov offensive in May 1942. When his unit was encircled by German forces, Iskrov was severely shell-

Viktor M. Iskrov

shocked during a breakout attempt, and was captured. He later escaped, however, and continued fighting as a member of a local partisan unit. Rejoining the Red Army in the summer of 1943, he fought in the Ukraine, and later participated in

192

Operation BAGRATION *in June 1944. On 23 June, he was wounded again, less severely this time. After participating in the conquest of the fortress of Königsberg in East Prussia (now Kaliningrad, Russia), his unit was transferred to Mongolia in June–July 1945. There, he took part in combat against the Japanese until the end of the war shortly thereafter.*

After the war, Colonel Iskrov served in positions of increasing responsibility in field artillery units stationed in the vicinity of Leningrad. He retired from active duty in 1958, and lives in St. Petersburg. He has two daughters, two grandchildren, and one great-granddaughter.

His military awards and decorations include the Order of the Red Banner; the Order of the Great Patriotic War, 1st and 2nd Degrees; two Orders of the Red Star; the Medal "For Merit in Battle"; the Campaign Medal "For the Capture of Königsberg"; and many commemorative medals.

Here is Colonel Iskrov's account of his successful action against the Tigers of Heavy Tank Battalion 506. . . .

Fighting in the 116th Guards "Order of Lenin" Artillery Regiment as commanding officer of the 2nd Battalion, on September 26, 1943 at the village of Shevchenko we encountered a column of German armor. The events unfolded in the following manner.

I was at the battalion's CP with the commander of the 4th Battery, Senior Lieutenant D. S. Gaidaenko when we spotted a group of German tanks that were advancing toward the battery from the flank. Apparently, they had broken through our infantry defenses and were now going for us. I immediately contacted the regimental commander over the radio and asked for orders. His answer was short, "Act on your own!"

I left the chief of forward observers, Senior Lieutenant M. M. Yakovlev, at the CP, and we (Senior Lieutenant Gaidaenko and I) ran as fast as our feet would carry us to the 4th Battery. I recalled faces of all my family and my relatives. In my thoughts I said farewell to them all: to my mother (I did not yet know that she had been dead for over a year, dying of starvation in besieged Leningrad), to my wife Maria, and others. This was a very brief farewell. In front of us were the advancing German tanks and four ZIS-3 76.2mm field guns of the 4th Battery to stop them. The guns, camouflaged in the hedgerows at Shevchenko, were turned 90 degrees to the right to repel the assault.

Inexperienced or green gun-layers were replaced by experienced officers. I found a place on a hillock behind the battery to have a good view of the battlefield and so that my crews could see me. I told the crews to fire at the tracks and side armor, and ordered them to open fire only on my command, when I waved a small red flag.

Tanks appeared from behind the hills that were in front of us. One of the gun-layers, Sergeant Serdyuk, became unnerved and fired as soon as the tanks appeared on the hilltops. He missed, and the German tanks immediately spotted his gun. It was blasted with a direct hit. We found Sergeant Serdyuk's head lying some 15–20 meters from the gun after the battle. We were all very sorry about his death, but, in fact, he himself was to blame.

I saw the advancing German tanks very well. As soon as I saw that they started turning a little bit, exposing their side armor to us, I waved the small red flag, which served as a command for opening fire. After this, each individual crew fought independently. It was a real duel against the German armor. We knocked out four of them, including two Tigers. The Germans could not take this and started to retreat. Our losses were also high. Killed in this battle were Senior Lieutenant Semen Markin from Leningrad, platoon leader Lieutenant Vladimir Kolymagin, Sergeant Serdyuk, and ten privates and sergeants.

Markin was killed when the German tanks started to retreat and his 6th Battery opened fire on them, knocking out two tanks. The German tanks were returning fire as they retreated. An armor-piercing shell killed Markin at the firing position. The solid steel shell tore his body into two parts—body and head were one piece, and legs were another piece. This is how Lieutenant Markin died, having fulfilled his duty to the utmost. We used to talk with him for a long time, recalling Leningrad. He often told me, "I would like to meet a little Tiger! (that is, German Tiger tank.) I would answer, "When you become commander of the 6th Battery, you will get to meet your Tiger cub!" That's exactly how it happened, but this was the last battle for Markin.

After the battle, the senior officer of the 6th Battery, Lieutenant Danilenko, called me and said, "We buried Lieutenant Markin right here, at the battlefield." I was outraged and ordered, "Immediately dig up the corpse, wrap it in a rain cape and transport it to the battalion HQ, and then to the regimental HQ, to bury him with full military honors!" This order was followed. Lieutenant Markin was buried in Svatovo in a mass grave. On the day of his death, the battalion received an order from the commanding general of our corps (1st Guards Mechanized Corps), General Major Russiyanov, about the promotion of Markin to the rank of senior lieutenant.

I did not even notice that during the battle the sleeve of my tunic (we had just received new uniforms) was torn into pieces by small fragments and a tiny fragment had become lodged under my skin.

Soon after the end of engagement I received a message that General Major Russiyanov was about to visit our battery. I was not surprised, as this general often visited the battlefield. He was always driving around in his Willys Jeep.

When he saw the nightmare at our positions after the battle—wounded screaming, dead lying right at the guns, some crew members torn apart by direct hits—General Russiyanov took off his cap, took a deep bow and, with tears in his eyes, said, "Eternal memory and glory be with the defenders of our Fatherland!" I, as battalion commander, tried to maintain military formalities, salute the general, and make an official report, but my nerves were so shaken by the battle that I did not succeed. Russiyanov, in turn, did not require any military ceremony at that moment. Right on the spot, on the battlefield, he handed Senior Lieutenant Gaidaenko and me medals, Orders of the Red Banner, and ordered me to recommend all the men of the 4th Battery for decorations.

An American View

AUTHOR'S NOTE: Heavy Tank Battalion 504 arrived at the front in Italy on 20 June 1944. It was formed from the remnants of one of its companies whose personnel managed to escape from Sicily and from Tank Company 314, a unit with radio-controlled, tracked demolition vehicles. The remainder of the battalion had been destroyed fighting in North Africa the previous year. The Tigers of Heavy Tank Battalion 504 arrived at the front in Italy, just north of Rome, while the situation was still very fluid, with American and British forces continuing their attacks to the north and German forces attempting to stabilize the front. Two days after being first employed, on 22 June 1944, Heavy Tank Battalion 504 lost two Tigers in an engagement with American forces. Over its first ten days of combat, involving withdrawals over very rugged terrain, Heavy Tank Battalion 504 lost 28 Tigers, going from a combat strength of 45 tanks, its full authorization, to having only 17 on hand by the end of the day on 1 July 1944. The vast majority of these losses were from self-destruction by the crews. Possibly as few as three Tigers were lost to direct fire.

One of those was Tiger 221, commanded by Leutnant Keitel, who attacked in the eastern portion of the town of Cecina. He and another Tiger were supported by a reinforced platoon (or a weak company) of infantry from the 16th SS-Panzer-Grenadier Division, "Reichsführer-SS." His tank was destroyed by the crew of a Sherman driven by Technician 4th Grade Ray Holt of the American 752nd Tank Battalion, supporting the 34th Infantry Division.

Raymond L. Holt was born on 7 March 1918 in Hartford, Connecticut. He joined the US Army on 8 September 1941. After basic training, he was assigned to the 752nd Tank Battalion, which was one of the first separate tank battalions to be formed, and one of the first to be shipped overseas. He received armored training at Fort Knox, Kentucky, and Fort Lewis, Washington, and then

*underwent desert training under General George S.
Patton, Jr. near Indio, California, in preparation for combat in North Africa.*

*Ray Holt was a tank driver during his first months of
combat. His first tank was lost to German 88s on the outskirts of Rome, and in this action he saved the life of a fel-
low tanker in a field riddled by machine-gun bullets.
Sergeant Holt was awarded command of his own tank on
9 July 1944, one week after his crew destroyed a Tiger at
Cecina. He and his comrades fought up the west coast of
Italy during the summer of 1944, and also fought in the*

Raymond L. Holt

*Northern Apennine mountains during the following fall
and the bitter winter of 1944–45. Sergeant Holt earned his first home leave in late
February 1945, and upon reporting back to duty in April 1945, he learned that
he had accumulated enough "points" to remain stateside. While home on fur-
lough, his tank was knocked out by a German wielding a Panzerfaust in the Po
Valley, just three days before the war in Italy ended. Sergeant Holt was honorably
discharged from the US Army on 15 May 1945, after three and a half years of
service.*

*After the war, Ray Holt worked as a plumber until his retirement in the 1970s,
and was blessed with four children and six grandchildren. He passed away in
1997.*

*Sergeant Holt's military awards include the Good Conduct Medal, the
American Defense Medal, the American Campaign Medal, the European-
African-Middle Eastern Campaign Medal with four campaign stars and assault
landing arrowhead, and the WWII Victory Medal.*

*Here is Ray Holt's account of his successful action against the Tigers of Heavy
Tank Battalion 504, as told to his son, Bob Holt. . . .*

I was a tank driver with the 752nd Tank Battalion. My tank was commanded
by Lieutenant Cox, who led the 3rd Platoon of Company B.

The company supported an attack by the 133rd Infantry Regiment to the
eastern edge of Cecina, Italy, on the third day of the battle. It took us all morning just to advance a few hundred yards, knocking out pillboxes and machine-
gun nests along the way. We still had not encountered any German armor,
although we knew there were Tiger tanks in the area.

We finally reached our objective in the early afternoon. A little later, our
company was ordered to move out to support an attack on the other side of
town. We started to move, but at the last minute the decision was made to
leave the 3rd Platoon in the center of town to support the infantry in the event
of a counterattack.

Around dusk, we received word over the radio that the Germans were counterattacking our sector with infantry and Tiger tanks. When I heard that, I thought, "Oh, my God, this is it." Just a few weeks earlier, our platoon had lost three of its five tanks to German 88s on the outskirts of Rome. We knew that we were a pretty poor match for Tiger tanks.

Lieutenant Cox advanced the platoon up a dirt road along the edge of town to meet the German force. We got to the center of Cecina before making contact, so Lieutenant Cox dispersed the four other tanks in the streets to maximize coverage of the Germans' most likely advance routes. Then he took our tank, which was an earlier model with a 75mm main gun, further up the street to meet the Germans. We still did not know exactly where the Germans were, because the terrain and buildings blocked our view.

As we approached a slight curve in the road, I saw a German infantryman, who stood up to wave to someone who was out of our view. I called Lieutenant Cox on the interphone and asked him if he saw the German, and he said, "Yeah, I'm watching him."

Suddenly we realized that the German soldier was guiding a Tiger tank. When you see a Tiger tank coming from the flank, the first thing you see is the gun barrel. It looks like a telephone pole on its side. Well, we saw that telephone pole coming around from behind a building on the curve, and we knew we were about to run into the lead Tiger. The infantryman stood up again to signal the Tiger, and we machine gunned him.

The Tiger came around the curve, and now we were face to face at about 75 yards. We both fired simultaneously. The Tiger's shot hit the ground next to us, and the concussion lifted my side of the tank off the ground. Our gunner fired a 75mm armor-piercing shell, which hit the Tiger on the front hull. The armor is extremely thick on the front of a Tiger, so our shell merely chipped the Zimmerit coating and bounced off.

Fortunately for us, the movement of the tanks and the exploding shells kicked up a huge dust cloud, so it was impossible to see much of anything. Lieutenant Cox shouted "Back up! Back up! Back up!" so I put it in reverse and started backing as fast as I could. Then he told me "OK, turn left onto that side street." This positioned our tank next to a two story building on the corner of a perpendicular street. The front of our tank was facing away from the road that the Tiger was on, and Lieutenant Cox traversed the main gun over the rear of the tank to cover the main road. We did not know where the Tiger was.

Lieutenant Cox knew that the best way to knock out a Tiger tank was by hitting its thin side armor at close range. He assumed that the Tiger would continue to advance along the same road. If it did, its crew would be blind to the sides of the street, and they would not be able to see us hiding next to that building on the corner. If they did see us when they passed, they would not be able to manually traverse their turret quickly enough to fire a shot before we hit them. If we failed to stop the Tiger, the position of our tank allowed a clear escape route in the opposite direction. So the plan was to wait and hope that the Tiger crossed our path.

The Tiger shelled the buildings near us for several minutes in an attempt to locate us and draw us out. We held our position, though, and after a while the Tiger slowly lumbered in front of us. Lieutenant Cox told the gunner, "Hold on. . . . Hold on. . . . Now!" and at that moment the gunner fired a 75mm armor-piercing round into the side of the Tiger from a range of only 25 or 30 yards.

The round penetrated the Tiger's side armor and hit the fuel tank, causing the Tiger to burst into a huge ball of flames. Its crew bailed out before the ammunition exploded, and sought cover in the ditch on the side of the road. With the destruction of the lead Tiger, the other German armor withdrew and the counterattack collapsed.

The Tiger was still smoldering when we inspected it the next day. The interior was burned out, and the roof above the radio operator's position had buckled upward from the ammunition explosion. Now the reality of what we had accomplished set in, and we realized that we were very fortunate to have survived this engagement.

Appendix: Comparative Analysis of Heavy Tank Doctrines

The German Army, and its armor forces specifically, is widely regarded as the model of military forces during the World War II era in terms of doctrine, equipment, and organization. The Tiger and King Tiger tanks, in addition to the Panther, are venerated as the "best" tanks produced during the war. A comparative analysis of other country's doctrine, organizations, and equipment will help to better evaluate the German heavy tank battalions and their associated doctrine concerning breakthroughs. This comparison will help to determine, on a relative and admittedly subjective scale, the overall combat effectiveness of German heavy tank battalions. This comparison is necessarily generalized because doctrine, organizations, and equipment evolved during the war.

France

If the German doctrine and organization could be characterized as armor-centric, French doctrine was definitely artillery-centric. The German solution for overcoming the static, positional war of 1914–18 was centered around the tank. The French solution for the same problem was centered around artillery. This led them both to adopt different doctrines and different organizations to accomplish those doctrinal concepts.

The French General Staff departed from the Foch principle of World War I that stated that the best defense was in attack. The French military before World War II was faced with France's low birth rate. This resulted in a great disparity in populations capable of supporting a modern war: 80,000,000 Germans against 40,000,000 Frenchmen.[1] This, combined with several political decisions that disavowed any strategic offensive objectives, led the French to an extremely and almost exclusively defensive doctrine. The French military design aimed at using the power of the defense to save their men and wait for the Germans to break their strength before the French assumed the offense.

The French doctrine evolved between the world wars and ultimately became known as "Methodical Battle."[2] This name implies a rigidly-controlled operation in which all units and weapons were carefully marshaled and then employed in combat.[3] The French developed this doctrine—which was characterized by time-consuming preparation and thorough pre-planning—

because they believed that artillery dominated the modern battlefield.[4] In an attempt to best support the artillery, they centralized command in order to synchronize the infantry and armor with the artillery. In the offense or the defense, the French favored a step-by-step battle, with units obediently moving between phase lines and adhering to strictly-scheduled timetables.[5] The focus of decision making was kept at higher command levels, because they believed that a centralized command system was necessary to coordinate the actions of numerous subordinate units.

French doctrine was predicated on the assumption that there was little chance of conducting a successful breakthrough of an enemy's defenses. They predicted that the defender would be able to establish subsequent defensive positions quicker than the attacker would be able to exploit the breakthrough. In keeping with the model of World War I, they thought that only after successive offensive operations—ones that would "grind down" the defender— would a successful exploitation of a breakthrough be possible. In other words, only a successive series of attrition-oriented "methodical battles," facilitated by artillery, would lead to the ability to conduct any operational maneuver.

French armor doctrine underwent numerous changes throughout the inter-war period, but it all revolved around the best way to implement the methodical battle. French classification of tanks became confused, as did other countries' classifications throughout the inter-war period, and did not always conform with the doctrinal mission a tank was to perform. The French did not always adhere to the classic definitions of breakthrough or rupture tanks being heavy, exploitation tanks being medium, and reconnaissance tanks being light.

A 1919 tank program study outlined three types of tank: the accompanying, battle, and rupture. These tanks loosely corresponded to light, medium, and heavy tanks except that the accompanying tanks were to accompany the infantry during the methodical battle. The reason for this was that light tanks were cheaper and easier to make and there would thus be more of them to support the infantry. Also, because of the conceptual constraints of methodical battle, it is unclear what doctrinal role was envisioned for the medium tanks. In other words, if a breakthrough was theoretically impossible, then medium tanks were unnecessary because a breakthrough was a necessary precondition for exploitation forces.

A 1921 commission concluded that only two types of tanks were needed: a battle and a heavy, or rupture tank. A new commission in 1925 changed this view again, and recommended three types of tanks: light, battle, and heavy. The light and heavy tank roles remained the same doctrinally. The role of the battle tank was less well defined, but in general, it was to protect the light tanks from enemy anti-tank weapons and other tanks as they accompanied the infantry.

In 1934 the Superior War Council eliminated the heavy tank, leaving only two tank types in accordance with French doctrine: the light and battle tanks. This was done based upon the recognition that, because of the size and high-maintenance requirements of heavy tanks that were being produced at that time, they were highly vulnerable. The council assumed that the new models of medium tanks could fulfill the doctrinal role of the heavy tank as well as defending the light tanks.

In deliberately calling it a battle tank instead of a medium tank, the French were either unsure or deliberately unclear, possibly because of a lack of agreement, on the specific doctrinal role of the tank. On the other hand, they may have purposely called it a battle tank because they envisioned a truly multi-purpose tank capable of performing multiple roles. In the years prior to World War II, however, the doctrine for the employment of the battle tank in the French military came to resemble the doctrinal employment originally envisioned in the heavy tank.

Despite the doctrinal change, by the late 1930s, the battle tank was referred to as the "heavy" tank.[6] This came about because the French, when faced with the increasing defensive firepower in terms of antitank weapons, slowly added more and more armor protection for the battle tank. They choose the greater protection afforded by additional armor over greater speed, obviously because they were only concerned with supporting and staying with the infantry during the methodical battle. Having a tank that was fast was not needed and in fact was looked down upon as a weakness because greater control would be needed to ensure that the tanks and infantry stayed in close proximity to each other to support one another.

French doctrine saw tanks as vehicles to assist the maneuver of the infantry. Infantry maneuver, in turn, would be facilitated by massed artillery. Some French theorists did realize that tanks were much more mobile than the infantry, but did not see a need to change their doctrine, however, and conformed emerging technology to fit their doctrine of methodical battle. They only saw that tanks would be able to take advantage of the fire of artillery at a quicker rate. Instead of waiting for infantry to occupy an area "conquered" by the artillery, this occupation could be done much more rapidly with tanks.

Both German and French doctrine focused on and addressed the problem of defeating the enemy's artillery. The responsibility of defeating enemy artillery in German doctrine was assigned to the leading waves of tanks. Specifically, after defeating the enemy tank counterattack that German doctrine theorized would be launched in order to save the enemy artillery, German heavy tanks were to destroy that artillery before it could withdraw. This would be accomplished by conducting a quick and deep thrust through the enemy's defensive depth.

French doctrine sought to reach the enemy's artillery, but envisioned that it would be accomplished through successive, methodical bounds. The infantry support/heavy tanks would be protected by the suppressive effects of French artillery fire, but were not assigned a specific task to destroy enemy artillery.

The numerous changes in French doctrine and the continual debate throughout the inter-war period meant that tanks were produced and fielded with a wide variety of roles in mind. They were also organized in a variety of ways, with the primary focus being on how they could best be integrated into the methodical battle.

The French initially developed and fielded the B-model (*Char B*) tank as their battle tank.[7] Throughout its life, the B-model was referred to as a battle tank, a medium tank, and eventually by many in the French Army as a heavy tank. It was armed with a low-velocity 75mm main gun, had 60mm armor plating and weighed 33 tons.[8] Although this tank suffered from many mechanical problems, it was fielded and operating at a time in the war when the German Army did not field any heavy tanks. The most heavily-armed German tank at the time of their attack into France in 1940 was the Panzer IV. At the time, this tank was armed with a low-velocity 75mm *KwK* 37 L/24 main gun and had only 30 millimeters of frontal armor.

Although the B-model tank was to be used as a tank in massed formations, such as an armored division, constant modifications through its development, and slow production, reduced its availability.[9] In 1936, a plan was proposed to produce enough B-model tanks to field twelve battalions.[10] These were intended to be organized into two armored divisions of six battalions each. By the time the Germans attacked in 1940, the French Army had only created three armored divisions.[11] B-model tanks comprised less than half of the strength of these armored divisions, with the remainder of the tanks being light H-39 model tanks.[12]

The armored divisions were intended to assist the maneuver of a larger infantry formation such as an infantry corps or army.[13] This would increase the offensive power of the infantry, which remained the decisive branch of the army. French doctrine envisioned the armored division operating in several echelons of two or three battalions each. The lead echelon's flanks were to be protected by the following echelon of tanks that would also reduce any bypassed enemy positions or units.

French theorists also saw a role for the armored division in the defense. They noted that it could be used in a counterattack role, although the methodical battle doctrine saw artillery as the primary means of defeating breakthrough attempts.

French doctrine differed radically from German doctrine in that it did not accept the possibility of successfully breaking through enemy defenses without a long period of attrition. French offensive doctrine saw the "break-through" as being a long series of highly-coordinated and synchronized methodical battles, dominated by the artillery, conducted by the infantry, and supported by tanks. This doctrine led to a continual debate within the French Army about the various roles of the tank. The variety of ideas on the employment of armor prevented the French from developing a coherent concept that enabled armor to achieve its fullest potential. The emphasis upon methodical battle ensured that the development, production, and fielding of tanks and armor units were all focused upon supporting the methodical battle doctrine. The deficiencies in this doctrine were highlighted during the Battle of France in 1940.

United Kingdom and United States

United States and British doctrine closely mirrored each other, although there were notable differences in several aspects of doctrine and in the labeling of tanks based upon their envisaged doctrinal role. By the time the war began, the official British policy called for two types of tanks: one, with heavy armor protection to give close support to the infantry; and the other, with lighter armor but with a high degree of mobility to exploit success.[14] In neither case did armor-penetrative capability or tank-killing capability appear to have been of major importance initially.

The first type of tank was called the infantry tank. These tanks were slower and more heavily armored than other tanks and were similar to other country's heavy classification of tanks. They were intended to precede the infantry in the attack and support them in overcoming the enemy's defenses.[15] Throughout the war, the British developed several subcategories of infantry-type tanks for specific roles. Although they were called different things, such as assault tanks or close-support tanks, their doctrinal role was still similar to the overall concept of infantry tanks.

British doctrine did see a role for tanks in fighting other tanks. Early in the war, however, this was not the case for infantry tanks that were intended to deal with enemy infantry, machine-gun emplacements, bunkers, and other minor fortifications.[16] As such, infantry tanks did not have main guns with armor-defeating ability until later in the war.

The British developed and fielded several infantry support tanks, including the Matilda, the Valentine, and the Churchill. The earliest Matildas were armed only with two .303-caliber machine guns and although fairly well armored, were useless against other tanks. Later marks of the Matilda were much more heavily armored and equipped with a turret-mounted 2-pounder (40mm) main gun. The most common and widely-fielded tank was the Churchill. Each infantry tank underwent many modifications and was fielded in several different variations. For example, the Matilda had at least six variants, and the Valentine and the Churchill had at least twelve different variants![17] Most, but not all, of the modifications involved increasing the caliber and the velocity of the main gun.

Infantry tanks were grouped into army tank brigades and were normally assigned to support an infantry division.[18] Usually, these army tank brigades were then further broken up within the infantry division, with a regiment supporting an infantry brigade, a squadron supporting a battalion, and a troop supporting a company.[19]

Infantry tank tactics early in the war saw two waves of tanks preceding the infantry.[20] These tanks were to secure the objective area and remain on the objective until the infantry arrived with their own organic antitank guns. Later in the war, infantry tanks coordinated their attack closely with armored vehicles that were equipped with higher-velocity guns capable of defeating enemy armor.[21] These were either tank destroyers or up-gunned Shermans, which supported the infantry tanks from an overwatch position.[22] Except under unusual circumstances, infantry tanks operated under the control of the infantry unit that they supported. When faced with an enemy armor threat, a company might combine and fight as a unit, but the occasions when a battalion or the brigade of infantry tanks fought as a combined unit were rare.

The British saw the infantry, supported by infantry tanks, as the primary means with which to conduct a breakthrough of the enemy defenses. Once this breakthrough was made, the other type of British tank would exploit that breakthrough. These tanks, which the British labeled as cruiser tanks, were more balanced, and were much faster and capable of long-range operations.[23] These fulfilled a doctrinal role similar that envisioned for the medium tanks of other countries and were combined together in armored divisions.

U.S. doctrine was very similar to British doctrine in that medium tanks were grouped together into armored divisions to be employed primarily to exploit breakthroughs in the enemy's defenses.[24] U.S. doctrine also called for a heavy emphasis on reconnaissance and therefore included a number of light tanks. They were also to be used in conjunction with the medium tanks during exploitation of breakthroughs, moving quickly and operating across vast distances.

The U.S. stands alone—unlike Germany, England, and the Soviet Union—in rejecting the need for a special tank type to assist the infantry in the attack. Adherence to this doctrine is largely to blame for the lack of development, and inability to field, a U.S. heavy tank capable of defeating the German heavy tanks in direct combat until late in the war.

Like the British, U.S. doctrine saw the infantry as the primary means for conducting a breakthrough of the enemy's defenses.[25] Although U.S. doctrine did incorporate and discuss many different branches of the service—including armor, artillery, and engineers—the infantry were viewed as being the supported branch. To assist infantry forces in the attack, the U.S. Army fielded independent tank battalions.[26] These units were equipped with medium tanks, and just like British infantry-tank-equipped brigades, were attached to infantry divisions and further subdivided down to infantry brigades and battalions.

Although the 1941 version of Field Manual 100-5, *Operations*, mentioned the employment of these battalions in echelons similar to the German waves, the manual portrays the idea that they were to accomplish their mission by incorporating the basic infantry tactics of fire and movement. In other words, one section of tanks would overwatch and suppress enemy forces if necessary, while another section maneuvered to a position of advantage. Using these tactics, U.S. tanks did not need to be heavily armored because doctrine did not envision them frontally attacking enemy defenses. Those defenses would either be suppressed or attacked from a flank or other position of advantage, or both. Regardless of how supporting tanks helped accomplish the breakthrough, U.S. doctrine rejected the need for a tank in the traditional heavy classification because the job of creating the breakthrough fell primarily to infantry forces.[27]

U.S. Army doctrine led them to develop, field, and manufacture a massive number of medium tanks. By far, the most common and ubiquitous model was the M4 Sherman. This tank was used in both armored divisions for exploitation purposes, and in independent tank battalions for infantry support. It was mass produced and exported in incredible quantities to the British Army as well as to the Red Army.

In March 1942, U.S. and British tank experts met in Washington, D.C. to discuss and develop a combined tank program. They agreed to reduce the number of tank designs to as few as possible and discussed production potential to meet with the requirements. The official U.S. Army history relates the results of this combined effort and highlights the differences between the two country's doctrines:

> The Americans had already agreed among themselves that the principal item of tank production in the United States should be the M4 medium tank series, with a subsidiary production of light tanks. The British accepted this decision since the Sherman met their requirement for a

"cruiser" tank to fulfill the mobile role in armored divisions. However, they also had large requirements for an "assault" tank—heavier and less mobile than the cruiser though armed with the same guns—which they thought necessary for use in support of infantry or in attack on fortified positions. The Americans agreed to develop experimental models of an assault tank, though their own doctrine recognized no need for the type.[28]

Later in the war, British armor development shifted to fielding a universal tank. This tank would fulfill the roles of both the cruiser and the infantry tanks in the same way that the U.S. medium tanks fulfilled both doctrinal roles of heavy and medium tanks.

Based upon American encounters between their medium tanks and German heavy tanks during the war, it was unfortunate for the U.S. Army that they did not embrace the need for a heavy tank in some form within their doctrine. Even though a heavy tank was not identified as necessary within U.S. doctrine, development of a heavy tank began prior to the war and continued throughout the war.[29] A prototype of a U.S. heavy tank labeled the T1E2 underwent testing by the Army Ordnance Department beginning in August 1941.[30] Initially, this tank had many problems and deficiencies, especially in the transmission. It was originally armed with only a 76mm main gun, but was eventually upgraded to a 90mm and even a 105mm main gun.[31] When compared with the development of the German Tiger, whose first prototype did not undergo initial testing until May 1942, one wonders what might have been accomplished with this headstart in development and potential production had U.S. doctrine identified a need for a heavy tank.

The end result of the lack of a heavy tank in U.S. doctrine and the valid reasons for their rejection, is best summed up by the Chief of Staff of the Army, General George C. Marshall, after the war in Europe ended:

Another noteworthy example of German superiority was in the heavy tank. From the summer of 1943 to the spring of 1945 the German Tiger and Panther tanks outmatched our Sherman tanks in direct combat. This stemmed largely from different concepts of armored warfare held by us and the Germans, and the radical difference in our approach to the battlefield. Our tanks had to be shipped thousands of miles overseas and landed on hostile shores amphibiously. They had to be able to cross innumerable rivers on temporary bridges, since when we attacked we sought to destroy the permanent bridges behind the enemy lines from the air. Those that our planes missed were destroyed by the enemy when he retreated. Therefore our tanks could not well be of the heavy type. We designed our armor as a weapon of exploitation. In other words, we desired to use our tanks in long-range thrusts deep into the enemy's rear where they could chew up his supply installations and communications. This required great endurance—low consumption of gasoline and ability to move great distances without breakdown.[32]

British, Soviet, and even German sources validate the fact that the Sherman was highly reliable mechanically.[33] German heavy tank battalions in Italy, for example, went out of their way to capture Shermans to use as recovery vehicles. A British major with extensive armor experience stated that, "The commander of a unit equipped with Shermans can be confident of taking 99 percent of his vehicles into battle [while] if he were equipped with Cromwells or Centaurs he would be in a continuous state of anxiety as to whether enough of his tanks would reach the battlefield to carry out the normal tasks expected of his unit."[34]

Even the leaders within the U.S. Army armor community rejected the need for a heavy tank throughout the war. Writing on 7 December 1942, the Commanding General of the Armored Forces, General Jacob Devers stated that "Due to its tremendous weight and limited tactical use, there is no requirement in the Armored Force for the heavy tank." During the war, the U.S. Army never identified a doctrinal requirement for a heavy tank, although they did realize the need for tanks with increased firepower to effectively defeat German heavy tanks.

Efforts to develop a U.S. heavy tank never stopped and the Ordnance Department designed, produced, and tested several prototypes. Eventually, the U.S. Army realized that their medium tanks were at a distinct disadvantage against German heavy tanks, no matter what large-caliber and high-velocity main gun was mounted on them.

But while that [exploitation] was the most profitable use of the tank, it became unavoidable in stagnant prepared-line fighting to escape tank-to-tank battles. In this combat, our medium tank was at a disadvantage, when forced into a head-on engagement with the German heavies. Early in 1944 it was decided that a heavy American tank, on which our Ordnance experts had been continuously experimenting since before the war, must be put into mass production. As a result the M-26 (Pershing) tank began to reach the battle lines last winter [the winter of 1944–45]. This tank was equal in direct combat to any the Germans had and still enjoyed a great advantage in lighter weight (43 tons), speed, and endurance. At the same time, work was begun on two new models, the T-29 and T-30, which weighed 64 tons, one mounting a high-velocity 105mm rifle, the other a 155mm rifle.[35]

The M-26 Pershing reached Europe too late to have any real impact upon the by-then inevitable course of the war. There were only a handful of instances in which the Pershing encountered and engaged a Tiger in combat.[36]

An interesting aspect of the Pershing is that, even though it was a direct descendant of several heavy tank prototypes and was classified as a heavy tank throughout its development, when the U.S. Army finally fielded it, it was classified as a medium tank. Although there may well be another reason, one possible explanation is that official U.S. Army doctrine still did not see any doctrinal role for a heavy tank and it was thus designated as a medium tank in accordance with that doctrine.

An interesting and auxiliary aspect of British and U.S. tanks during World War II is the development of super-heavy assault tanks. The requirement for these was established before the Allied invasion of Normandy. These massively-armored, powerfully-armed, and turretless vehicles were to be used to break through the formidable defensive line expected along the German border, the Westwall (known to the Allies as the "Siegfried Line"). The British vehicle was called the Tortoise and the U.S. vehicle was designated as Superheavy Tank T-28. Although neither of these vehicles was fielded before the end of the war, they were awe inspiring when finally built. The thickness of the frontal armor of the U.S. tank was 304 millimeters, it was armed with a high-velocity 105mm main gun, and it weighed over 85 tons.[37]

In the end, despite the absence of a heavy tank, the sheer number of medium tanks produced by the Americans, along with a wide variety of other mechanized and motorized vehicles, allowed them to achieve a level of mechanization unmatched by the Germans. German tanks could not be everywhere on the battlefield at the same time and the mechanization of the American forces allowed them to overcome the superior firepower of German tanks like the Panther and King Tiger.[38]

The British also managed to achieve a remarkable level of production, given their relatively limited natural resources, compared to the remainder of the continent of Europe. In the three and a half years between September 1939 and March 1943, the United Kingdom actually produced 3,000 more tanks than did Germany.[39] From 1940 to the end of the war, they produced a total of 24,803 tanks of all types.[40] Although of superior quality, during the same time period, Germany produced only 23,967 tanks.[41]

American and British breakthrough operations developed a high degree of coordination of all arms throughout the war. Although their doctrine called for infantry to make the primary effort in conducting breakthroughs, armor, engineer, and artillery forces were eventually incorporated into an efficient team. The element that added the undeniably decisive piece to the breakthrough operations conducted by U.S. and British forces in World War II was the effective incorporation of air power, and sometimes even strategic air power.[42] Although there were several mistakes made, especially during the initial attempts, later use of strategic bombers was characterized by highly-innovative coordination measures that effectively broke through enemy defenses with ease. Even if one ultimately judges American and British doctrine and tank quality to be inferior to their German counterparts, the incorporation of strategic bombers and tactical ground support aircraft more than compensated for these shortcomings by bringing massive and overwhelming firepower to bear on the German defenses.

Another aspect of American and British equipment development, eventually incorporated as a key element of breakthrough operations, was armored vehicles capable of breaching minefields. Both countries developed, tested, and fielded an impressive variety of mine rollers, mine flails, and other mechanical mine-breaching devices capable of being mounted on an armored vehicle. These armored vehicles breached minefields without requiring engineers or other troops to dismount under fire to clear a path through the mines, thus saving many lives. Additionally, they were able to breach a minefield without a high number of tanks being disabled from mines. This stands in stark contrast to German heavy tank battalions whose combat power was reduced quickly on many occasions after encountering a minefield.

Soviet Union

Throughout most of the 1930s, the Soviet Union developed a theory of warfare that was conceptually advanced, which incorporated all technical means, branches, and arms of service. They then took measures to field the weapons that would allow them to accomplish the concepts established in that theory. Although there were obvious inadequacies in Soviet doctrine, or at least in the implementation of that doctrine due to the purges of the Soviet officer corps in the years preceding hostilities, they ultimately adapted their basic concepts to the realities of war against the Germans. Ultimately, Soviet doctrine was implemented with a high degree of effectiveness by the end of the war.[43]

During the pre-war years, Marshal Mikhail Tuchachevskiy played a prominent role in developing the doctrine that the Soviet Union used during World War II.[44] Before being murdered in 1937 during Stalin's purges, his ideas were codified in the publication of the Soviet Army's field service regulations, PU-36 (*Vremennyi Polevoi Ustav*), in 1936.[45]

Many of the concepts found in this manual are similar in wording to those found in Guderian's *Achtung Panzer,* or more accurately, the concepts found in *Achtung Panzer* are similar to those found in PU-36, because Guderian's book was published a year after PU-36. Where the Soviet concepts differed from any other country's doctrine, and as their subsequent operations in World War II demonstrated, was in the scale and scope of operations.

Tuchachevskiy wrote about two techniques for destroying an enemy, namely, the envelopment and the breakthrough.[46] Although he saw the envelopment as the preferred form, he and other Soviet theorists realized that modern warfare would be vast in breadth, and that envelopments would rarely be possible without first conducting breakthrough operations.[47] Tuchachevskiy, PU-36, as well as other Soviet theorists like V. K. Triandafillov, were explicit in continually emphasizing the successive nature of operations.[48]

The Soviets theorized that modern mechanized warfare would extend in breadth across one border or natural barrier to another, similar to World War I. They also theorized that the battlefield would extend in depth, with successive tactical zones as well as subsequent operational, and even strategic, levels.[49] In light of this appraisal of the future battlefield, they developed offensive concepts that addressed the breadth and depth of those defenses.

Soviet doctrine and thought essentially divided their forces, conceptually at least, into "holding" and "striking" forces.[50] In the offense, the holding force attacked the enemy across the breadth of the defense, effectively fixing them in place to prevent them from repositioning to the threatened breakthrough sector. The striking force conducted the breakthrough and continued on into the depth of the enemy defenses as quickly as possible to accomplish subsequent missions such as envelopment, pursuit, exploitation, and so on.[51] Soviet doctrine emphasized conducting wide breakthroughs rather than narrow ones.[52] V. K. Triandafillov addressed the breadth, depth, and successive nature of operations in relation to a breakthrough:

> A breakthrough can count upon success only in the event that it involves a significant portion of the enemy forces occupying a given front and when the direction of the blow is selected so that the penetrating forces will break out to an advantageous operational position relative to the remaining enemy front, if the attacker's shock grouping will break out on routes from which it is possible to develop the blow against the flank and rear area of the enemy front not involved directly in the offensive. . . . The first blow must engage at least half, minimum one-third, of the enemy forces occupying a given front to deprive the enemy of the capability of making a wide maneuver with reserves. To do so, the attack frontage must be so wide that liquidation of the resultant breakthrough will require forces equal to another third or the other half of his forces.[53]

Soviet doctrine called for armies, or specially-reinforced armies called "shock armies," to be assigned the mission of breaking through the enemy's defenses.[54] These were combined arms organizations that contained robust tank and/or mechanized forces, as well as large quantities of field artillery. In accordance with the theory of the deep offensive operation, these units were required to penetrate not only through the tactical depth of the enemy's defenses, but to the operational depth of his defense. In doing so, it was essential that the speed of the attackers' advance surpass the rate of defenders' withdrawal.[55] Armored/mechanized forces were ideal for this.

The composition of a shock army normally included 3 to 4 rifle corps consisting of a total of 12 to 15 rifle divisions; 1 to 2 mechanized corps or a cavalry corps; and army air units consisting of 3 to 4 air divisions.[56] Additionally, other reinforcements could include between 10 to 12 artillery regiments, several tank regiments, and engineer battalions. Although the initial attacks could incorporate all branches of the military, the mechanized forces were specifically assigned to overtake the retreating enemy to prevent him from establishing a subsequent defensive line.[57]

Soviet commanders organized their assault groups by integrating infantry, tanks, artillery, and engineer units for the breakthrough of the tactical zone. The assault commanders formed special mobile groups in the lead rifle divisions to seize deep tactical objectives quickly. During the latter part of the war, Soviet assault forces usually broke through the main positions of the German tactical defensive zone within 24 hours of the start of the offensive and passed second echelon units forward.[58] These units continued the attack deep into the German rear, even while the remainder of the German defensive line was being held.

The width of the sector of the main attack, or the breakthrough area, of a shock army, was 20 to 30 kilometers.[59] The shock army was expected to penetrate the enemy defenses to a depth of between 75 and 100 kilometers.[60] On several occasions, fronts attacked with as many as three shock armies. These could be employed in different sectors to break through on several axes or in adjacent sectors to further widen the breakthrough sector.[61]

Tuchachevskiy proposed that armored units be divided into different categories, depending upon the characteristics of the tanks and the specific mission they were to accomplish. Prior to World War II, he advocated the creation of three types of tanks: (1) tanks for close support of infantry, which could be slower models of relatively limited range; (2) tanks for distant support of infantry, which could move faster and farther; and (3) independent long-range striking armor.[62] PU-36 mentions only two tank types, infantry support tanks and "strategic" tanks.[63] The discussion in the manual associated with these tank types reveals a close conceptual correlation with the traditional definition of heavy and medium tanks.[64]

When World War II started, the Soviet Union fielded a wide array of tanks that are not easily classified, but can loosely be associated into the heavy, medium, and light categories.[65] In the early stages of the war, their primary heavy tank was the "KV."[66] The standard model, the KV-1, was heavily armored and was armed with a 76mm main gun. The Red Army, based upon experience during the Russo-Finnish War, identified the need for a "bunker-busting" tank.[67] This led the Soviet Army to field the large-turretted KV-2 which was armed with a low-velocity 152mm howitzer. During the initial stages of the war, these tanks suffered from mechanical breakdowns, poor crew training, and fuel shortages, but achieved spectacular results in the defense on several occasions.[68]

By the summer of 1942, the KV tanks were even less effective. They continued to suffer mechanically, but their two largest deficiencies were that they were extremely slow and that they were only armed with a 76mm gun. The result of this was that they could not keep up with the much faster T-34s, and even when they could, they did not add an increase in firepower over the T-34 armed with the same 76mm gun.

Beginning in 1943, after encountering the German Tiger, the Soviets began converting their KVs into turretless assault guns called SU-152s. Although SU-152s served primarily as an assault gun in the direct-fire support role, this vehicle, by most accounts, was an effective interim measure in dealing with the Tiger.

By late 1943, the Soviets developed and fielded a new heavy tank, the Josef Stalin. The initial tank, the JS-1, was armed with an 85mm main gun, but was never issued to any units and never saw combat.[69] Instead, the 107 JS-1s produced were converted to JS-2s, armed with 122mm main guns.[70] This change was promulgated from a debate within the Soviet Army about the appropriate roles for heavy tanks. The adoption of the 122mm gun gave the JS-2 the ability to accomplish its primary role of supporting infantry forces during breakthrough operations. Although not designed for tank-to-tank battle, the massive size of the projectile made the JS-2 a capable tank in destroying German armor.[71] This allowed it to be employed in a tank-killing role when needed.

JS-2s were fielded in similar fashion to German heavy tanks, in separate heavy tank regiments, beginning in early 1944.[72] These were smaller in size than American and German battalions. Soviet heavy tank regiments possessed a total of 21 JS-2 tanks, formed into 4 companies with 5 tanks each, with 1 tank for the regimental commander.[73]

Augmenting the heavy tank regiments, but performing a similar tactical role were the heavy assault guns built on the JS-2 chassis. These turretless vehicles, known as the JSU series, were armed with either a 152mm or 122mm gun and were produced in much greater numbers than the JS-2 tank.[74] The JSU-152 was intended to be the primary heavy assault gun, but because of a shortage of 152mm howitzers and a surplus of 122mm gun tubes, the Soviet Army fielded a significant number of JSU-122s.[75] Like the JS-2s, JSUs were organized as separate regiments. These heavy assault gun regiments were homogenous, being equipped with either the JSU-122 or the JSU-152, but not both.

Although tactics and employment varied depending upon the mission, both heavy tank regiments and heavy assault gun regiments were normally attached to a larger combined arms unit to assist in breaking through German defenses. Both types of regiments appear to have worked in close cooperation with each other to perform their tactical roles of suppressing infantry strong-points and destroying enemy antitank guns and armor. The JSUs were used to overwatch the attacking JS-2s from stationary positions.[76] When the JS-2s reached a specified point, the JSUs would move forward and the bounding overwatch process was repeated.

Soviet doctrine differed from German doctrine in its higher degree of emphasis upon the integration of artillery into the breakthrough operation. PU-36, and Soviet theorists such as V. K. Triandafillov, emphasized the role of artillery in achieving tactical breakthroughs of enemy defenses.[77] The density of artillery firepower advocated by pre-war sources in support of a break-through, although high, steadily increased throughout the war.[78] The increase in the density of artillery firepower supporting the breakthrough has been attributed by several sources as a primary reason for the continual improve-ment in the performance of the Red Army throughout the war.[79]

During Soviet breakthrough operations, the infantry/tank attack was pre-ceded by a massive artillery barrage.[80] This preparation was intended to destroy the enemy artillery and observation posts, antitank weapons, and areas heavily fortified by the enemy infantry.[81] In addition to achieving these specific tasks, the artillery preparation was supposed to generally disrupt the enemy defenses throughout their tactical depth. Prior to the war, Soviet theo-rists envisioned artillery being replaced by assault guns, tanks, and other mobile direct-fire weapons during the breakthrough. After much practical experience, however, Red Army leaders found that, primarily because of the proliferation of antitank weapons throughout the defensive depth, the densi-ty of artillery could not be decreased no matter how many tanks and assault guns were assigned to the breakthrough.[82] In fact, artillery densities continued to increase throughout the war while breakthrough operations were weighted with more and more tanks and assault guns.[83]

German doctrine and actions after 1943 focused on tactical breakthroughs, presumably in the hopes of conducting tactical envelopments. The Soviets saw the potential of continuing a tactical breakthrough into an operational break-through, which in turn could be exploited to achieve operational-level results. This distinction allowed the Soviets to achieve spectacular success on the bat-tlefield. At the same time, after 1943, the Germans failed to successfully break through Soviet defenses through even their tactical depth and consequently were never able to achieve more than minor tactical envelopments. This rep-resented a major turnabout from the first two years of the war, in which the Germans had been able to break through Soviet defenses consistently, and subsequently effect the envelopment and destruction of whole Soviet field armies.

Soviet operations, especially in the latter part of the war, harmoniously integrated artillery, tanks, infantry, air power, and engineers to achieve breakthroughs. These breakthroughs were accomplished rapidly across a wide front, which allowed a following echelon force, such as a Guards Tank Army, to conduct a subsequent operation deep into the German defenses. The rapidity and depth of the breakthrough prevented German forces from repositioning forces to block the lead elements of the breakthrough. The width of the breakthrough prevented German forces from restoring the main defensive line by attacking into the flank of the breakthrough.

When German armor was encountered, the Red Army's heavy tanks and heavy assault guns were sufficiently armed and armored to dispose of most German armored vehicles. Beyond the 53,000 T-34s produced by the Soviets (and the roughly 10,000 British, Canadian, and American tanks transferred as military aid), the Soviets also produced heavy tanks and heavy assault guns in numbers that dwarfed the relatively miniscule production of late-model German tanks such as the King Tiger. Soviet doctrine required the rapid introduction of exploitation forces after the tactical breakthrough. These forces, equipped with armored vehicles like the highly mobile and fast T-34 medium tank, penetrated as quickly and deeply as possible. In many cases, this rendered inconsequential the counter-efforts of ponderous German heavy tank battalions.

The Char B1-bis was France's principal heavy tank in 1940. Its design, with a limited-traverse 75mm main gun mounted in a sponson in the hull and a 47mm gun in the turret combined with excellent armor would have made it a formidable foe if employed differently.
(Patton Museum of Cavalry and Armor)

The Matilda II replaced the earlier Matilda I Infantry Tank, which was only armed with machine guns. The Matilda II was slow and lightly armed, equipped with only a 2-pounder (40mm) main gun, but it was very heavily armored. Until the appearance of the Panzer IV and *Sturmgeschütz* assault guns with the longer 75mm guns, it was practically invulnerable on the battlefield, except to the 88mm antiaircraft gun.
(Patton Museum of Cavalry and Armor)

The Valentine Infantry Tank was developed from the cruiser series, but was more heavily armored. Like some other British tanks, the earliest versions were armed with a 2-pounder (40mm) main gun, but later marks were equipped with 6-pounders (57mm), such as the Valentine VIII in the photo above. The final version even mounted a 75mm gun. The Valentine saw action with British forces in the battle for Tunisia in 1943, but most were ultimately either supplied to the Soviets, used against the Japanese, or used as chassis for self-propelled guns. *(Patton Museum of Cavalry and Armor)*

A Churchill III of the 14th Canadian Tank Regiment. Heavily armored but slow, this
Churchill is armed with a 6-pounder (57mm) main gun. Later variants were even more heavi-
ly armored and were reequipped with a 75mm main gun.
(*The Tank Museum, Bovington*)

The T1E2 (later, M6 series) Heavy Tank was an early US Army design for a heavy tank. The
first prototypes were tested on the day after the attack on Pearl Harbor. In contrast, the first
Tigers were not available for testing until over five September 1942. Armed with a three-inch
(76mm) gun and well armored, the design never saw combat.
(*Patton Museum of Cavalry and Armor*)

The Medium Tank M26 was introduced in combat in the European Theater in early 1945. Its 90mm main gun, based upon an anti-aircraft gun, was capable of defeating all German tanks at extended ranges. Very few—probably not more than 20—ever saw action in WWII. (*US Army Signal Corps Photo*)

The U.S. T-28 Super Heavy Tank was to be used to break through the *Westwall*. Even though available components were used when possible, the first vehicle was not available for testing prior to the end of the war in Europe. Only two of these were ever produced, and the only surviving example is outside the Patton Museum at Fort Knox, Kentucky. (*Patton Museum of Cavalry and Armor*)

The KV-1 (above) was very heavily armored, moderately well-armed (a medium-velocity 76mm main gun), but slow. The KV-2 (below), armed with a 152mm howitzer, was meant for bunker busting rather than fighting other tanks, but otherwise suffered from the same lack of agility and mechanical unreliability as the KV-1. More KV tanks were abandoned due to breakdowns than were lost in battle. Still, in 1941, the Germans could only hope to destroy one by using an 88mm antiaircraft gun in the direct-fire mode. Experience with the KV series spurred the acceleration of tank development that resulted in the introduction of the Panther and Tiger series. *(Patton Museum of Cavalry and Armor)*

Although it was more than a match for the Tiger, and about the equal to the Tiger II, the JS-2 was produced in far greater quantities. The Soviets built about 3,850 JS-2s, compared with the Germans' roughly 500 Tiger IIs. Supported by assault guns which shared a common chassis—thereby making maintenance much easier—the JS-2 was especially effective in the offensive role for which it was designed. *(Patton Museum of Cavalry and Armor)*

Two variations of the Josef Stalin (JS) heavy tank were built in assault gun versions. These were armed with either a 122mm gun or a 152mm gun. (The one in this photo is a JSU-122). These were more economical to manufacture than the tank versions because they did not have a turret. When used in conjunction with JS-2s, the JSUs would provide overwatch for the JS-2s during attacks. *(Patton Museum of Cavalry and Armor)*

Notes

Chapter 1

1. *Militärwochenblatt*, 11 November 1936, No. 30, in *Attack: A Study of Blitzkrieg Tactics*, Major Ferdinand Otto Miksche (New York: Random House, 1942), 42.

2. John Keegan, *The Second World War* (New York: Penguin, 1990), 402.

3. Thomas L. Jentz and Hilary L. Doyle, *Germany's Tiger Tanks, D.W. to Tiger I: Design, Production and Modifications* (Atglen, Pa.: Schiffer, 2000), 10.

4. Thomas L. Jentz, *Panzertruppen: The Complete Guide to the Creation and Combat Employment of Germany's Tank Force, 1933–1942* (Atglen, Pa.: Schiffer, 1996), 220.

5. Both the Tiger and Tiger II's numerical classification was *Panzerkampfwagen VI* or *Panzer VI*.

6. Thomas L. Jentz, *Germany's Tiger Tanks, Tiger I and II: Combat Tactics* (Atglen, Pa.: Schiffer, 1997), 38.

7. Ibid., 7.

8. Danny S. Parker, "German Tiger Tanks Were at the Battle of the Bulge, but Not in the Numbers Usually Cited for Them." *World War II* (March 1990): 8.

9. Jean Restayn, *Tiger I on the Eastern Front*, trans. Alan McKay (Paris: Histoire and Collections, 1999), 101.

10. Jean Restayn, *Tiger I on the Western Front* (Paris: Histoire and Collections, 2001), 4.

11. Ibid.

12. Peter Gudgin, *The Tiger Tanks* (London: Arms and Armour, 1991), 133.

13. In the summer of 1944, there were two heavy tank battalions operating in Italy and there would ultimately be three heavy tank battalions committed against the Allied beachhead at Normandy from June to August 1944.

14. Wolfgang Schneider, *Tigers in Combat II* (Winnipeg, Manitoba: J. J. Fedorowicz, 1998), 263.

15. Remarks by Colonel Stoves, "1st Panzer Division Attempts to Relieve the Cherkassy Pocket" (in Art of War Symposium, From the Dnepr to the Vistula: Soviet Offensive Operations, November 1943–August 1944. David Glantz, Chairman, Washington, D.C.: Center for Land Warfare, U.S. Army War College, 1985), 179.

16. For a good discussion on this, see David M. Glantz, *American Perspectives on Eastern Front Operations in World War II* (Fort Leavenworth, Kans.: U.S. Army Combined Arms Center, Soviet Army Studies Office, April 1987), 9–13.

17. There are many different definitions of the operational level of warfare. This is only one simplified definition intended to provide a conceptual foundation. Since the Soviets were masters of the operational level by 1944, it is helpful to view their concept. The definition espoused by the Soviet Frunze Academy prior to World War II was, "An operation is the sum total of the maneuvers and battles in a given sector of a theater of military operations and is directed toward the attainment of a general goal established as the final objective during the given phase of the campaign. The conduct of operations is a subject of operational art and occupies an intermediate position

between tactics and strategy." See Ministry of Defense of the USSR, *History of the Great Patriotic War of the Soviet Union, 1941–1945,* vol. 1, *Preparation for the Unleashing of the War by Imperialistic Powers,* unedited translation (Moscow: Military Publishing House of the Ministry of Defense of the USSR, 1960), 565.

Chapter 2

1. Heinz Guderian, *Achtung-Panzer! The Development of Armoured Forces, Their Tactics and Operational Potential,* trans. Christopher Duffy with an introduction by Paul Harris (London: Arms and Armour, 1995), 168.

2. Bryan Perret, *A History of Blitzkrieg,* with a foreword by John Hackett (New York: Jove, 1989), 66.

3. Examples of follow-on exploitation operations are an envelopment of the enemy's front line forces, or pursuit of fleeing enemy forces, or they could be tasked with seizing a deep objective.

4. Many country's medium tanks evolved to become universal tanks, which eventually became the main battle tank.

5. Range in this instance means radius of operation.

6. James S. Corum, *The Roots of Blitzkrieg: Hans von Seeckt and German Military Reform* (Lawrence, Kans.: University of Kansas Press), 140.

7. Reichswehrministerium, *Die Truppenfuhrung* (Troop Leading), (Berlin: 1933) trans. by the U.S. War Department, in the Combined Arms Research Library, Fort Leavenworth, Kans., 57.

8. Ibid., 62.

9. Ibid., 63.

10. Ibid., 76–77.

11. Ibid., 69. *Die Truppenfuhrung* also included antiaircraft elements following closely behind the leading elements.

12. Ibid., 63.

13. Ibid.

14. Ibid., 82–92.

15. Ibid., 87.

16. Ibid., 89.

17. Ibid.

18. Ibid

19. Ibid., 90–91.

20. Heinz W. Guderian, *Panzer Leader,* trans. Constantine Fitzgibbon, with a foreword by B. H. Liddell Hart (New York: E. P. Dutton, 1952), 20.

21. Guderian references Soviet thought and compares his ideas to Soviet theory in *Achtung Panzer!* 190–91. The *Militärwochenblatt* translated and published the writings of many foreign theorists.

22. *"Nutzanwendungen aus der Tankschlacht von Cambrai II," Militärwochenblatt* No. 24, (1929), in *Imagining War: The Development of Armored Doctrine in Germany and the Soviet Union, 1919–1939,* ed. Mary Ruth Habeck (Ann Arbor, MI: UMI Dissertation Services, 1996), 153.

23. Ludwig Beck, *"Nachträgliche Betrachtungen zu dem Einsatz des Panzerkorps in der Lage der Truppenamsreise vom 13.6.1935,"* in Habeck, *Imagining War*, 313–14.

24. Heinz W. Guderian, *"Die Panzertruppen und ihr Zusammenwirken mit den anderen Waffen,"* in Habeck, *Imagining War*, 335.

25. See Guderian, *Achtung Panzer!* 190–91 for his views on the different waves and their missions.

26. Shimon Naveh, *In Pursuit of Military Excellence: The Evolution of Operational Theory* (London: Frank Cass, 1997), 157.

27. Guderian, *Achtung-Panzer!* 170.

28. Ibid.

29. Ibid.

30. Ibid., 179.

31. Ibid.

32. Ibid.

33. Ibid.

34. Ibid.

35. Albert Kesselring and others, eds., "Manual for Command and Combat Employment of Smaller Units." MS #P-060b. trans. G. Weber and W. Luetzkendorf, ed. G. C. Vanderstadt [Washington, D.C.: Department of the Army, Office of the Chief of Military History (CMH), 1952], 115.

36. Ibid., 115–16.

37. Ibid., 116.

38. Ibid., 175.

39. Ibid.

40. Jentz, *Panzertruppen, 1933–1942*, 63.

41. Ibid., 64–65.

42. Ibid., 69.

43. Rolf Möbius, "German Heavy Armor," MS #D-226. Draft Translation (Washington, D.C.: CMH, 1954), 2.

44. Ibid., 3.

45. Jentz, *Tiger I and II*, 23.

46. Gudgin, *Tiger Tanks*, 91.

47. Egon Kleine and Volkmar Kuhn, *Tiger: The History of a Legendary Weapon, 1942–45*, trans. David Johnston (Winnipeg, Manitoba: J. J. Fedorowicz, 1989), 9.

48. Gudgin, *Tiger Tanks*, 91.

49. Jentz, *Tiger I and II*, 24–25.

50. These are essentially the U.S. Army equivalent of Tables of Organization and Equipment.

51. Jentz, *Tiger I and II*, 24–25.

52. Ibid., 25–26.

53. Wolfgang Schneider, *Tigers in Combat I* (Winnipeg, Manitoba: J. J. Fedorowicz, 2000), 147.

54. Ibid., 79, 228, 264, 312.

55. Gudgin, *Tiger Tanks*, 93.

56. Jentz, *Tiger I and II*, 24.

57. Schneider, *Tigers in Combat I*, 79, 147, 264.

58. Dr. Franz-Wilhelm Lochmann and others, eds., *The Combat History of schwere Panzer-Abteilung 503: In Action in the East and West with the Tiger I and Tiger II* (Winnipeg, Manitoba: J. J. Fedorowicz, 2000), 14.

59. Jentz and Doyle, *Tiger Tanks: D.W. to Tiger I,* 69.

60. Ibid, 27.

61. Hans-Joachim Jung, *Panzer Soldiers for "God, Honor, Fatherland," The History of Panzerregiment "Grossdeutschland:" The German Army's Elite Panzer Formation,* trans. David Johnston (Winnipeg, Manitoba: J. J. Fedorowicz, 2000), 145.

62. Others, like Heavy Tank Battalions 501 and 504, were attached temporarily to the 10th Panzer Division during operations in Tunisia.

63. Schneider, *Tigers in Combat II,* 3. The Panzer Regiment already had a heavy tank company assigned that was fighting in the battle of Kursk when the rest of the battalion was forming in Germany.

64. Schneider, *Tigers in Combat I,* 443.

65. Schneider, *Tigers in Combat II,* 3, 6–7.

66. Ibid., 7.

67. Patrick Agte, *Michael Wittmann and the Tiger Commanders of the Leibstandarte,* trans. David Johnston (Winnipeg, Manitoba: J. J. Fedorowicz, 1996), 216.

68. Lochmann et al., *schwere Panzer-Abteilung 503,* 309.

69. Ibid. The title *Feldherrnhalle* ("Field Commanders' Hall," a memorial to fallen German military leaders) refers to the building on the Odeonsplatz in Munich where the attempted Nazi *Putsch,* or *coup d'etat,* of 1923 was defeated by government forces. Several Nazis died in the fray, and the building became a shrine of the Nazi Party.

70. Jentz, *Tiger I and II,* 27.

71. Gudgin, *Tiger Tanks,* 133.

72. See Schneider, *Tigers in Combat I,* 82, 152, 231, 314, 346–47, 374, 441; idem, *Tigers in Combat II,* 364, 324–25, 397.

73. Jentz and Doyle, *Tiger Tanks: D.W. to Tiger I,* 9.

74. Ibid.

75. Ibid., 10.

76. Ibid., 12.

77. Ibid., 25, 30.

78. Kleine and Kuhn, *Tiger,* 4.

79. *Flak* was a German abbreviation for antiaircraft guns. The L/74 suffix referred to the length of the gun that measured 74 calibers from the muzzle to the rear face of the breech ring. The caliber is the diameter of the bore of the gun, in this case, 88mm. Increasing the length of the gun tube increased the velocity of the round fired, which in turn increased the armor-penetrative capability of kinetic energy rounds.

80. Kleine and Kuhn, *Tiger,* 4.

81. Jentz and Doyle, *Tiger Tanks: D.W. to Tiger I,* 12, 23.

82. Directives began bearing the stamp of "Hitler's Order. All deadlines must be met unconditionally!"

83. Jentz and Doyle, *Tiger Tanks: D.W. to Tiger I,* 19–20, 67, 69.

84. 88mm *KwK* 36 L/56 means that the diameter of the projectile is 88mm; it is a tank gun (*Kampfwagen Kanone*); its development was finalized in 1936; and the length of the gun tube is 56 times the diameter of the projectile, or 56 x 88mm.

85. Jentz, *Tiger I and II,* 9–10.

86. Thomas L. Jentz, *Panzertruppen: The Complete Guide to the Creation and Combat Employment of Germany's Tank Force, 1943–1945* (Atglen, Pa.: Schiffer, 1997), 295.

87. Thomas L. Jentz and Hilary L. Doyle, *Germany's Tiger Tanks: VK45.02 to Tiger II* (Atglen, Pa.: Schiffer, 2000), 10.

88. Ibid., 16.

89. Jentz and Doyle, *Tiger Tanks: VK45.02 to Tiger II,* 59.

90. Jentz, *Panzertruppen: 1943–1945,* 296.

91. Jentz and Doyle, *Tiger Tanks: VK45.02 to Tiger II,* 59.

92. David Fletcher, *Tiger! The Tiger Tank: A British View* (London: Her Majesty's Stationary Office, 1986), 228.

93. Jentz, *Panzertruppen: 1943–1945,* 294–95.

94. Gudgin, *Tiger Tanks,* 49.

95. Major Lüder, Commander of the Heavy Tank Battalion 501, "Tiger Experiences in Tunisia," dated 18 March 1943, in Jentz, *Tiger I and II,* 59.

96. These railcars were called Ssyms Cars.

97. See Heinz Guderian, Generalinspektur der Panzertruppen, *Tiger Fibel, D656/27,* written by Josef von Glatter-Goetz (n.p., 1943), 91; Taylor Downing, *Heavy Metal: Tiger!* written and directed by Patrick King. (n.p., The History Channel, 2002).

98. Guderian, *Tiger Fibel,* 91.

99. Ibid.

100. See Gudgin, *Tiger Tanks,* 77; Jentz and Doyle, *Tiger Tanks: VK45.02 to Tiger II,* 68.

101. Gudgin, *Tiger Tanks,* 93–94.

102. Schneider, *Tigers in Combat I,* 315, 349, 375.

103. Kleine and Kuhn, *Tiger,* 39.

104. Gudgin, *Tiger Tanks,* 107.

105. Jentz, *Tiger I and II,* 23, 31–37.

106. Merkblatt 47a/29 (20 May 1943) in Jentz, *Tiger I and II,* 31–32.

107. Ibid., 32–33.

108. Ibid., 34–35.

109. Ibid., 34.

110. Ibid., 36.

111. Ibid.

112. Ibid.

113. Merkblatt 47a/30 (20 May 1943) in Jentz, *Tiger I and II,* 36–37.

114. Ibid.

115. Ibid., 37.

116. Ibid.

117. Ibid.

118. Kleine and Kuhn, *Tiger,* 41–42.

119. Ibid.

120. Ibid.

121. Ibid.

122. Ibid.

Chapter 3

1. Jentz, *Tiger I and II*, 40.

2. Ibid., 24–26.

3. Jentz, *Panzertruppen: 1943–1945*, 32.

4. Schneider, *Tigers in Combat I*, 43, 83–85, 234.

5. Ibid., 83–85.

6. Ibid., 83–85.

7. Guderian, *Panzer Leader*, 280.

8. "Armee-Oberkommando 18 Summary," dated 2 April 1943, in Jentz, *Tiger I and II*, 40.

9. Ibid., 39.

10. Ibid., 40.

11. See Ibid., 41; Schneider, *Tigers in Combat I*, 84.

12. Schneider, *Tigers in Combat I*, 83–85.

13. Jentz, *Panzertruppen: 1943–1945*, 13.

14. Gudgin, *Tiger Tanks*, 107, 111.

15. Schneider, *Tigers in Combat I*, 42.

16. Ibid., 43.

17. George F. Howe, *Northwest Africa: Seizing the Initiative in the West*, United States Army in World War II, The Mediterranean Theater of Operations (Washington, D.C.: CMH, 1957), 311.

18. In addition to elements of the 10th Panzer Division and Heavy Tank Battalion 501, he added elements of a separate panzer battalion, the 190th.

19. Howe, *Northwest Africa*, 314.

20. See Schneider, *Tigers in Combat I*, 41; Howe, *Northwest Africa*, 314.

21. Jentz, *Tiger I and II*, 42.

22. Ibid.

23. Howe, *Northwest Africa*, 317.

24. Schneider, *Tigers in Combat I*, 41.

25. See Schneider, *Tigers in Combat I*, 41; Jentz, *Tiger I and II*, 42–43. Schneider claims 15, but an after-action report from Heavy Tank Battalion 501 only mentions eight tanks destroyed during this time period.

26. At the beginning of the operation there were probably about 50 German tanks available in all four combat groups, including Tigers and Panzer IIIs from Heavy Tank Battalion 501.

27. Schneider, *Tigers in Combat I*, 41.

28. See Howe, *Northwest Africa*, 331; Rick Atkinson, *An Army at Dawn: The War in North Africa, 1942–1943* (New York: Henry Holt, 2002), 231.

29. Records do not indicate what type of obstacle. Considering that movement was restricted primarily to the roads, it is plausible that a simple point minefield supported by accurate artillery fire would have sufficed to stop the attack.

30. Howe, *Northwest Africa*, 331.

31. The ten "Medium" German tanks were probably a mix of Panzer IIIs and IVs.

32. Howe, *Northwest Africa*, 332–33.

33. Schneider, *Tigers in Combat I*, 42.

34. This was the first time Heavy Tank Battalion 501 conducted an operation with the majority of the battalion. The battalion did not, however, operate as a unit, but was divided into three groups between two different combat groups. The honor of being the first battalion to conduct an operation as a cohesive unit went to Heavy Tank Battalion 503, operating with Army Group Don. They conducted an attack around Stavropol, southeast of Rostov, on 6 January 1943 with the entire battalion, 12 days prior to Operation EILBOTE.

35. I. S. O. Playfair, C. J. C. Molony; F. C. Flynn; and T. P. Gleave, *The Mediterranean and the Middle East: The Destruction of the Axis Forces in Africa,* vol. IV, History of the Second World War, United Kingdom Military Series (London: HMSO, 1966), 278.

36. Howe, *Northwest Africa,* 376–77.

37. Ibid.

38. Ibid., 377.

39. Major Lüder, "Combat Report for the Period from 18 to 22 January 1943," dated 27 January 1943, in Jentz, *Tiger I and II,* 48. The "suspension problems" were caused by "hits" from mines. The Tiger was later cannibalized because of a lack of spare parts for Tigers in Tunisia. See Schneider, *Tigers in Combat I,* 42.

40. Ibid.

41. See Howe, *Northwest Africa,* 377; Schneider, *Tigers in Combat I,* 42; Major Lüder, "Combat Report for the Period from 18 to 22 January 1943," dated 27 January 1943, in Jentz, *Tiger I and II,* 48.

42. See Major Lüder, "Report for 18 to 22 January 1943," 48; Schneider, *Tigers in Combat I,* 42. One of these Tigers was reportedly knocked out by a 6-pounder (57mm) antitank gun of 2 Troop, A Battery of the British 72d Antitank Regiment. It was the first Tiger captured by Allied forces and was subsequently used for testing to discover its weaknesses and strengths. See Gudgin, *Tiger Tanks,* 106–11, for numerous photos and Fletcher, *Tiger!* 11–27, for more pictures and copies of the tests conducted on this Tiger and the results. See also the report detailing this loss in Major Lüder, "Combat Report for the Period from 31 January to 1 February 1943," dated 3 February 1943, and Technical Reports No. 4 from the Engineer of the Panzer Battalion 501 on the "Tiger Situation in Tunisia for the operation during the period from 31 January to 1 February 1943" in Jentz, *Tiger I and II,* 51–53. These German reports misleadingly indicate that the Tiger was destroyed completely and nothing useful or of any consequence was captured by the British.

43. Major Lüder, "Report for 18 to 22 January 1943," 48.

44. Ibid.

45. Ibid.

46. Ibid.

47. Ibid.

48. Ibid.

49. See Schneider, *Tigers in Combat I,* 42. Howe, *Northwest Africa,* 382, lists total Allied losses of 87 machine guns, 16 antitank guns, 36 artillery pieces, 21 tanks, 4 armored reconnaissance cars, 4 self-propelled gun carriages, more than 200 other vehicles, and over 300 horses; Major Lüder in "Report for 18 to 22 January 1943," 49, lists Combat Group Lüder's total claims as 25 guns; 9 self-propelled guns or armored

half-tracks; 7 tanks (Sherman, Lee, Grant), about 125 trucks and cars; and 2 armored cars. Also listed are 235 prisoners, of which 8 were officers.

50. Major Lüder in "Report for 18 to 22 January 1943," 49. Presumably, the statement about one in nine Tigers being operational is a reference about one of the two companies and not the entire battalion. The battalion had 16 Tigers available at the end of this operation, not counting the one being used for spare parts.

51. Howe, *Northwest Africa*, 407.

52. Ibid., 411.

53. Ibid., 412.

54. Ibid.

55. See Schneider, *Tigers in Combat I*, 43; Jentz, *Tiger I and II*, 54. Jentz states that only 15 were claimed by Heavy Tank Battalion 501, while Schneider claims 20. Howe, *Northwest Africa*, 415, lists the total American losses from Combat Command A for the day as 44 tanks, all but 2 antitank guns, 9 of the 12 authorized 105-mm pieces of the 91st Armored Field Artillery Battalion, and the entire 2d Battalion, 17th Field Artillery.

56. This battalion, under Lieutenant Colonel Alger, lost 50 of their 54 tanks during the day.

57. Schneider, *Tigers in Combat I*, 43.

58. Howe, *Northwest Africa*, 415.

59. Ibid.

60. See Howe, *Northwest Africa*, 505–7; Playfair et al., *The Destruction of the Axis Forces in Africa*, vol. IV, 327–28.

61. British forces reportedly destroyed or disabled 40 of the 77 tanks in Combat Group Lang during the day, although many were repairable and were in action again in a short amount of time.

62. Howe, *Northwest Africa*, 506.

63. Schneider, *Tigers in Combat I*, 43.

64. Ibid.

65. Howe, *Northwest Africa*, 507.

66. Playfair et al., *The Destruction of the Axis Forces in Africa*, vol. IV, 328.

67. "Kampgruppe Lüder Operational Strengths during Operation OCHSENKOPF," and "Schwere Panzer-Abteilung 501 Operational Strength," dated 5 March 1943, in Jentz, *Tiger I and II*, 55–56.

68. Ibid., the battalion was issued with Panzer IVs to replace some lost Panzer IIIs.

69. Ibid.,

70. Restayn, *Tiger I on the Western Front*, 3.

71. Ibid., 41–43.

72. See Ibid, 43; Jentz, *Tiger I and II*, 50, 55; Gudgin, *Tiger Tanks*, 117. The battalion was authorized 20 Tigers in a two-company battalion and received two Tigers as replacements on 28 February 1943. Gudgin claims that there were 20 operational Tigers, but this is highly unlikely as the battalion never had more than 20 Tigers at any one time.

73. Jentz, *Tiger I and II*, 50.

74. Gudgin, *Tiger Tanks*, 104, 107.

75. "Technische Report Nr. 3 von Truppen-Ingenieur Panzer-Abteilung 501, 18–25 Januar 1943," in Jentz, *Tiger I and II*, 50.

76. "Technische Report Nr. 4 von Truppen-Ingenieur Panzer-Abteilung 501, 31 Januar–1 Februar 1943," in Jentz, *Tiger I and II*, 51.

77. "Tiger Experiences in Tunisia," dated 18 March 1943 in Jentz, *Tiger I and II*, 59.

78. Ibid.

79. In other words, a way to breach minefields mechanically without damaging the tanks by driving over them.

80. See Schneider, *Tigers in Combat I*, 47; David Rolf, *The Bloody Road to Tunis* (London: Greenhill, 2001), 127–31; Paul M. Robinett, *Armor Command* (Washington, D.C.: McGregor and Werner, 1958), 163–64; Charles Whiting, *Kasserine: First Blood* (New York: Stein and Day, 1984), 173–91. German claims cannot be verified in every instance, however, they do not appear to be exaggerated in the cases where some level of verification is possible. The Germans, for example, claim they destroyed 20 U.S. Sherman tanks on 14 February 1943 as part of Operation FRÜHLINGSWIND. This is a reasonable number considering the fact that a large portion of Combat Command A was destroyed during the operation, which the Americans called "the battle for Kasserine Pass."

81. Schneider, *Tigers in Combat I*, 41–43.

82. Ibid., 43.

83. Major Lüder, Commander of Heavy Tank Battalion 501, letter dated 16 February 1943, in Jentz, *Tiger I and II*, 54.

84. Lüder, "Combat Report, dated 16 December 1942," in Jentz, *Tiger I and II*, 43.

85. Ibid., 45.

86. Lüder, "Report for 18 to 22 January 1943," 48.

87. Schneider, *Tigers in Combat I*, 233–34.

88. Ibid., 233. German sources credit Heavy Tank Battalion 504 with destroying 35 U.S. tanks. American sources universally mention that this attack was halted—although rain and swampy conditions are usually given as the primary factors—while no losses are provided.

89. See Schneider, *Tigers in Combat I*, 233–34; Jack Coggins, *The Campaign for North Africa* (New York: Doubleday, 1980), 137, 155–57. In this attack, part of the Allied offensive Operation VULCAN, British losses within the 1st and 6th Armored Divisions on 21 April 1943 were 162 tanks. Heavy Tank Battalion 504 claims to have destroyed about 40 of them. Although they claim these tanks belonged to the British 9th Armored Division, only the 1st and 6th Armored Divisions attacked in the Medjez el Bab area on this day.

90. Jentz, *Tiger I and II*, 60.

91. Schneider, *Tigers in Combat I*, 234.

92. See Restayn, *Tiger I on the Western Front*, 44; Schneider, *Tigers in Combat I*, 234. Restayn lists the number as 150, but Schneider lists more than 250 enemy tanks destroyed. Verification from American and British sources leads one to the conclusion that 250 is an extreme over-estimate, and that 150 may, in fact, be accurate.

93. "Technischer Report Nr. 6 von Truppen-Ingenieur Panzer-Abteilung 501, 3 März–1 Mai 1943," in Jentz, *Tiger I and II*, 62.

94. Ibid.

95. Dana V. Sadarananda, *Beyond Stalingrad: Manstein and the Operations of Army Group Don* (New York: Praeger, 1990), 56.

96. Ibid., 60–61.

97. Schneider, *Tigers in Combat I*, 153.

98. Sadarananda, *Beyond Stalingrad*, 61.

99. Lange, Commander of 2d Company, Heavy Tank Battalion 502. "After Action Report, 29 January 1943," in Lochmann et al., *schwere Panzer-Abteilung 503*, 56.

100. Schneider, *Tigers in Combat I*, 153.

101. Ibid.

102. Kleine and Kuhn, *Tiger*, 48.

103. Ibid.

104. Ibid.

105. Ibid.

106. Schneider, *Tigers in Combat I*, 153.

107. Kleine and Kuhn, *Tiger*, 52.

108. Ibid.

109. Schneider, *Tigers in Combat I*, 154.

110. Ibid.

111. Ibid.

112. Ibid.

113. Ibid., 155.

114. Ibid.

115. Ibid., 153–55.

116. Ibid.

117. Ibid., 154, 226.

118. Ibid., 226.

119. Richard von Rosen, "Initial Employment with Heeresgruppe Don," in Lochmann et al., *schwere Panzer-Abteilung 503*, 44.

120. Ibid.

121. Jentz, *Tiger I and II*, 68.

122. von Rosen, "Initial Employment with Heeresgruppe Don," in Lochmann et al., *schwere Panzer-Abteilung 503*, 43.

123. Kleine and Kuhn, *Tiger*, 52.

124. Williamson Murray and Allan R. Millett, *A War To Be Won: Fighting the Second World War* (London: The Belknap Press of Harvard University Press, 2000), 292.

125. See David M. Glantz and Jonathan M. House, *The Battle of Kursk* (Lawrence, Kans.: University of Kansas Press, 1999), 19; Walter S. Dunn, Jr., *Kursk: Hitler's Gamble, 1943* (London: Praeger, 1997), 30.

126. Dunn, *Kursk*, 31.

127. Ibid., 28.

128. Ibid., 91.

129. Ibid., 91–92.

130. Ibid., 92.

131. Pavel Rotmistrov, "Tanks Against Tanks," in *Main Front: Soviet Leaders Look Back on World War II*, with a foreword by Marshal of the Soviet Union S. Sokolov and a commentary by John Erickson (New York: Brassey's, 1987), 110.

132. See Lüder, "Letter dated 16 February 1943," "Tiger Experiences in Tunisia, dated 18 March 1943," and "schwere Panzer-Abteilung 503 Combat Report for the Period 2 to 22 February 1943," in Jentz, *Tiger I and II*, 54–55, 59, 65; Captain Lange, "After Action Report of the 2./schwere Panzer-Abteilung 502, dated 29 January 1943," in Lochmann et al., *schwere Panzer-Abteilung 503*, 57–58.

133. "The 13.(Tiger) Company/Panzer-Regiment Grossdeutschland After Action Report on Employment 7–19 March 1943 in the area of Poltawa-Belgorad," Jentz, *Tiger I and II*, 75.

134. Guderian, Generalinspekteur der Panzertruppen, 14 May 1943, quoted in Jentz, *Tiger I and II*, 79.

135. Ibid.

136. "Infanterie-Division '*Grossdeutschland*' Report, Dated 3 April 1943" in Jentz, *Tiger I and II*, 74.

137. Guderian, Generalinspekteur der Panzertruppen, 27 April 1943, quoted in Jentz, *Tiger I and II*, 74.

138. Panzer officer on the staff of the Chief of the Army General Staff, "Comments on the reports from the Tiger Company of Infantry Division '*Grossdeutschland*', Dated 11 April 1943" in Jentz, *Tiger I and II*, 77.

139. Guderian, "Comments of the Experience Report from the 13.Company (Tiger)/Panzer-Regiment 'Grossdeutschland', Dated 14 May 1943" in Jentz, *Tiger I and II*, 79.

140. See Niklas Zetterling and Anders Frankson, *Kursk 1943: A Statistical Analysis* (London: Frank Cass, 2000), 134; Schneider, *Tigers in Combat I*, 156.

141. See Jentz, *Panzertruppen: 1943–1945*, 74; Schneider, *Tigers in Combat I*, 267.

142. Schneider, *Tigers in Combat I*, 156.

143. Jentz, *Tiger I and II*, 85.

144. Schneider, *Tigers in Combat I*, 267.

145. See Schneider, *Tigers in Combat I*, 267–68; Restayn, *Tiger I on the Western Front*, 138.

146. Karlheinz Münch, *Combat History of schwere Panzerjäger Abteilung 653, formerly the Sturmgeschutz Abteilung 197: 1940–1943*, trans. Bo H. Friesen. (Winnipeg, Manitoba: J. J. Fedorowicz, 1997), 51.

147. Jentz, *Tiger I and II*, 85–86.

148. Schneider, *Tigers in Combat I*, 268.

149. Dunn, *Kursk*, 55–56.

150. Hermann Breith, General der Panzertruppen, Commander of III Panzerkorps, "Breakthrough of a Panzer Corps Through Deeply Echeloned Russian Defenses During Battle of Kharkov [Kursk], July 1943." MS # D-258, Draft Translation (Washington, D.C.: CMH, 1947), 2.

151. Dunn, *Kursk*, 109.

152. Glantz and House, *Battle of Kursk*, 104.

153. Graf Kageneck, Commander of Heavy Tank Battalion 503 "Daily Report, dated 6 July 1943," in Jentz, *Panzertruppen: 1933–1942*, 92–93.

154. von Rosen, "ZITADELLE," in Lochmann et al., *schwere Panzer-Abteilung 503*, 107–8.

155. Dunn, *Kursk*, 137.

156. Jentz, *Panzertruppen: 1933–1942*, 87–91.

157. Glantz and House, *Battle of Kursk*, 136.

158. The corps' start line was essentially the Donets River southeast of Belgorod.

159. von Rosen, "*ZITADELLE*," in Lochmann et al., *schwere Panzer-Abteilung 503*, 108–9.

160. See Schneider, *Tigers in Combat I*, 156–57; Breith, "Breakthrough of a Panzer Corps," MS # D-258, 11.

161. Schneider, *Tigers in Combat I*, 226.

162. Jentz, *Tiger I and II*, 90.

163. Glantz and House, *Battle of Kursk*, 86.

164. Robin Cross, *Citadel: The Battle of Kursk* (New York: Sarpedon, 1993), 163.

165. Ibid. This is an overly optimistic assessment of the situation given that the Soviets had not committed any operational or strategic reserves at this point in the battle.

166. Schneider, *Tigers in Combat I*, 268. It is unclear whether the author used the word "front" in this statement to mean an echelon of the Soviet defenses or the Soviet Central Front, which was similar in size to a German Army Group. If the former, destruction of an echelon of the tactical defense was probably possible. If the latter, destruction of the entire Central Front by the commitment of one panzer division is a very optimistic and probably unrealistic assessment. Although the Central Front commander obviously saw penetration of the first defensive echelon as a threat, the Central Front stabilized the situation with operational reserves and did not require reinforcement from any strategic reserves at any time during the battle.

167. Glantz and House, *Battle of Kursk*, 89.

168. Ibid.

169. Ibid., 93.

170. Ibid., 91.

171. David M. Glantz and Harold S. Orenstein, eds., *The Battle for Kursk, 1943: The Soviet General Staff Study* (London: Frank Cass, 1999), 114.

172. See Ibid; Glantz and House, *Battle of Kursk*, 93.

173. Glantz and House, *Battle of Kursk*, 93.

174. Ibid., 117.

175. Schneider, *Tigers in Combat I*, 268.

176. Ibid.

177. Ibid.

178. See Ibid., 267–68; Glantz and House, *Battle of Kursk*, 18.

179. Schneider, *Tigers in Combat I*, 268.

180. Ibid.

181. Ibid.

182. Ibid., 311.

183. Jentz, *Tiger I and II*, 90.

184. Ibid.

185. Ibid.

186. Glantz and Orenstein, *Battle for Kursk, 1943*, 71.

Chapter 4

1. "R.A.C. Liaison Letter," issued April 1943 in Fletcher, *Tiger!* 28.

2. Robin Cross, *Citadel*, 234.

3. Jentz, *Tiger I and II*, 125.

4. Ibid.

5. See Major Gomille, "Report of III.(Tiger) Abteilung/Panzer Regiment *Gross-deutschland*," dated 31 August 1943; Captain Graf Kageneck, "Experience in Panzer Operations" by Heavy Tank Battalion 503, dated 10 October 1943; Major Withing, "Preliminary Experience Report for Tiger Abteilung 506," dated 30 September 1943; Major Gierka, "Tiger Abteilung 509 Report" [Extract], dated 17 December 1943 in Jentz, *Tiger I and II*, 124, 128–32, 135–37, 139–40, 142–44, 146, 148.

6. Withing, in Jentz, *Tiger I and II*, 135–37.

7. Ibid.

8. Ibid.

9. Ibid.

10. Ibid., 137.

11. Ibid.

12. Schneider, *Tigers in Combat I*, 316.

13. Lange, "Experience Report from Tiger Abteilung 506," dated 15 January 1944 in Jentz, *Tiger I and II*, 144.

14. Ibid.

15. Schneider, *Tigers in Combat I*, 159.

16. Alfred Rubbel, "The Operations of Schwere Panzer-Abteilung 503 in Opening the Tscherkassy Pocket," in Lochmann et al., *schwere Panzer-Abteilung 503*, 120.

17. Ibid., 118.

18. Ibid., 131.

19. Ibid., 118, 122.

20. See Franz Bäke, "The Balabanowka Pocket (25 January–30 January 1944)," in Lochmann et al., *schwere Panzer-Abteilung 503*, 122; Schneider, *Tigers in Combat I*, 160. These numbers are only from German sources and as such, are unconfirmed.

21. Schneider, *Tigers in Combat I*, 160, 226.

22. Rubbel, "Tscherkassy Pocket," 131.

23. Ibid.

24. Douglas F. Nash, *Hell's Gate: The Battle of the Cherkassy Pocket, January–February 1944* (Southbury, Conn.: RZM, 2002), 129.

25. Ibid. The overall relief operation was called Operation HOMECOMING by the *OKH*.

26. Ibid., 158.

27. See Rubbel, "Tscherkassy Pocket," 132; Nash, *Hell's Gate*, 125.

28. Nash, *Hell's Gate*, 160.

29. Ibid.

30. Ibid.

31. Franz Bäke, "Tcherkassy (3–20 February 1944) Advance Northeast Toward Medwin (3–9 February 1944)" in Lochmann et al., *schwere Panzer-Abteilung 503*, 123.

32. Nash, *Hell's Gate*, 161.

33. Franz Bäke quoted in Nash, *Hell's Gate*, 166.

34. Nash, *Hell's Gate*, 162.

35. Ibid., 163.

36. Rubbel, "Tscherkassy Pocket," 137.

37. Nash, *Hell's Gate,* 161.

38. Ibid., 166.

39. Ibid., 165.

40. Ibid., 174.

41. Rubbel, "Tscherkassy Pocket," 131. The two panzer divisions within the III Panzer Corps were also extremely weak. The 16th Panzer Division, for example, had 19 tanks and the 17th Panzer Division had 4 tanks operational on 9 February 1944. See remarks by David Glantz, 1985 Art of War Symposium, 153.

42. Five officers were authorized in the battalion headquarters or specialty platoons, and four were authorized in each tank company.

43. Rubbel, "Tscherkassy Pocket," 131.

44. Schneider, *Tigers in Combat I,* 318. This battalion also took part in the first attack (Operation WANDA). It was, like Heavy Tank Battalion 503, in the III Panzer Corps but was attached to the 16th Panzer Division that trailed the Heavy Panzer Regiment Bäke.

45. Schneider, *Tigers in Combat I,* 318.

46. Nash, *Hell's Gate,* 232.

47. Rubbel, "Tscherkassy Pocket," 132.

48. Ibid.

49. See Ibid.; Schneider, *Tigers in Combat I,* 160–61. A fifth Tiger was damaged but was repairable.

50. Rubbel, "Tscherkassy Pocket," 134.

51. See Ibid.; Schneider, *Tigers in Combat I,* 161.

52. Rubbel, "Tscherkassy Pocket," 134.

53. Ibid.

54. See Ibid.; Schneider, *Tigers in Combat I,* 161. Schneider claims 15 while Rubbel states the number as 14. Because Rubbel was present, I have chosen his number.

55. Rubbel, "Tscherkassy Pocket," 134.

56. Nash, *Hell's Gate,* 268–69.

57. Ibid., 267.

58. See Rubbel, "Tscherkassy Pocket," 135; Nash, *Hell's Gate,* 271.

59. Rubbel, "Tscherkassy Pocket," 134.

60. Nash, *Hell's Gate,* 295.

61. Leon Degrelle, *Campaign in Russia: The Waffen SS on the Eastern Front* (Costa Mesa, Calif.: Institute for Historical Review, 1985), 213–14.

62. Nash, *Hell's Gate,* 320–21.

63. Rubbel, "Tscherkassy Pocket," 135.

64. Ibid., 136.

65. Schneider, *Tigers in Combat I,* 160–61.

66. Remarks by David Glantz, 1985 Art of War Symposium, 166. Glantz states that 56,000 German soldiers were trapped inside the pocket, 35,000 attempted to break out on 17 February 1944, of which 30,000 men made it out safely.

67. If half of the kills are attributed to each battalion of Heavy Panzer Regiment Bäke, then Heavy Tank Battalion 503 destroyed 164 enemy tanks, a 7.5-to-1 kill ratio.

68. Schneider, *Tigers in Combat I,* 375.

69. Ibid., 380.

70. Ibid., 236, 242.

71. Kleine and Kuhn, *Tiger,* 247.

72. See Jentz, *Tiger I and II,* 93; Schneider, *Tigers in Combat I,* 236, 375.

73. Jentz, *Tiger I and II,* 93.

74. See Kleine and Kuhn, *Tiger,* 247; Schneider, *Tigers in Combat I,* 236, 375; Martin Schmidt, "Employment of Panzer Units in Central Italy in 1944, and Peculiarities Thereof." MS #D-204. (Washington, D.C.: CMH, 1947), 4.

75. Schneider, *Tigers in Combat I,* 236, 375.

76. Hans Bahr, "The 2./Schwere Panzer-Abteilung 508," in Kurt Hirlinger, ed. *The Combat History of schwere Panzer-Abteilung 508: In Action in Italy with the Tiger I* (Winnipeg, Manitoba: J. J. Fedorowicz, 2001), trans. David Johnston, 34.

77. Erich Amann, quoted in Hans Bahr, "2./s.P-Abt. 508," 34.

78. Hans Bahr, "2./s.P-Abt. 508," 34.

79. Schneider, *Tigers in Combat I,* 375–76.

80. Kleine and Kuhn, *Tiger,* 247.

81. Curt Riegel, "The Panzerwerkstatt-Kompanie (Tank Maintenance Company)," in Hirlinger, *schwere Panzer-Abteilung 508,* 142.

82. Ibid.

83. Schneider, *Tigers in Combat I,* 376.

84. "Report on activities of s.Pz.-Abt. 508 between 23 and 25 May 1944 in the area of Cisternia" in Jentz, *Tiger I and II,* 97–98.

85. See Ibid., 98; for a good description of the U.S. dispositions and the larger picture involving the commitment of Heavy Tank Battalion 508 see Ernest F. Fisher, Jr., *Cassino to the Alps,* United States Army in World War II, The Mediterranean Theater of Operations (Washington, D.C.: CMH, 1977), 137.

86. GMDS by a combined British, Canadian, and U.S. Staff, *The German Operation at Anzio: A Study of the German Operations at Anzio Beachhead from 22 Jan 44 to 31 May 44* (Camp Ritchie, Md.: German Military Documents Section, Military Intelligence Division, War Department, 9 April 1946), 107.

87. "Report of Activities of 3.Kompanie/schwere Panzer-Abteilung 508 between 23–25 May 1944," in Jentz, *Tiger I and II,* 97–98.

88. Schneider, *Tigers in Combat I,* 408.

89. Ibid., 377.

90. Restayn, *Tiger I on the Western Front,* 81.

91. AFV(T) G-H/JB, Technical Branch, "Who Killed Tiger?" dated August 1944 in Fletcher, *Tiger!* 215–18.

92. Ibid., 216.

93. Ibid., 236.

94. Ibid., 236–37, 263.

95. Fisher, 261.

96. George F. Howe, *The Battle History of the 1st Armored Division "Old Ironsides"* (Washington, D.C.: Combat Forces, 1954), 354.

97. Ibid., 354, 356. Both Company A and D were detached from the division during this operation.

98. Fisher, 262.

99. Schneider, *Tigers in Combat I,* 236–37.

100. See Ibid.; for an excellent description of a typical encounter between U.S. forces and German forces, supported by Tigers, during this operation, see Howe, *1st Armored Division,* 357–60.

101. Schneider, *Tigers in Combat I,* 377.

102. Ibid., 236–37, 376–77. From 23 May 1944 to 1 July 1944 Heavy Tank Battalion 508 lost 36 and Heavy Tank Battalion 504 lost 28 Tigers.

103. Ibid., 379, 408.

104. Ibid., 379.

105. Ibid., 378.

106. See Ibid., 381, 408; Restayn, *Tiger I on the Western Front,* 60; GMDS, *The German Operation at Anzio,* 64, 68, 107.

107. Schneider, *Tigers in Combat I,* 408.

108. Ibid., 263.

109. Ibid.

110. Ibid.

111. Jentz, *Tiger I and II,* 98–99.

112. This includes Heavy Tank Battalion 501 through 509 and 3d Battalion, Panzer Regiment *Grossdeutschland.*

Chapter 5

1. Hans-Joachim Schwaner, Battalion Commander, "After Action Report on the Employment of the 502d Heavy Panzer Battalion in the 16th Army Sector from 4 July to 17 August 1944," dated 20 August 1944 in Otto Carius, *Tigers in the Mud,* (Winnipeg, Manitoba: J. J. Fedorowicz, 1992), 240.

2. Jentz, *Panzertruppen: 1943–1945,* 204–5.

3. Schneider, *Tigers in Combat II,* 255, 327.

4. Schneider, *Tigers in Combat I,* 164, 443.

5. Operation OVERLORD is used here, but includes subsequent operations following the cross-channel attack until the breakout from Normandy.

6. Schneider, *Tigers in Combat I,* 45, 276, 319–20. Heavy Tank Battalion 501 was totally destroyed, Heavy Tank Battalion 505 transported 11 Tigers back to factories in Germany and Heavy Tank Battalion 506 handed its 6 remaining Tigers over to Heavy Tank Battalion 507.

7. See Schneider, *Tigers in Combat I,* 165.; idem, *Tigers in Combat II,* 260, 262, 333; Restayn, *Tiger I on the Western Front,* 88.

8. Overwatch is a basic principle of mounted movement where an element occupies a position, usually stationary, that offers cover and concealment, good observation, and clear fields of fire to support another element that moves under the "protection" of the overwatch element.

9. Generalinspekteur der Panzertruppen, Comments on "Report From a Tiger Company," Nachrichtenblatt der Panzertruppen, September 1944, in Jentz, *Tiger I and II,* 148–52.

10. See Curtis S. King, "Operation BAGRATION: A Soviet Victory." *Military Review* (April 1994): 89–90; Paul Adair, *Hitler's Greatest Defeat: The Collapse of Army Group*

Centre, June 1944 (London: Arms and Armour, 1998), 56–61, 177–80; William M. Connor, *Analysis of Deep Attack Operations: Operation* BAGRATION, *Belorussia, 22 June–29 August 1944* (Fort Leavenworth, Kans.: Combat Studies Institute, March 1987), 18–19. Connor states that at the beginning of the Soviet attack there may have been as few as 200 tanks and assault guns in all of Army Group Center. Although he says that the number may be double that, it is nothing compared to the 4,050 tanks and assault guns the Soviets fielded against them. Glantz also gives the number as 200 tanks/assault guns for the Germans, making the force ratio, initially at least, 20 to 1.

11. Jentz, *Panzertruppen: 1943–1945*, 205.

12. Ibid.

13. Schneider, *Tigers in Combat I*, 45.

14. See Ibid., 45; Steve Zaloga, BAGRATION *1944: The Destruction of Army Group Centre* (Hong Kong: Osprey, 1996), 54–55.

15. Schneider, *Tigers in Combat I*, 45.

16. Ibid., 45.

17. Zaloga, BAGRATION, 59.

18. Ibid.

19. See Ibid; Schneider, *Tigers in Combat I*, 275.

20. Schneider, *Tigers in Combat I*, 275.

21. Ibid.

22. Ibid.

23. See Ibid., 276, 311; Zaloga, BAGRATION, 69.

24. Schneider, *Tigers in Combat I*, 275.

25. See Ibid., 351; Zaloga, BAGRATION, 46–47.

26. Schneider, Tigers in Combat I, 352.

27. Ibid.

28. Ibid., 351–52, 372.

29. Zaloga, BAGRATION, 72–73.

30. Werner Haupt, *Army Group North: The Wehrmacht in Russia, 1941–1945.* (Atglen, Pa.: Schiffer, 1997), 228.

31. Ibid., 231.

32. Hans-Joachim Schwaner, Heavy Tank Battalion 502 Battalion Commander. "After Action Report on the Employment of the 502d Heavy Panzer Battalion in the 16th Army sector from 4 July to 17 August 1944," in Carius, *Tigers in the Mud*, 223. The divisions came primarily from the 18th Army sector and included several assault gun brigades and battalions, *Flak* and heavy artillery battalions, as well as Heavy Tank Battalion 502.

33. Ibid.; Schneider, *Tigers in Combat I*, 92.

34. Schwaner, "AAR from 4 July to 17 August 1944," in Carius, *Tigers in the Mud*, 224.

35. Ibid.

36. Ibid., 224–25.

37. Ibid., 225. The enemy forces were believed to be in regimental strength and were located in Garniai (two kilometers south of Daugailiai).

38. Ibid.

39. Ibid., 226.

40. Ibid., 228. The length of the roadmarch was not the shortest route because the shortest route contained bridges incapable of supporting Tigers.

41. Ibid.; Schneider, *Tigers in Combat I*, 92.

42. Schwaner, "AAR from 4 July to 17 August 1944," 234.

43. Ibid., 235. Carius personally destroyed 10 of the 17. Three Soviet tanks managed to escape to the east. Carius received the Oak Leaves to the Knight's Cross for his actions this day.

44. Ibid., 237.

45. This action was northwest of Dünaburg where the Düna River flows southeast to northwest instead of straight east to west.

46. Schwaner, "AAR from 4 July to 17 August 1944," 243.

47. Schneider, *Tigers in Combat I*, 164–65.

48. Rubbel, "The Battalion Receives the Königstiger (King Tiger)" in Lochmann et al., *schwere Panzer-Abteilung 503*, 234.

49. Late in August elements of Heavy Tank Battalion 503 did defend against U.S. forces.

50. L. F. Ellis, G. R. G. Allen, A. E. Warhurst, and James Robb, *Victory in the West: The Battle of Normandy*. History of the Second World War, United Kingdom Military Series, vol. I (London: HMSO, 1962), 546.

51. Ibid. Further research developed a discarding sabot (DS) round that was issued later in the war. This round had a tungsten core enclosed in a light metal casing or 'sabot' that was discarded as the projectile left the gun and resulted in greatly increased velocity and penetration ability.

52. Additionally, the Tiger had a lower probability of making a hit than the 17-pounder at that range.

53. A British regiment was a U.S.-battalion-sized unit. Companies were called squadrons and platoons were called troops.

54. Ellis, *Victory in the West*, 541.

55. See Constance McLaughlin Green, Harry C. Thomson, and Peter C. Roots, "The Search for Increased Fire Power: Ammunition" in *The Ordnance Department: Planning Munitions for War*, in United States Army in World War II, The Technical Services (Washington, D.C.: CMH, 1955), 355–61.

56. Agte, *Michael Wittmann*, 313–16.

57. Schneider, *Tigers in Combat II*, 256.

58. Agte, *Michael Wittmann*, 317–18.

59. See Ibid., 318; Daniel Taylor, *Villers-Bocage: Through the Lens of a German War Photographer* (London: Battle of Britain, 1999), 18. Taylor states that Möbius's 1st Company had ten Tigers. The discrepancy in numbers could be the difference between what was available in the morning and what was committed to the battle later in the day. Taylor's account of the Battle of Villers-Bocage is by far the most comprehensive and thoroughly researched of all available publications.

60. Taylor, *Villers-Bocage*, 9. This operation was codenamed Operation PERCH.

61. Michael Wittmann, quoted in Agte, *Michael Wittmann*, 318.

62. Taylor, *Villers-Bocage*, 9.

63. Agte, *Michael Wittmann*, 319.

64. Taylor, *Villers-Bocage*, 17.

65. Ibid., 16.

66. Ibid., 38.

67. Ibid., 76. Several of these tanks were light reconnaissance tanks (Stuarts) that were no match for a Tiger and one was an artillery observer's tank. This Cromwell tank had the gun removed in order to provide room for more radios. In order for it to "blend in" with other tanks so as not to highlight itself as a high priority target, it had a "fake" wooden gun tube installed.

68. See Taylor, *Villers-Bocage*, 76; Ellis et al., *Victory in the West*, 254. The British official history lists their total losses as 25 tanks, 14 armored trucks, and 14 Bren carriers.

69. Michael Reynolds, *Steel Inferno: 1st SS Panzer Corps in Normandy* (New York: Dell, 1997), 126.

70. Agte, *Michael Wittmann*, 325–26.

71. Ellis et al., *Victory in the West*, 254–55.

72. See Taylor, *Villers-Bocage*, 76; Agte, *Michael Wittmann*, 324; Schneider, *Tigers in Combat II*, 256–57. This records for this engagement are unclear in terms of Tiger losses. Taylor claims that the Germans lost 5 Tigers while Schneider claims only 3. Agte provides the most extensive account that identifies losses by tank commander. He claims the Germans lost 6 Tigers in the town of Villers-Bocage and another 1 outside of the town. Agte could, however, be listing the total number destroyed and disabled instead of delineating the Tigers totally destroyed.

73. Taylor, *Villers-Bocage*, 19. Wittmann's own Tiger was still en route to Normandy and he actually used Unterscharfuhrer Kurt Sowa's Tiger.

74. See Taylor, *Villers-Bocage*, 56; Schneider, *Tigers in Combat II*, 256–57; Agte, *Michael Wittmann*, 324.

75. See Taylor, *Villers-Bocage*, 76; Schneider, *Tigers in Combat II*, 256.

76. Agte, *Michael Wittmann*, 326.

77. If only six Tigers from Möbius's company entered the town, then every single Tiger that entered the town was damaged or destroyed.

78. Taylor, *Villers-Bocage*, 83. The British reserve crews were called Left Out of Battle, or LOB, crews.

79. Jentz, *Panzertruppen: 1933–1942*, 110.

80. Guderian, Tactical Analysis of the Situation in Normandy, to Adolf Hitler, 19 June 1944, in Jentz, *Tiger I and II*, 177, 180–82.

81. Guderian, Situation Report Presentation to Adolf Hitler, 28 June 1944, in Jentz, *Panzertruppen: 1933–1942*, 182.

82. von Rosen, "Operation GOODWOOD 18 July 1944: The Darkest Day for schwere Panzer-Abteilung 503," in Lochmann et al., *The Combat History of schwere Panzer-Abteilung 503*, 239.

83. Ellis et al., *Victory in the West*, 336.

84. See Restayn, *Tiger I on the Western Front*, 34; Schneider, *Tigers in Combat I*, 164–65; von Rosen, "Operation GOODWOOD," in *schwere Panzer-Abteilung 503*, 239–42.

85. See Ellis et al., *Victory in the West*, 337; von Rosen, "Operation GOODWOOD," in *schwere Panzer-Abteilung 503*, 239.

86. See Schneider, *Tigers in Combat I,* 164; von Rosen, "Operation GOODWOOD," in *schwere Panzer-Abteilung 503,* 239. The 3d Company was still equipped with the Tiger I, but the 1st Company had the King Tiger/Tiger II at this time.

87. von Rosen, "Operation GOODWOOD," in *schwere Panzer-Abteilung 503,* 239.

88. Ibid., 241.

89. Ibid.

90. See Ellis et al., *Victory in the West,* 340–41; von Rosen, "Operation GOODWOOD," in *schwere Panzer-Abteilung 503,* 241; Hans von Luck, *Panzer Commander: The Memoirs of Colonel Hans von Luck* (New York: Dell, 1989), 193–99. Von Luck was the commander of the 21st Panzer Division and literally forced the *Luftwaffe* captain in charge of the battery to begin engaging the British tanks after he refused because his "concern is enemy planes, fighting tanks is your job." Von Luck drew his pistol, aimed it at the captain and said, "Either you're a dead man or you can earn yourself a medal." The *Luftwaffe* captain obviously chose the latter.

91. von Rosen, "Operation GOODWOOD," in *schwere Panzer-Abteilung 503,* 241.

92. Ibid.

93. Four tanks reportedly made it all the way to the village of Demouville. Taking and holding this town would have been a huge undertaking as it was on the primary route of British attack. This would have stopped the British attack from advancing and cut off any British forces that had already passed by and continued toward Cagny. See von Rosen, "Operation GOODWOOD," in *schwere Panzer-Abteilung 503,* 242.

94. See von Rosen, "Operation GOODWOOD," in *schwere Panzer-Abteilung 503,* 242; Schneider, *Tigers in Combat I,* 164–65.

95. See "The Gorman Story" and "The Thaysen Story" in *schwere Panzer-Abteilung 503,* 242–43. The British account has the Sherman ramming the Tiger and the German account has the King Tiger inadvertently backing into the Sherman.

96. von Rosen, "Operation GOODWOOD," in *schwere Panzer-Abteilung 503,* 241.

97. Ibid.

98. Schneider, *Tigers in Combat II,* 258.

99. Agte, *Michael Wittmann,* 404.

100. See Schneider, *Tigers in Combat II,* 258; Agte, *Michael Wittmann,* 404.

101. British sources give high credit to Tigers, usually equating their "suffered heavy losses" with "Tigers and 88s." See Ellis et al., *Victory in the West,* 340–43, 347.

102. Ellis et al., *Victory in the West,* 345.

103. von Luck, 197. The 21st Panzer Division commander states that "In the extensive cornfields to the north of the village stood at least 40 British tanks, on fire or shot up. I saw how the tanks that had already crossed the main road were slowly rolling back." He fails to provide an exact time, but based upon the remainder of his narrative, this was probably still early in the afternoon. Schneider, *Tigers in Combat I,* 165, claims that Heavy Tank Battalion 503 destroyed 40 British tanks on 18 July 1944.

104. Ellis et al., *Victory in the West,* 317.

105. Ibid.

106. Will Fey, *Armor Battles of the Waffen SS, 1943–45 (Panzerkampf),* trans. Harri Henschler. (Winnipeg, Manitoba: J. J. Fedorowicz, 1990), 148.

107. Schneider, *Tigers in Combat II*, 328–29.

108. Ibid.

109. Ellis et al., *Victory in the West*, 419.

110. Ibid., 420. The U.S. self-propelled guns were known as the "Priest" because of the offset sponson that resembled a pulpit. The Canadians removed the guns as well as the seats and ammunition bins and welded steel sheets across the openings in the front of the vehicle. The troops then referred to these vehicles as "unfrocked priests" or "holy rollers."

111. Ibid.

112. Ibid.

113. Ibid.

114. Kurt Meyer, *Grenadiers* (Winnipeg, Manitoba: J. J. Fedorowicz, 1994), Translated by Michael Mende, 157–58. After seeing German soldiers from the 89th Infantry Division retreating along the Caen-Falaise road, he wrote, "I suddenly realize that the fate of Falaise and the safety of both [German] armies depends on my decision."

115. Ibid., 158.

116. Agte, *Michael Wittmann*, 406, 423.

117. See Schneider, *Tigers in Combat II*, 259; Agte, *Michael Wittmann*, 423. Agte states that the number was eight and not ten.

118. Agte, *Michael Wittmann*, 401.

119. Ibid., 423–33. First Lieutenant Heurich never commanded a tank company and this was his first combat action.

120. Ibid., 423.

121. Meyer, 159.

122. Ken Tout, *A Fine Night for Tanks: The Road to Falaise* (Gloucestershire, UK: Sutton), 133.

123. Agte, *Michael Wittmann*, 424.

124. Ibid.; Tout, *Fine Night for Tanks*, 129.

125. Tout, *Fine Night for Tanks*, 129. Tout, who was present at this battle, stated "If there was a flaw in the German dispositions, it must have been the failure to integrate fully a tiny but potentially deadly Tiger force with other counterattacking Panthers and Mark IVs, supported by Panzergrenadiers." He concludes his assessment by saying "had they been used in a more elusive and better supported role the delay to the Allies could have been far worse."

126. Agte, *Michael Wittmann*, 424.

127. Tout, *Fine Night for Tanks*, 130.

128. See Ibid., 130; Taylor, *Villers-Bocage*, 6. This number includes three tank companies of 19 tanks each in each regiment as well as 4 tanks in the Headquarters element and 11 Stuarts in the reconnaissance troop.

129. Tout, *Fine Night for Tanks*, 130. Tout puts the number of Fireflys at 34, but if each platoon had one firefly, the number would be 36.

130. For a synopsis see Tout, *Fine Night for Tanks*, 131.

131. Ibid., 89.

132. Ibid.

133. See Tout, *Fine Night for Tanks,* 89; Agte, *Michael Wittmann,* 424. According to Tout, the gunner of this Firefly, Trooper Joe Ekins, is definitely credited with three Tigers and another tank at the range of 1,200 yards (1,100 meters). Agte states that four of the six Tigers traveling on the east side of the road were destroyed (Dollinger's, Wittmann's, Iriohn's, and Kisters' Tigers were destroyed. Blase and the new company commander Heurich survived). The fifth Tiger destroyed during this attack was traveling on the west side of the road (Hoflinger's Tiger was destroyed and von Westernhagen survived).

134. Tout, *Fine Night for Tanks,* 102. Altogether, this one U.S.-battalion-sized unit claimed the destruction of five Tigers, four Panthers, six Panzer IVs, and five assault guns. This accounted for 20 of the fewer than 50 armored vehicles included in the German counterattack. In doing so, they lost 16 tanks.

135. The destruction of the Tigers can only be credited to the gunner because the original tank commander, Sergeant Gordon, was injured by return fire after the first Tiger was destroyed and Lieutenant James took over during the engagement and destruction of the final two Tigers.

136. Tout, *Fine Night for Tanks,* 164.

137. See Schneider, *Tigers in Combat II,* 259; Meyer, 160; Ellis et al., *Victory in the West,* 419. The British official history states that only six were destroyed.

138. Schneider, *Tigers in Combat II,* 259.

139. Ibid.

140. Agte, *Michael Wittmann,* 432. SS Captain Dr. Rabe wrote, "Toward evening I drove to Major General Kraemer [Chief of Staff of the 1st SS Panzer Corps] and reported the day's events to him. As I was the battalion's senior serving officer he instructed me to lead back the remnants of the battalion and placed me under Wunsche's command."

141. See Meyer, 163; Schneider, *Tigers in Combat II,* 259.

142. See Schneider, *Tigers in Combat I,* 164–65, 226–27; idem, *Tigers in Combat II,* 259–61, 320, 332–33, 365.

143. Schneider, *Tigers in Combat I,* 164–65, 226–27.

144. Schneider, *Tigers in Combat II,* 259–61, 320, 332–33, 365.

145. Ibid., 365.

146. Ibid., 259–61, 320, 332–33, 365.

147. Restayn, *Tiger I on the Western Front,* 34, 88, 116.

148. Normandy: SS-Heavy Tank Battalions 501 and 503, Heavy Tank Battalion 503. Italy: Heavy Tank Battalions 504 and 508.

149. Army Group North: Heavy Tank Battalions 502 and 510, and 3d Battalion, Panzer Regiment *Grossdeutschland.* Poland: Heavy Tank Battalion 507 in the north and Heavy Tank Battalion 509 in the south.

150. Ohdruf: Heavy Tank Battalions 501. 505, and 506.

151. The fact that three heavy tank battalions were operating in East Prussia and Lithuania was probably due to the emphasis on protecting German territory.

152. Schneider, *Tigers in Combat I,* 45.

153. Ibid., 276.

154. Ibid., 319–20.

155. Ibid., 276.

156. See Ibid., 45; "The Royal Opponent", 2002, unpublished manuscript, based upon article in *Tankomaster*, No. 6, 1999.

157. Schneider, *Tigers in Combat I*, 276.

158. Ibid., 45.

159. "The Royal Opponent," 2.

160. See Ibid., 3; Lieutenant Colonel Shapar, 71st Independent Guards Heavy Tank Regiment Commander, *Report about Operations of the 71st Independent Guards Heavy Tank Regiment from 14 July to 31 August 1944*, 1.

161. "The Royal Opponent," 6.

162. Ibid., 6. Sources indicate that this King Tiger had only operated a total of 444 kilometers.

163. Shapar, *Operations of the 71st Independent Guards Heavy Tank Regiment*, 1.

164. "The Royal Opponent," 3.

165. Shapar, *Operations of the 71st Independent Guards Heavy Tank Regiment*, 2.

166. Ibid.

167. Schneider, *Tigers in Combat I*, 46.

168. "Was the Tiger Really 'King': Testing the King Tiger at Kubinka," 2002, unpublished manuscript, based upon article in *Tankomaster*, No. 6, 1999, translated by Douglas Rauber, 1.

169. Ibid.

170. Ibid.

171. Ibid., 2.

Chapter 6

1. The *Combat History of schwere Panzer-Abteilung 507: In Action in the East and West with the Tiger I and II*, 116.

2. See Schneider, *Tigers in Combat I*, 166; von Rosen, "Employment in Hungary" in Lochmann et al., *schwere Panzer-Abteilung 503*, 282.

3. Schneider, *Tigers in Combat I*, 166.

4. von Rosen, "Employment in Hungary," 282.

5. The pro-Nazi elements were composed of some pro-German elements in the Hungarian Army and units of the Arrow-Cross, a Hungarian Fascist organization. The other primary German unit involved in overthrowing Admiral Horthy was the 8th SS-Cavalry Division "Florian Geyer."

6. See von Rosen, "Employment in Hungary," and Hauptmann Fromme, "After Action Report dated 25 November 1944," in Lochmann et al., *schwere Panzer-Abteilung 503*, 284, 300.

7. von Rosen, "Employment in Hungary," 284.

8. Ibid.

9. Ibid.

10. Ibid.

11. During the Battle of the Bulge, SS-Heavy Tank Battalion 501 penetrated 60 kilometers on 17 and 18 December 1944, although they did not lead the attack, but formed the trail element of Combat Group Peiper and followed as best they could.

12. von Senger und Etterlin, quoted in Lochmann et al., *schwere Panzer-Abteilung 503*, 283.

13. Fromme, "After Action Report dated 25 November 1944," in Lochmann et al., *schwere Panzer-Abteilung 503*, 300–301.

14. von Rosen, "Employment in Hungary," 285.

15. Schneider, *Tigers in Combat I*, 167.

16. Ibid.

17. Ibid.

18. For an overview of these operations, see Remarks by Glantz, 1985 Art of War Symposium, 155, 160.

19. Schneider, *Tigers in Combat I*, 168.

20. von Rosen, "Employment in Hungary," 292.

21. For an overview of these operations, see Remarks by Glantz, 1985 Art of War Symposium, 167, 170, 175.

22. Schneider, *Tigers in Combat I*, 168.

23. von Rosen, "Employment in Hungary," 293.

24. Schneider, *Tigers in Combat I*, 168–69.

25. See Schneider, *Tigers in Combat II*, 263; Agte, *Michael Wittmann*, 505–7.

26. Michael Reynolds, *Men of Steel, I SS Panzer Corps: The Ardennes and Eastern Front 1944–45* (New York: Sarpedon, 1999), 42–43, 48.

27. See Agte, *Michael Wittmann*, 507; Parker, "German Tiger Tanks," 54; Kleine and Kuhn, *Tiger*, 219.

28. Agte, *Michael Wittmann*, 506.

29. Ibid., 508.

30. Ibid., 506.

31. See Ibid., 508; Schneider, *Tigers in Combat II*, 263.

32. Schneider, *Tigers in Combat II*, 263–65. It was again "destroyed" by a Sherman of the 740th (U.S.) Tank Battalion on 25 December 1944.

33. Agte, *Michael Wittmann*, 508–9. The 2d and 3d Companies, as well as the battalion command element, followed Combat Group Peiper's route. 1st Company, starting in the trail of the battalion, ended up taking a more southerly route.

34. See Agte, *Michael Wittmann*, 509–11; Hugh M. Cole, *The Ardennes: Battle of the Bulge*, United States Army in World War II, The European Theater of Operations (Washington, D.C.: CMH, 1965), 265–69.

35. Agte, *Michael Wittmann*, 510.

36. Ibid.

37. Ibid. SS-Unterscharfuhrer Wortmann says that two vehicles emptied their tanks to supply the other two so that the ones with fuel could tow the ones without fuel.

38. Schneider, *Tigers in Combat I*, 321.

39. See Schneider, *Tigers in Combat I*, 321; Cole, *The Ardennes*, 162.

40. See Schneider, *Tigers in Combat I*, 321; Cole, *The Ardennes*, 404–5.

41. Cole, *The Ardennes*, 404–5.

42. See Schneider, *Tigers in Combat I*, 321–22, 344; idem, *Tigers in Combat II*, 263–65, 320.

43. Schneider, *Tigers in Combat I*, 321–22, 344.

44. Schneider, *Tigers in Combat II*, 263–65, 320.

45. Schneider, *Tigers in Combat I,* 322.

46. See Ibid., 321–22, 344; idem, *Tigers in Combat II,* 263–65, 320.

47. Rubbel, "The End of Separate Unit Status: Incorporation into Panzer-Korps 'Feldherrnhalle'," in Lochmann et al., *schwere Panzer-Abteilung 503,* 309.

48. *The Combat History of schwere Panzer-Abteilung 503* states that they did not want to refer to themselves as *FHH* because of the name's Nazi implications. Another reason may have been that they were justifiably proud of their accomplishments as Heavy Tank Battalion 503 and were reluctant to change unit designations. See Rubbel, "The End of Separate Unit Status: Incorporation into Panzer-Korps 'Feldherrnhalle'," in Lochmann et al., *schwere Panzer-Abteilung 503,* 309.

49. The other army heavy tank battalion assigned to a corps was 3d Battalion, Panzer Regiment *Grossdeutschland,* which was actually assigned down to the divisional level. All three Waffen SS heavy tank battalions were assigned directly to a corps HQ.

50. von Rosen, "Employment in Hungary," 282.

51. Remarks by Glantz, 1985 Art of War Symposium, 670–708.

52. Ibid., 670–718. A German counteroffensive—which could be viewed as a limited fourth German offensive—occurred 3–18 February.

53. Ibid., 670–84.

54. See Ibid; Schneider, *Tigers in Combat I,* 169.

55. Dr. Nordewin von Diest-Koerber, "Diary Entries from 14 December 1944 to May 1945 as Commander of schwere Panzer-Abteilung 503," in Lochmann et al., *schwere Panzer-Abteilung 503,* 312.

56. See Schneider, *Tigers in Combat I,* 169; von Rosen, "Employment in Hungary," 295.

57. Remarks by Glantz, 1985 Art of War Symposium, 686–92.

58. Ibid., 688–89.

59. See Remarks by Glantz, 1985 Art of War Symposium, 686–92; Schneider, *Tigers in Combat I,* 169; von Diest-Koerber, "Diary Entries," 313; and von Rosen, "Employment in Hungary," 296–97.

60. See Schneider, *Tigers in Combat I,* 169; von Diest-Körber, "Diary Entries," 313–14; and von Rosen, "Employment in Hungary," 296–97.

61. Ibid.

62. von Rosen, "Employment in Hungary," 296–97.

63. Ibid.

64. Remarks by Glantz, 1985 Art of War Symposium, 684, 686, 717–18. The Germans were able to achieve a superiority in armor of 1.5:1 in the offensive sectors. The overall strength, in personnel, of Army Group South was less than 450,000 while the combined strength of the 2d and 3d Ukrainian Fronts was about 850,000 to 900,000. In the attack sectors the Soviets had about 200,000 troops while the combined strength of the IV SS Panzer Corps, the III Panzer Corps, and the 1st Cavalry Corps was about 100,000.

65. von Rosen, "Employment in Hungary," 296–97.

66. von Diest-Körber, "Diary Entries," 313.

67. See von Diest-Körber, "Diary Entries," 314; and von Rosen, "Employment in Hungary," 297. The airplanes were destroyed attempting to take off from a forward Soviet airfield that the battalion overran.

68. See von Diest-Körber, "Diary Entries," 314; von Rosen, "Employment in Hungary," 297; and Schneider, *Tigers in Combat I,* 169.

69. Schneider, *Tigers in Combat I,* 417.

70. Ibid.

71. Remarks by Glantz, 1985 Art of War Symposium, 684.

72. Ibid.

73. Kleine and Kuhn, *Tiger,* 208.

74. Ibid.

75. For example, Heavy Tank Battalion 503 during Operation ZITADELLE and during their first employment in Hungary, and Heavy Tank Battalion 501 during Operation WACHT AM RHEIN.

76. For example Heavy Tank Battalion 505 during Operation ZITADELLE; SS-Heavy Tank Battalion 501 and Heavy Tank Battalion 503 (*FHH*) during Operation SÜDWIND; Heavy Tank Battalion 506 during Operation WACHT AM RHEIN, and SS-Heavy Tank Battalion 501 and Heavy Tank Battalion 509 during Operation FRÜHLINGSERWACHEN.

77. Kleine and Kuhn, *Tiger,* 208.

78. It is unfortunate that there is no mention made of the other platoons in the battalion (such as the antiaircraft platoon, the scout and engineer Platoon, and so on) and what their actions were during the attack.

79. Schneider, *Tigers in Combat I,* 417.

80. Kleine and Kuhn, *Tiger,* 208.

81. Schneider, *Tigers in Combat I,* 417.

82. Kleine and Kuhn, *Tiger,* 208.

83. Ibid.

84. Schneider, *Tigers in Combat I,* 417.

85. Because the German attack continued to make substantial progress past the Sarviz Canal, it is apparent that other vehicles were able to ford the canal and continue the attack. On 19 January 1945, German engineers built a bridge across the Sarviz, but it was not strong enough for the King Tigers. Engineers finally made a ford site reinforced with railroad ties for the King Tigers to cross.

86. See Schneider, *Tigers in Combat I,* 418; remarks by Glantz, 1985 Art of War Symposium, 708; Kleine and Kuhn, *Tiger,* 209–10.

87. See Schneider, *Tigers in Combat I,* 418; Kleine and Kuhn, *Tiger,* 209–10. The Soviet tank brigade was either from the 23d Tank Corps, the 1st Guards Mechanized Corps, or the 5th Guards Mechanized Corps. These Soviet tank losses, like literally all on the Eastern Front, have not been verified by Soviet sources. A careful examination of the German account reveals that the four King Tigers probably did not "own the battlefield" after their successful defense and thus did not themselves check out each destroyed Soviet tank to confirm that it was totally destroyed. Given the fact that elements of three Soviet corps did attack in this area on 27 January 1945, however, the number of destroyed Soviet tanks is totally plausible.

88. Schneider, *Tigers in Combat I,* 418.

89. Reynolds, *Men of Steel,* 187.

90. Ibid.

91. von Rosen, "Employment in Hungary," 299.

92. See Reynolds, *Men of Steel,* 190; Schneider, *Tigers in Combat II,* 265.

93. See von Rosen, "Employment in Hungary," 299; Schneider, *Tigers in Combat I*, 170.

94. von Rosen, "Employment in Hungary," 299.

95. Ibid.

96. See Ralf Tiemann, *The Leibstandarte*, vol. IV/2. Translated by Frederick Steinhardt (Winnipeg, Manitoba: J. J. Fedorowicz, 1998), 188; Schneider, *Tigers in Combat II*, 265.

97. von Rosen, "Employment in Hungary," 299.

98. See Ibid., 300; Schneider, *Tigers in Combat I*, 171.

99. Ibid.

100. Reynolds, *Men of Steel*, 197.

101. Ibid., 188.

102. Schneider, *Tigers in Combat II*, 266.

103. Ibid.

104. Schneider, *Tigers in Combat I*, 419.

105. Schneider, *Tigers in Combat II*, 266.

106. Ibid., 267.

107. Schneider, *Tigers in Combat I*, 419.

108. Ibid.

109. Ibid., 353–54. Prior to the battle, Heavy Tank Battalion 501 was officially renamed Heavy Tank Battalion 424 to confuse Soviet intelligence.

110. See Schneider, *Tigers in Combat I*, 45–46; Kleine and Kuhn, *Tiger*, 145.

111. Major Krebs, "General Staff Officer of the 17th Panzer Division, Situation Evaluation," in 1986 Art of War Symposium, David Glantz, Chairman (Washington, D.C.: Center for Land Warfare, U.S. Army War College, 1986), 610–15.

112. See Ibid; Schneider, *Tigers in Combat I*, 45–46.

113. Ibid.

114. See Ibid., 46; Kleine and Kuhn, *Tiger*, 145; Russ Schneider, *Götterdämmerung 1945: Germany's Last Stand in the East* (Philomont, Va.: Eastern Front Warfield, 1998), 47. Estimates from sources vary from between 20 and 27, although most state that 27 were destroyed. Schneider states that this battalion destroyed a further 50 to 60 Soviet tanks fighting in and around Lissow.

115. Kleine and Kuhn, *Tiger*, 145.

116. See Ibid; Schneider, *Tigers in Combat I*, 46.

117. Schneider, *Tigers in Combat I*, 354.

118. Ibid.

119. Ibid., 355.

120. Ibid., 446. As late as 10 April 1945, Heavy Tank Battalion 510 still had 13 operational Tigers in Kurland.

121. Schneider, *Tigers in Combat II*, 370–71.

122. Ibid., 375.

Chapter 7

1. Paul Carrel, *Foxes of the Desert* (New York: Bantam Dell, 1967), 318; quoted in Charles Whiting, *Kasserine*, 174.

2. Alfred Rubbel. "Technical Services and Supply/Logistics" in Lochmann et al., *schwere Panzer-Abteilung 503*, 27.

3. Heavy Tank Battalion 505's attack as part of the northern pincer of Operation ZITADELLE; SS-Heavy Tank Battalion 501 and Heavy Tank Battalion 503's attacks during Operation SÜDWIND; and Heavy Tank Battalion 509's attack during Operation FRÜHLINGSERWACHEN were all successful at penetrating the first or second echelons of the Soviet defenses.

4. In all the books listed in the bibliography, only two mention a mine roller for the Tiger as a counter to the increased use of mines. Only one of these is from a German source. Otto Carius mentions a mine roller, but states that they were not used, probably because of the swampy terrain that Heavy Tank Battalion 502 operated in as part of Army Group North. The Soviet General Staff also mentions Tiger tanks mounting mine rollers during the Battle of Kursk. In terms of antitank guns, Joachim Peiper provides good insight when he stated, "by all rights the destruction of a dug-in antitank gun should have been valued higher than the destruction of an enemy tank." See Kleine and Kuhn, *Tiger*, 219.

5. Joachim Peiper endorsed including heavy tank companies in the panzer regiment of a panzer division, "I am of the opinion that the Tiger would have fared better if the army had not formed independent battalions, but rather incorporated an organic heavy company in every regiment. The Tigers would then have been part of a firm structure and their employment in conjunction with the light tanks would have been more flexible and tactically more sensible." See Kleine and Kuhn, *Tiger*, 219.

6. The 1st and 2d SS Division's heavy tank companies formed the nucleus of SS-Heavy Tank Battalions 501 and 502. *Grossdeutschland*'s heavy tank company expanded to become a full battalion.

7. Patrick King, *Heavy Metal: Tiger!* Narrated by Greg Stebner, produced by Taylor Downing, edited by Andrew Mason (The History Channel, 2002).

8. Michael Swift and Michael Sharpe. *Historical Maps of World War II: Europe* (London: PRC, 2000), 85. The map shows eight heavy tank battalions when in fact there were only 2 in the west at this time.

9. While many Tigers were lost because they could not be recovered or broke down during extensive withdrawals and must be included in the ratio to obtain an accurate picture, the total Tiger losses includes all Tigers issued to the heavy tank battalions, or total annihilation.

10. To discover how many enemy tanks each Tiger had to destroy, to be cost-effective at the national level, would require a macroeconomic study of all countries involved in WWII, incorporating labor, time, and natural resources/minerals.

11. Franz Bäke, quoted in Kleine and Kuhn, *Tiger*, 97; Dr. Bäke cites the limited radius of action as the greatest disadvantage of the Tiger. He took part in nearly 500 missions in virtually every type of German tank and was one of the few WWII German tank commanders who was involved in the tank battle at Cambrai during WWI. He was a dentist by profession, and passed away in 1978.

12. For a good discussion of the inability of the Germans to develop a plan to fully utilize and maximize the resources they had available, see Richard Overy, "A Genius for Mass-Production: Economies at War" in *Why the Allies Won* (New York: W. W. Norton, 1995), 180–207.

13. The majority of heavy tanks and heavy tank battalions were built and fielded after the battle of Kursk in the summer of 1943.

Appendix

1. Gordon Waterfield, *What Happened to France* (London: Butler and Tanner, First edition 1940, Reprinted 1941), 21.

2. Robert A. Doughty, *The Seeds of Disaster: The Development of French Army Doctrine, 1919–1939*, (Hamden, Conn.: Archon Books, 1985), 3–4. In French the term is *bataille conduite*.

3. Ibid., 4.

4. Ibid., 154–55.

5. Ibid., 4.

6. Ibid., 143.

7. Ibid., 141.

8. Ibid.

9. Ibid., 162.

10. Ibid., 164.

11. Ibid., 177.

12. Ibid.

13. Ibid., 168. In 1939, the Inspector General of Tanks in the French Army published *The Provisional Notice on the Use of Units of the Armored Division*. This document continued the emphasis on tank support of infantry during the methodical battle.

14. Ellis, et.al., *Victory in the West*, 254–55.

15. Chris Ellis and Peter Chamberlain, eds., *Handbook on the British Army 1943* (Reprint of the U.S. Army Technical Manual 30-410, Handbook on the British Army, first published in 1943) (New York: Hippocrene, 1976), 164.

16. See Bryan Perrett, *The Churchill Tank*, (London: Osprey, 1980), 15; David Fletcher, *The Great Tank Scandal: British Armour in the Second World War, Part 1* (London: HMSO, 1989), 6.

17. Gudgin, *Armoured Firepower: The Development of Tank Armament, 1939–1945.* (Gloucestershire, U.K.: Sutton, 1997), 74–75.

18. See Ellis and Chamberlain, eds., *Handbook on the British Army 1943*, 42; Perrett, *The Churchill Tank*, 14. The Army tank brigade had a total strength of 178 tanks, almost all of which were infantry tanks.

19. Perrett, *The Churchill Tank*, 14. British regiments were U.S.-battalion equivalents, a squadron was company-sized, and a troop was platoon-sized.

20. Ibid.

21. Ibid.

22. Ibid., 14–15. Some tank brigades were equipped with both upgunned Shermans, which provided overwatch support, and traditional infantry tanks like the Churchill, which "bounded" forward under the protective fire of the stationary Shermans.

23. See Ellis and Chamberlain, eds., *Handbook on the British Army 1943*, 41, 164–65; Gudgin, *Armoured Firepower*, 44–59.

24. See Christopher R. Gabel, "World War II Armor Operations in Europe" in *Camp Colt to Desert Storm: The History of U.S. Armored Forces* (Lexington, Ky.: The University Press of Kentucky, 1999), 145; U.S. War Department, *Field Manual 100-5, Field Service Regulations, Operations* (Washington, D.C.: GPO, 22 May 1941), 127, 263–76; idem, *Field Manual 100-5, Field Service Regulations, Operations* (Washington, D.C.: GPO, 15 June 1944), 305–12.

25. U.S. War Department, *Field Manual 100-5* (1941 edition), 5–6, 97–111, 120–23, 127; idem, *Field Manual 100-5*, (1944 edition), 305–12. In the 1941 manual, U.S. doctrine sees two forms of the offense: the penetration and the envelopment. The word "breakthrough" is discussed in Chapter 12, "Special Operations" when talking about attacks against strong, prepared enemy defenses (called fortified localities in the manual). Although no specific taxonomy is provided, it appears that the breakthrough was seen as a specialized form of a penetration. For the sake of consistency, the word breakthrough is used when discussing doctrine, for the U.S. Army as well as other countries, although in some instances the doctrinally precise wording would be the penetration.

26. U.S. War Department, *Field Manual 100-5* (1941 edition), 278–80; idem, *Field Manual 100-5*, (1944 edition), 316–18. The 1941 manual refers to these units as General Headquarters (GHQ) Tank Units and the 1944 manual calls them nondivision armored units.

27. U.S. War Department, *Field Manual 100-5*, (1944 edition), 115. The only exception was when wide gaps were identified in the defense or when the defense was extremely weak. Only then were mobile forces, including armor units, to lead the breakthrough. This type of "breakthrough" cannot be classified in the same category as other country's breakthrough doctrine which saw a World-War-I-type breakthrough of a prepared defense. The exception is the French doctrine, which saw an eventual breakthrough of a weak defense based upon massive prior attrition through failed enemy attacks and preparatory artillery fire.

28. Richard M. Leighton and Robert W. Coakley, *Global Logistics and Strategy: 1940–1943*, United States Army in World War II, The War Department (Washington, D.C.: CMH, 1955), 288.

29. R. P. Hunnicutt, *Firepower: A History of the American Heavy Tank* (Novato, Calif.: Presidio, 1988), 27.

30. Ibid., 28–30.

31. Ibid., 28–59.

32. George C. Marshall, *General Marshall's Report, The Winning of the War in Europe and the Pacific: Biennial Report of the Chief of Staff of the United States Army: July 1, 1943 to June 30, 1945, to the Secretary of War* (Washington, D.C.: GPO, 1 September 1945), 95–96.

33. Green, Thomson, and Roots, *The Ordnance Department*, 286–87. In the European Theater, Shermans lasted five times longer mechanically than their German adversaries. Soviet tank designers held a different view of the importance of mechanical reliability than U.S. designers. On the assumption that a tank was almost certain

to be knocked out after a brief period of fighting, the Soviets considered a lifetime of fourteen hours for its mechanical components to be excellent. U.S. tanks, by comparison, were required to last for a minimum of forty hours. This was an intelligent design requirement considering that U.S. equipment was employed thousands of ocean kilometers away from any factory-level repair facilities. This ruled out transporting tanks back to the U.S. for major overhauls like German, Soviet, and British armies were able to do with their tanks.

34. David Fletcher, *The Universal Tank: British Armour in the Second World War, Part 2* (London: HMSO, 1993), 81.

35. Marshall, *The Winning of the War in Europe and the Pacific*, 96.

36. George Forty, *United States Tanks of World War II in Action* (Dorset, U.K.: Blandford, 1983), 138–41. Forty provides several interesting stories of Pershings in combat against Tigers.

37. Superheavy Tank T.28 Pamphlet, Archive copy available in the Patton Museum of Cavalry and Armor, Fort Knox, Kentucky.

38. As General Omar Bradley wrote, "our tank superiority devolved primarily from a superiority in the number rather than the quality of tanks we sent into battle."

39. Ellis, et.al., *Victory in the West*, 254–55.

40. Forty, *Tanks of World War II*, 21.

41. Ibid.

42. Operations GOODWOOD, COBRA, and BUCKLAND are three examples of the use of strategic bombers to affect a breakthrough of German defenses.

43. One of the primary reasons that the Soviets fared so poorly during the initial stages of the war was the purges of the senior military leadership undertaken by Josef Stalin in the late 1930s. Any army would have had trouble recovering from the severe losses in professional leadership. Only a few years before the war began, 3 out of 5 marshals, 13 out of 15 army commanders, 57 out of 85 corps commanders, 110 out of 195 division commanders, and 220 out of 406 brigade commanders were killed. See Bryan I. Fugate, *Operation BARBAROSSA: Strategy and Tactics on the Eastern Front, 1941* (Novato, Calif.: Presidio, 1984), 28.

44. For an interesting overview of Marshall Tukhachevskiy and his background, see J. F. C. Fuller, *A Military History of the Western World*, vol. 3, *From the Seven Days Battle, 1862, to the Battle of Leyte Gulf* (New York: Funk and Wagnalls, 1956), 339–40.

45. Daniel K. Malone, "Introduction" in *Foundation of Military Theory* (Fort Leavenworth, Kans.: U.S. Army Command and General Staff College, School of Advanced Military Studies, Course 1), v.

46. Mikhail N. Tukhachevskiy, *Problems of the Higher Command* (first published in 1924), excerpts contained in "Foundation of Military Theory," (Fort Leavenworth, Kans.: U.S. Army, Command and General Staff College, School of Advanced Military Studies, 1983), 45.

47. Ibid.

48. See Tukhachevskiy, *Problems of the Higher Command*, 45; Soviet Commissariat of Defense, *Field Service Regulations, Soviet Army, 1936* (Tentative). Originally published in Moscow: Soviet Military Publication Division, 1937, Translated by Charles

Borman, U.S. Army War College Translation Section (Washington, D.C.: GPO, 1937), 63, 66, 75, 77. Ministry of Defense of the USSR, *History of the Great Patriotic War of the Soviet Union, 1941–1945,* vol. 1, *Preparation for the Unleashing of the War by Imperialistic Powers,* unedited translation (Moscow: Military Publishing House of the Ministry of Defense of the USSR, 1960), 565–67; V. K. Triandafillov, *The Nature of the Operations of Modern Armies (Kharakter operatsii sovremennykh armiy,* first published in 1929), edited and with a foreword by Jacob W. Kipp and an introduction by James J. Schneider, (London: Frank Cass, 1994), 115–18, 127–36. Tukhachevskiy wrote "But the breakthrough itself makes no sense without the further applications of the enveloping movement. Both forms serve to surround the enemy, that is, the most effective of all means of destruction."

49. Although he took the opposite view of Tukhachevskiy in the "destruction versus attrition" debate within the Soviet military prior to World War II, Aleksandr A. Svechin provides good insight into the Soviet military thought in the levels of the defense up to the strategic level. See Aleksandr A. Svechin, *Strategy,* 2d Ed. (first published in 1927) with a foreword by the Russian First Deputy Minister, Andrei A. Kokoshin and introductory essays by Valentin V. Larionov, Vladimir N. Lobov, and Jacob W. Kipp (Minneapolis, Minn.: East View, 1997), 175–96, 239–56.

50. PU-36 labels these as the assault group and containing group. See Soviet Commissariat of Defense, *Field Service Regulations 1936,* 35–36.

51. PU-36 stated, in part, that "the enemy is to be paralyzed in the entire depth of his deployment, surrounded, and destroyed." See Soviet Commissariat of Defense, *Field Service Regulations 1936,* 35–36.

52. Triandafillov, *Modern Armies,* 113. Triandafillov wrote "Given today's elongation of the fronts of million-man armies and stability of the defense, it is impossible to break open these fronts by means of breakthroughs in a narrow sector."

53. Ibid., 113–14.

54. See Connor, *Analysis of Deep Attack Operations,* 15; Ministry of Defense of the USSR, *History of the Great Patriotic War,* vol. 1, 568.

55. Ministry of Defense of the USSR, *History of the Great Patriotic War,* vol. 1, 566.

56. Ibid., 568.

57. Ibid.

58. Connor, *Analysis of Deep Attack Operations,* 32.

59. Ministry of Defense of the USSR, *History of the Great Patriotic War,* vol. 1, 568.

60. See Ministry of Defense of the USSR, *History of the Great Patriotic War,* vol. 1, 568; Triandafillov, *Modern Armies,* 109. The depth increased throughout the war. Prior to the war, V. K. Triandafillov theorized that a tactical breakthrough would need to penetrate 25–35 kilometers.

61. Ibid.

62. Fugate, *Operation* BARBAROSSA, 25.

63. Soviet Commissariat of Defense, *Field Service Regulations 1936,* 38, 63–66, 71–72.

64. The only mention of heavy and medium tanks in the manual is made in discussing attacks against fortified areas, see Soviet Commissariat of Defense, *Field Service Regulations 1936,* 79.

65. These included several types of heavy tank, medium tanks, cavalry tanks, and amphibian tanks to name just a few.

66. Named after Klimenti Voroshilov, the murderous Defense Commissar in the late 1930s and later Soviet President.

67. Steven J. Zaloga, Jim Kinnear, Andrey Aksenov, and Aleksandr Koschchavtsev, *Stalin's Heavy Tanks, 1941–1945: The KV and IS Heavy Tanks* (Hong Kong: Concord, 1997), 3.

68. See "The Armored Roadblock, June 1941" in *Armor in Battle, Fort Knox Supplemental Material 17-3-2* (Fort Knox, Ky.: U.S. Army Armor School, Leadership Branch, Leadership and Training Division, Command and Staff Department, March 1986), 2-1 to 2-7; Zaloga et al., *Stalin's Heavy Tanks*, 4–5. During Army Group North's attack during the initial stages of Operation BARBAROSSA, a single KV-2 succeeded in blocking the advance of a reinforced Panzer Division (the 6th Panzer Division) for two days in Lithuania. Massed German armor, attacking from three sides, eventually managed to distract the KV-2 while an 88mm antiaircraft gun was brought up behind the KV-2. After eight shots from the 88mm, the KV-2 was finally knocked out. Throughout the two days, it does not appear that the KV-2 ever moved from its key position on the road.

69. Zaloga et. al., *Stalin's Heavy Tanks*, 8.

70. Ibid.

71. Ibid., The JS-2 fired a 55-pound (25 kilogram) projectile. This is more than double the weight of a round fired from a Tiger whose round was under 25 pounds (9 kilograms).

72. Ibid.

73. Ibid.

74. Ibid., 8–9.

75. Ibid.

76. Ibid., 9.

77. See Fugate, *Operation* BARBAROSSA, 26; Soviet Commissariat of Defense, *Field Service Regulations 1936*, 38–39, 70–72; Triandafillov, *Modern Armies*, 76–79, 92, 118; Mikhail Nokolayevich Tukhachevskiy, *New Problems in Warfare* (believed to have been written in 1931), excerpts contained in "Foundation of Military Theory," (Fort Leavenworth, Kans.: U.S. Army, Command and General Staff College, School of Advanced Military Studies, 1983), 14; Ministry of Defense of the USSR, *History of the Great Patriotic War*, vol. 1, 568, 572.

78. Ministry of Defense of the USSR, *History of the Great Patriotic War*, vol. 1, 568, 572.

79. Remarks by Glantz, *1985 Art of War Symposium*, 535.

80. Ministry of Defense of the USSR, *History of the Great Patriotic War*, vol. 1, 569.

81. Soviet Commissariat of Defense, *Field Service Regulations 1936*, 70.

82. Ministry of Defense of the USSR, *History of the Great Patriotic War*, vol. 1, 568.

83. Ibid.; remarks by Glantz, *1985 Art of War Symposium*, 535.

Bibliography

Books

Adair, Paul. *Hitler's Greatest Defeat: The Collapse of Army Group Centre, June 1944.* London: Arms and Armour, 1996.

Agte, Patrick. *Michael Wittmann and the Tiger Commanders of the Leibstandarte* (Michael Wittman erfolgreichster Panzerkommandant in Zweiten Weltkrieg und die Tiger der Leibstandarte SS Adolf Hitler). Translated by David Johnston. Winnipeg, Manitoba: J. J. Fedorowicz, 1996.

Armstrong, Richard N. *Red Army Tank Commanders: The Armored Guards.* Atglen, Pa.: Schiffer, 1994.

Atkinson, Rick. *An Army at Dawn: The War in North Africa, 1942–1943.* New York: Henry Holt, 2002.

Babadjanyan, Amazasp. "Tank and Mechanised Forces." In *The Battle of Kursk.* 2d ed. Translated by G. P. Ivanov-Mumjiev. Moscow: Progress, 1976.

Badsey, Stephen, *Normandy 1944: Allied Landings and Breakout.* London: Osprey, 1990.

Caidin, Martin. *The Tigers Are Burning: The Story of the Battle of Kursk—The Greatest Single Land and Air Combat Engagement in Military History.* New York: Hawthorn, 1974.

Carius, Otto. *Tigers in the Mud.* Translated by Robert Edwards. Winnipeg, Manitoba: J. J. Fedorowicz, 1992.

Coggins, Jack. *The Campaign for North Africa.* Garden City, N.Y.: Doubleday, 1980.

Corum, James S. *The Roots of Blitzkrieg: Hans von Seeckt and German Military Reform.* Lawrence, Kans.: University of Kansas Press, 1992.

Cross, Robin. *Citadel: The Battle of Kursk.* New York: Sarpedon, 1993.

Degrelle, Leon. *Campaign in Russia: The Waffen SS on the Eastern Front.* Costa Mesa, Calif.: Institute for Historical Review, 1985.

Deighton, Len. *Blitzkrieg: From the Rise of Hitler to the Fall of Dunkirk.* Edison, N.J.: Castle, 2000.

Doughty, Robert Allan. *The Seeds of Disaster: The Development of French Army Doctrine, 1919–1939.* Hamden, Conn.: Archon, 1985.

Duffy, Christopher. *Red Storm on the Reich: The Soviet March on Germany, 1945.* New York: De Capo, 1993.

Dunn, Walter S., Jr. *Kursk: Hitler's Gamble, 1943.* London: Praeger, 1997.

———. *Soviet Blitzkrieg: The Battle for White Russia, 1944.* Boulder, Colo.: Lynne Rienner, 2000.

Ellis, Chris, and Peter Chamberlain, eds. *Handbook on the British Army 1943* (Reprint of the U.S. Army Technical Manual 30-410, *Handbook on the British Army,* first published in 1943), New York: Hippocrene, 1976.

Fey, Will. *Armor Battles of the Waffen-SS, 1943–45* (Panzerkampf). Translated by Harri Henschler. Winnipeg, Manitoba: J. J. Fedorowicz, 1990.

Fletcher, David. *The Great Tank Scandal: British Armour in the Second World War,* Part 1. London: HMSO, 1989.

———. *The Universal Tank: British Armour in the Second World War,* Part 2. London: HMSO, 1993.

———. *Tiger! The Tiger Tank: A British View.* London: HMSO, 1986.

Forty, George. *United States Tanks of World War II in Action.* Dorset, U.K.: Blandford, 1983.

Franks, Clifton R., John A. Hixson, David R. Mets, Bruce R. Pirnie, James F. Ransone, Jr., and Thomas E. Griess, eds. Department of History, United States Military Academy. *The Second World War: Europe and the Mediterranean.* Wayne, N.J.: Avery, 1984.

Fugate, Brian I. *Operation* BARBAROSSA: *Strategy and Tactics on the Eastern Front, 1941.* Novato, Calif.: Presidio, 1984.

Fuller, J. F. C. *A Military History of the Western World.* Vol. 3, *From the Seven Days Battle, 1862, to the Battle of Leyte Gulf.* New York: Funk and Wagnalls, 1956.

Glantz, David M. *From the Don to the Dnepr: Soviet Offensive Operations, December 1942–August 1943.* London: Frank Cass, 1991.

Glantz, David M., and Jonathan M. House. *The Battle of Kursk.* Lawrence, Kans.: University of Kansas Press, 1999.

Glantz, David M., and Harold S. Orenstein, eds. *Belorussia 1944: The Soviet General Staff Study.* London: Frank Cass, 2001.

———. *The Battle for Kursk, The Soviet General Staff Study.* London: Frank Cass, 1999.

Guderian, Heinz. *Achtung-Panzer! The Development of Armoured Forces, Their Tactics, and Operational Potential.* Translated by Christopher Duffy with an introduction by Paul Harris. London: Arms and Armour, 1995.

———. *Panzer Leader* (Erinnerungen eines Soldaten). Translated by Constantine Fitzgibbon with a foreword by B. H. Liddell Hart. New York: E. P. Dutton, 1952.

Gudgin, Peter. *Armoured Firepower: The Development of Tank Armament, 1939–1945.* Gloucestershire, U.K.: Sutton, 1997.

———. *The Tiger Tanks.* London: Arms and Armour, 1991.

Habeck, Mary Ruth. *Imagining War: The Development of Armored Doctrine in Germany and the Soviet Union, 1919–1939.* Ann Arbor, Mich.: UMI Dissertation Services, 1995.

Haupt, Werner. *Army Group North: The Wehrmacht in Russia, 1941–1945* (Heeresgruppe Nord). Translated by Joseph G. Welsh. Atglen, Pa.: Schiffer, 1997.

Hirlinger, Kurt, ed. *The Combat History of schwere Panzer-Abteilung 508: In Action in Italy with the Tiger I.* trans. David Johnston. Winnipeg, Manitoba: J. J. Fedorowicz, 2001.

Hoffmann, George F., and Donn A. Starry, eds. *Camp Colt to Desert Storm: The History of U.S. Armored Forces.* Lexington, Ky.: University Press of Kentucky, 1999.

Howe, George F. *The Battle History of the 1st Armored Division "Old Ironsides."* Washington, D.C.: Combat Forces, 1954.

Hunnicutt, R. P. *Firepower: A History of the American Heavy Tank.* Novato, Calif.: Presidio, 1988.

Jentz, Thomas L. *Germany's Tiger Tanks, Tiger I and II: Combat Tactics.* Atglen, Pa.: Schiffer, 1997.

———. *Panzertruppen: The Complete Guide to the Creation and Combat Employment of Germany's Tank Force, 1933–1942.* Atglen, Pa.: Schiffer, 1996.

———. *Panzertruppen: The Complete Guide to the Creation and Combat Employment of Germany's Tank Force, 1943–1945/Formation, Organizations, Tactics, Combat Reports, Unit Strengths, Statistics.* Atglen, Pa.: Schiffer, 1996.

Jentz, Thomas L., and Hilary L. Doyle. *Germany's Tiger Tanks, D.W. to Tiger I: Design, Production and Modifications.* Atglen, Pa.: Schiffer, 2000.

———. *Germany's Tiger Tanks, VK45.02 to Tiger II: Design, Production and Modifications.* Atglen, Pa.: Schiffer, 2000.

Jung, Hans-Joachim. *Panzer Soldiers for "God, Honor, Fatherland": The History of Panzerregiment "Grossdeutschland": The German Army's Elite Panzer Formation.* Translated by David Johnston. Winnipeg, Manitoba: J. J. Fedorowicz, 2000.

Keegan, John. *The Second World War.* New York: Penguin, 1990.

Kleine, Egon, and Volkmar Kuhn. *Tiger: The History of a Legendary Weapon, 1942–45* (Tiger: Die Geschichte einer Legendaren Waffe 1942–45). Translated by David Johnston. Winnipeg, Manitoba: J. J. Fedorowicz, 1989.

Le Tissier, Tony. *Zhukov at the Oder: The Decisive Battle for Berlin.* Westport, Conn.: Praeger, 1996.

Lochmann, Franz-Wilhelm, Nordewin von Diest-Koerber, Clemens Kageneck, Ulrich Koppe, Richard von Rosen, and Alfred Rubbel, eds. *The Combat History of schwere Panzer-Abteilung 503: In Action in the East and West with the Tiger I and II.* Translated by Fred Steinhardt. Winnipeg, Manitoba: J. J. Fedorowicz, 2000.

Macksey, Kenneth. *Tank Warfare: A History of Tanks in Battle.* New York: Stein and Day, 1972.

————. *The Tank Pioneers*. New York: Jane's, 1981.

Meyer, Kurt. *Grenadiers*. Translated by Michael Mende. Winnipeg, Manitoba: J. J. Fedorowicz, 1994.

Miksche, Ferdinand Otto. *Attack: A Study of Blitzkrieg Tactics*. With an introduction by Tom Wintringham. New York: Random House, 1942.

Münch, Karlheinz. *The Combat History of schwere Panzer-Jäger-Abteilung 653, Formerly the Sturmgeschütz Abteilung 197, 1940–1943*. Translated by Bo H. Friesen. Winnipeg, Manitoba: J. J. Fedorowicz, 1997.

————. *The Combat History of schwere Panzer-Jäger-Abteilung 654, In Action in the East and West with the Ferdinand and the Jagdpanther*. Translated by Bo H. Friesen. Winnipeg, Manitoba: J. J. Fedorowicz, 2001.

Murray, Williamson, and Allan R. Millet. *A War to be Won: Fighting the Second World War*. London: The Belknap Press of Harvard University Press, 2000.

Nafziger, George F. *The German Order of Battle: Panzer and Artillery in World War II*. London: Greenhill, 1999.

Nash, Douglas E. *Hell's Gate: The Battle of the Cherkassy Pocket, January–February 1944*. Southbury, Conn.: RZM, 2002.

Naveh, Shimon. *In Pursuit of Military Excellence: The Evolution of Operational Theory*. London: Frank Cass, 1997.

Nipe Jr., George M. *Decision in the Ukraine, Summer 1943: II. SS and III. Panzerkorps*. Winnipeg, Manitoba: J. J. Fedorowicz, 1996.

Ogorkiewicz, R. M. *Armored Forces: A History of Armoured Forces and Their Vehicles*. New York: Arco, 1970.

Overy, Richard. *Why the Allies Won*. New York: W. W. Norton, 1995.

Perrett, Bryan. *A History of Blitzkrieg*. Introduction by General Sir John Hackett. New York: Jove, 1989.

————. *The Churchill Tank*. London: Osprey, 1980.

Piekalkiewicz, Janusz. *Operation "Citadel": Kursk and Orel, the Greatest Tank Battle of the Second World War*. Translated by Michaela Nierhaus. Novato, Calif.: Presido, 1987.

Restayn, Jean. *Tiger I on the Eastern Front*. Translated by Alan McKay. Paris: Histoire and Collections, 1999.

————. *Tiger I on the Western Front*. Paris: Histoire and Collections, 2001.

Reynolds, Michael. *Men of Steel, I SS Panzer Corps: The Ardennes and Eastern Front, 1944–45*. New York: Sarpedon, 1999.

————. *Steel Inferno: 1st SS Panzer Corps in Normandy*. New York: Dell, 1997.

Robinett, Paul McDonald. *Armor Command: The Personal Story of a Commander of the 13th Armored Regiment, of CCB, 1st Armored Division, and of the Armored School during World War II*. Washington, D.C.: McGregor and Werner, 1958.

Rolf, David. *The Bloody Road to Tunis: Destruction of the Axis Forces in North Africa, November 1942–May 1943.* With a foreword by Julian Thompson. London: Greenhill, 2001.

Rotmistrov, Pavel. "Tanks Against Tanks." In *Main Front: Soviet Leaders Look Back on World War II.* With a foreword by Sergey Sokolov and a commentary by John Erickson. New York: Brassey's, 1987.

———. "The Role of Armoured Forces in the Battle of Kursk." In *The Battle of Kursk.* 2d ed. Translated by G. P. Ivanov-Mumjiev. Moscow: Progress, 1976.

Sadarananda, Dana V. *Beyond Stalingrad: Manstein and the Operations of Army Group Don.* New York: Praeger, 1990.

Saunders, Tim. *Hill 112: Battles of the Odon.* Conshohocke, Pa.: Combined, 2001.

Schneider, Russ. *Götterdämmerung 1945: Germany's Last Stand in the East.* Philomont, Va.: Eastern Front Warfield,1998.

Schneider, Wolfgang. *Tigers in Combat I.* 2d ed. Winnipeg, Manitoba: J. J. Fedorowicz, 2000.

———. *Tigers in Combat II.* Winnipeg, Manitoba: J. J. Fedorowicz, 1998.

Solovyov, Boris. *The Battle of Kursk: 1943.* Moscow: Novosti Press Agency, 1988.

Spaeter, Helmuth. *The History of the Panzerkorps Grossdeutschland.* Vol. 2. (Die Geschichte der Panzerkorps Grossdeutschland 2). Translated by David Johnston. Winnipeg, Manitoba: J. J. Fedorowicz, 1995.

Steiger, Rudolf. *Armour Tactics in the Second World War: Panzer Army Campaigns of 1939–41 in German War Diaries.* New York: Berg, 1991.

Svechin, Aleksandr A. *Strategy.* 2d Ed. First published in 1927. With a foreword by the Russian First Deputy Minister, Andrei A. Kokoshin and introductory essays by Valentin V. Larionov, Vladimir N. Lobov, and Jocob W. Kipp. Minneapolis, Minn.: East View, 1997.

Swift, Michael, and Michael Sharpe. *Historical Maps of World War II: Europe.* London: PRC, 2000.

Taylor, Daniel. *Villers-Bocage: Through the Lens of the German War Photographer.* London: Battle of Britain International Limited Church House, 1999.

Tiemann, Ralf. *The Leibstandarte,* Vol. IV/2. Translated by Frederick Steinhardt. Winnipeg, Manitoba: J. J. Fedorowicz, 1998.

Tout, Ken. *A Fine Night for Tanks: The Road to Falaise.* Gloucestershire, U.K.: Sutton, 1998.

Triandafillov, V. K. *The Nature of the Operations of Modern Armies* (Kharkter operatsiisovremennykh armiy). First published in 1929. Edited and with a foreword by Jacob W. Kipp and an introduction by James J. Schneider. London: Frank Cass, 1994.

Vashurin, Pyotr. "Tactics Employed by Ground Forces in the Battle of Kursk." In *The Battle of Kursk*, 2d ed. Translated by G. P. Ivanov-Mumjiev. Moscow: Progress, 1976.

von Luck, Hans. *Panzer Commander: The Memoirs of Colonel Hans von Luck.* New York: Dell, 1989.

von Mellenthin, F. W. *Panzer Battles: A Study of the Employment of Armor in the Second World War.* Translated by H. Betzler and edited by L. C. F. Turner. New York: Ballantine, 1956.

Waterfield, Gordon. *What Happened to France.* London: Butler and Tanner, 1941.

Whiting, Charles. *Kasserine: First Blood.* New York: Stein and Day, 1984.

Zaloga, Steven J. BAGRATION *1944: The Destruction of Army Group Centre.* London: Osprey, 1996.

Zaloga, Steven J., and James Grandsen. *Soviet Tanks and Combat Vehicles of World War Two.* London: Arms and Armour, 1984.

Zaloga, Steven J., Jim Kinnear, Andrey Aksenov, and Aleksandr Koschchavtsev. *Stalin's Heavy Tanks, 1941–1945: The KV and IS Heavy Tanks.* Hong Kong: Concord, 1997.

Zetterling, Niklas, and Anders Frankson. *Kursk 1943: A Statistical Analysis.* London: Frank Cass, 2000.

Government Documents: All Countries

Art of War Symposium, 1985. "From the Dnepr to the Vistula: Soviet Offensive Operations, November 1943–August 1944." With a Foreword by James E. Thompson and an introduction by David M. Glantz. Washington, D.C.: Department of the Army, Center for Land Warfare U.S. Army War College, August 1985. Reprinted, with additional maps included, by the Foreign Military Studies Office, Combined Arms Command, Fort Leavenworth, Kans. March 1992. Typewritten.

Art of War Symposium, 1986. "From the Vistula to the Oder: Soviet Offensive Operations, October 1944–March 1945." With a Foreword by James E. Thompson and a preface by David M. Glantz. Washington, D.C.: Department of the Army, Center for Land Warfare U.S. Army War College, July 1986. Typewritten.

Beck, Ludwig. *Army Regulation 300: Die Truppenführung* (Troop Leading). Translated by the U.S. War Department. Available in the Combined Arms

Research Library, Fort Leavenworth, Kans. Berlin: Reichswehrministerium, 1933.

Breith, Hermann. "Breakthrough of a Panzer Corps through Deeply Echeloned Russian Defenses during the Battle of Kharkov (Kursk) in July 1943." MS #D-258. Draft Translation. Washington, D. C.: Department of the Army, Office of the Chief of Military History (CMH), 1947.

Buell, Thomas B., Clifton R. Franks, John A. Hixson, David R. Mets, Bruce R. Pirnie, and James F. Ransone, Jr. *The Second World War: Europe and the Mediterranean*, Vol. I. West Point, N.Y.: Department of History, United States Military Academy, 1979.

Cole, Hugh M. *The Ardennes, Battle of the Bulge.* Washington, D.C.: GPO, 1965.

Connor, William M. *Analysis of Deep Attack Operations, Operation BAGRATION, Belorussia: 22 June–29 August 1944.* Fort Leavenworth, Kans.: Combat Studies Institute, U.S. Army Command and General Staff College, 1987.

Daniel, K. R. "Examination of Causes of Rendering Tanks Inoperative, dated 19 March 1945." In *Kasserine Pass Battles, Doctrines and Lessons Learned,* Vol. II, Part 3. Washington, D.C.: CMH, 1995.

Department of the Army, Historical Division. *Anzio Beachhead—1944. American Forces in Action Series,* ed. John Bowditch, III, and Robert W. Komer. Washington, D.C.: GPO, 1 October 1947.

Department of the Army, 12th Army Group. Report of Operations (Final After Action Report) 12th Army Group, Vol. 11, Antiaircraft Artillery, Armored, Artillery, Signal and Chemical Warfare Sections. n.p.: n.d.

Eisenhower, Dwight D., Supreme Commander Allied Expeditionary Force. Report by the Supreme Commander to the Combined Chiefs of Staff on the Operations in Europe of the Allied Expeditionary Force: 6 June 1944 to 8 May 1945. Washington, D.C.: GPO, 1946.

Ellis, L. F., C. R. G. Allen, A. E. Warhurst, and Sir James Robb. *History of the Second World War: Victory in the West.* Vol. 1, *The Battle of Normandy.* London: HMSO, 1962.

Ellis, L. F., and A. E. Warhurst. *History of the Second World War: Victory in the West.* Vol. 2, *The Defeat of Germany.* London: HMSO, 1968.

Fisher, Ernest F., Jr. *Cassino to the Alps.* Washington, D.C.: GPO, 1977.

Generalinspekteur der Panzertruppen. D656/27, Tigerfibel. Ober Kommando des Heer, August, 1943.

Glantz, David. *American Perspectives on Eastern Front Operations in World War II.* Fort Leavenworth, Kans.: U.S. Army Combined Arms Center, Soviet Army Studies Office, April 1987.

———. CSI Report No. 11: *Soviet Defensive Tactics at Kursk, July 1943.* Combined Arms Research Library, Fort Leavenworth, Kans.: Combat

Studies Institute, U.S. Army Command and General Staff College, 1986. Text-fiche.

GMDS by a combined British, Canadian, and U.S. Staff. *The German Operation at Anzio: A Study of the German Operations at Anzio Beachhead from 22 Jan 44 to 31 May 44.* Camp Ritchie, Md.: German Military Document Section, Military Intelligence Division, War Department, 1946.

Green, Constance McLaughlin, Harry C. Thomson, and Peter C. Roots. *United States Army in World War II, The Technical Services: The Ordnance Department, Planning Munitions for War.* Washington, D.C.: GPO, 1955.

Guderian, Heinz. "An Interview with Genobst Heinz Guderian." Interview by Robert W. Fye. Panzer Tactics in Normandy. ETHINT 38. Washington, D.C.: CMH, 1948.

———. "An Interview with Genobst Heinz Guderian." Interview by Kenneth W. Hechler. Employment of Panzer Forces on the Western Front. ETHINT 39. Washington, D.C.: CMH, 1945.

Howe, George F. *Northwest Africa, Seizing the Initiative in the West.* Washington, D.C.: GPO, 1957.

Jackson, William, and T. P. Gleave. *History of the Second World War: The Mediterranean and Middle East.* Vol. 6, *Victory in the Mediterranean, Part III: November 1944 to May 1945.* London: HMSO, 1988.

Kesselring, Albert, Ernst K. H. Doll, Curt Gailenkamp, Kurt Maelzer, Max Simon, Kurt Wolff. "Manual for Command and Combat Employment of Smaller Units." MS #P-060b. Translated by G. Weber and W. Luetzkendorf and edited by G. C. Vanderstadt. Washington, D.C.: CMH, 1952.

Leighton, Richard M., and Robert W. Coakley. *Global Logistics and Strategy, 1940–1943.* Washington, D.C.: GPO, 1955.

Marshall, George C. *General Marshall's Report, The Winning of the War in Europe and the Pacific: Biennial Report of the Chief of Staff of the United States Army, July 1, 1943 to June 30, 1945, to the Secretary of War.* Washington, D.C.: GPO, 1 September 1945.

Ministry of Defence of the USSR. *History of the Great Patriotic War of the Soviet Union, 1941–1945,* Vol. 1, *Preparation for the Unleashing of the War by Imperialistic Powers.* Unedited translation. Moscow: Military Publishing House of the Ministry of Defence of the USSR, 1960.

Möbius, Rolf. "German Heavy Armor." MS #D-226. Draft Translation. Washington, D.C.: CMH, 1954.

Mueller-Hillebrand, Herman Burkhart, and Oskar Munzel. "Tactics of Individual Arms (Russian Armored Command, Examples from World War II, Part 1)." With a preface by Franz Halder. MS #P-060f. Translated by N. Franke and edited by L. Schafer. Washington, D.C.: CMH, 1951.

Playfair, I. S. O., C. J. C. Molony, F. C. Flynn, and T. P. Gleave. *History of the Second World War: The Mediterranean and Middle East.* Vol. 4, *The Destruction of the Axis Forces in Africa.* London: HMSO, 1966.

Schmidt, Martin. "Employment of Panzer Units in Central Italy in 1944, and Peculiarities Thereof." MS #D-204. Translated by G. Kohler. Washington, D.C.: CMH, 1948.

Soviet Commissariat of Defense. *Field Service Regulations, Soviet Army, 1936* (Tentative). Originally published in Moscow, Soviet Military Publication Division, 1937. Translated by Charles Borman, U.S. Army War College Translation Section. Washington, D.C.: GPO, 1937.

U.S. Army, Armor School. *Armor in Battle, Fort Knox Supplemental Material 17-3-2.* Fort Knox, Ky.: U.S. Army Armor School, Leadership Branch, Leadership and Training Division, Command and Staff Department, March 1986.

U.S. Army, Command and General Staff College. *Foundation of Military Theory.* Fort Leavenworth, Kans.: U.S. Army Command and General Staff College, School of Advanced Military Studies, 1983.

U.S. War Department. *Field Manual 100-5, Field Service Regulations, Operations.* Washington, D.C.: GPO, 22 May 1941.

U.S. War Department. *Field Manual 100-5, Field Service Regulations, Operations.* Washington, D.C.: GPO, 15 June 1944.

von Brauchitsch, Walther, "Provisional Instructions for Leadership and Action of the Tank Regiment and Tank Battalion, dated 18 January 1941" British translation of captured German document. In *Kasserine Pass Battles, Doctrines, and Lessons Learned,* Vol. II, Part 4. Washington, D.C.: CMH, 1995.

von Manteuffel, Hasso, "Fast Mobile and Armored Troops." MS #B-036. Translated by Mysing. Washington, D.C.: CMH, 1945.

Ziemke, Earl F. *Stalingrad to Berlin: The German Defeat in the East.* Washington, D.C.: CMH, 1987.

Video Recordings

Carruthers, Bob. *Achtung Panzer! Steel Tigers: The Evolution of a Legend, 1939–1945.* Produced by Vanessa Tovell. 90 minutes. Cromwell Productions, 1999. Videocassette.

King, Patrick. *Heavy Metal: Tiger!* Produced by Taylor Downing. 60 minutes. The History Channel, 2002. Cable broadcast.

Journals and Magazines

King, Curtis S. "Operation BAGRATION: A Soviet Victory." *Military Review,* April 1994, 89–93.

Nipe, Jr., George M. "Kursk Reconsidered, Germany's Lost Victory?" *World War II,* February 1998, 26–32, 76.

Parker, Danny S. "German Tiger Tanks Were at the Battle of the Bulge, but Not in the Numbers Usually Cited for Them." *World War II,* March 1990, 8, 54, 56, 58, 60–61.

Unpublished Material

Rauber, Douglas. Translator. "Was the Tiger Really 'King': Testing the King Tiger at Kubinka," Unpublished manuscript based upon an article in Tankomaster, No. 6, 1999.

Shapar. Lieutenant Colonel, 71st Independent Guards Heavy Tank Regiment Commander. Report about Operations of the 71st Independent Guards Heavy Tank Regiment from 14 July to 31 August 1944. n.p., n.d.

Superheavy Tank T.28 Pamphlet, Archive copy available in the Patton Museum of Cavalry and Armor. Fort Knox, Ky.

"The Royal Opponent," Unpublished manuscript based upon an article in Tankomaster, No. 6, 1999.

About the Author

Chris Wilbeck is a serving US Army armor officer assigned to the 1st Cavalry Division. He is a veteran of Operations DESERT SHIELD and DESERT STORM, in which he served as a Scout Platoon Leader in the 3d Armored Division. He has also completed tactical assignments with the 1st Armored Division and the 3d Infantry Division. Major Wilbeck is a graduate of the US Army Command and General Staff College and the School of Advanced Military Studies. He holds a Masters in Business Administration, and Master of Military Arts and Sciences degrees in Military History and Theater Operations. At the time of publication, Major Wilbeck is serving in the 1st Cavalry Division in Iraq.